The Genius of Scotland

Scottish Cultural Review of Language and Literature

The titles published in this series are listed at *brill.com/scrl*

The Genius of Scotland

The Cultural Production of Robert Burns, 1785–1834

By

Corey E. Andrews

BRILL

RODOPI

LEIDEN | BOSTON

Cover illustration: Framed engraving by William Giller titled 'Robert Burns' after Charles Hancock, 1853.

Library of Congress Cataloging-in-Publication Data

Andrews, Corey.
  The genius of Scotland : the cultural production of Robert Burns, 1785-1834 / by Corey E. Andrews.
    pages cm. -- (Scottish cultural review of language and literature series)
  Includes bibliographical references and index.
  ISBN 978-90-04-29436-3 (pbk. : alk. paper) -- ISBN 978-90-04-29437-0 (e-book) 1. Burns, Robert,
1759-1796--Criticism and interpretation. 2. Burns, Robert, 1759-1796--Appreciation. 3. Literature and
society--Scotland--History--18th century. 4. Literature and society--Scotland--History--19th century.
5. Creation (Literary, artistic, etc.)--History--18th century. 6. Creation (Literary, artistic, etc.)--History--
19th century. I. Title.

  PR4338.A64 2015
  821'.6--dc23

                                                            2015006479

ISSN 1571-0734
ISBN 978-90-04-29436-3 (paperback)
ISBN 978-90-04-29437-0 (e-book)

This book is printed on acid-free paper.

MIX
Paper from
responsible sources
FSC
www.fsc.org   FSC® C109576

Printed by Printforce, the Netherlands

To my father Ronald and my daughter Lillian

Contents

Acknowledgements

I would first like to thank the University of South Carolina Thomas Cooper Library Department of Rare Books and Special Collections for its generous support of my research in the G. Ross Roy Collection of Burnsiana and Scottish Literature; receiving the W. Ormiston Roy Memorial Fellowship twice was essential for the completion of this book. I would also like to thank Elizabeth Sudduth, the Director of Rare Books and Special Collections, as well as the Rare Books staff for their help during my stays at the library. In addition, I would like to thank Youngstown State University for its recognition and financial support of my scholarship, as well as acknowledge the aid and encouragement of the English Department, especially my chair Julia Gergits and colleagues Steven Brown and Rebecca Barnhouse.

I am particularly indebted to Patrick Scott, Distinguished Professor of English Emeritus at the University of South Carolina, for his invaluable advice during the research and writing of this book; he has been a great supporter and mentor over the years. I would also like to recognise the contributions of the late G. Ross Roy and Lucie Roy to my research during my stays at the University of South Carolina; their generosity was only matched by their hospitality. In the same spirit, I would like to recognise the gracious and unremitting support of the late Kenneth Simpson; he and Ross will be greatly missed.

I would also to thank the following people for their kind assistance and support of my work: Alex Benchimol, Gerard Carruthers, John Corbett, Bill Dawson, Henry Fulton, Hans de Groot, Scott Hames, Gillian Hughes, Nigel Leask, Kirsteen McCue, Margery Palmer McCulloch, Carol McGuirk, Liam McIlvanney, Ralph McLean, Steve Newman, Murray Pittock, David H. Radcliffe, Richard Sher, Jeremy Smith, and Ronnie Young. Many thanks also go to the following for their friendship and help: Charles Boris, Jean-Marc Kehres, Thomas Keith, James E. May, Brooke McLaughlin-Mitchell,P Linda Merians, Susan Oliver, Eric Parisot, Carla Sassi, Frank Shaw, Geoffrey Sill, Brijraj Singh, and Linda Zionkowski.

I am deeply grateful for the help of my editor Rhona Brown at SCROLL for her unfailing aid and direction; her role has been instrumental and much appreciated. I would also like to thank Gillian Sargent at SCROLL, as well as my research assistants Bradley Dubos and Caitlyn Ryan, for their roles in preparing the manuscript for publication.

Lastly, I would like to acknowledge the constant support of my family during the process of writing this book; my wife Elaine and children Louis and Lillian deserve much gratitude for their love and understanding. I would also thank my parents Ronald and Pamela and my sister Jennifer for their encouragement over the years.

I would like to thank the editors of the following journals for allowing the republication of parts of the introduction, chapter two, and chapter five:
"The Genius of Scotland: Robert Burns and His Critics, 1796-1828," *The International Journal of Scottish Literature* 6 (Spring/Summer 2010): 1-16.
"'Far-fam'd RAB': Scottish Labouring-Class Poets Writing in the Shadow of Robert Burns, 1785-1792," *Studies in Hogg and His World* 23 (2013): 41-67.
"Venders, Purchasers, Admirers: Burnsian 'Men of Action' from the Nineteenth to the Twenty-First Century," *Scottish Literary Review* 2.1 (Spring/Summer 2010): 97-115.

Introduction

The Genius of Scotland

1. Literary and National Origins of Genius

Contemporary notions of *genius* in the literary field frequently invoke conceptions of prodigious talent exhibited by young writers, whose knowledge and skills seem to have appeared 'naturally' – that is, without the aid of extensive education.[1] While *genius* in science is internationally recognised in often quantitative fashion, the writer as *genius* is often more difficult to characterise and evaluate. Whether their works enter the domain of popular culture or remain in the rarified air of the academy typically influences the public reception of such figures. For example, writers like Jonathan Safran Foer and David Foster Wallace achieved success at an early age, with their initial works commended as 'works of genius'; however, both also became subjects of popular interest as well, perhaps more for their biographies than their writing.[2]

In an obituary for Wallace entitled 'Death of a Genius', Lev Grossman writes that after the success of *Infinite Jest* (Wallace's acclaimed second novel), 'Wallace became a reluctant literary pinup, with his stubbly outsize chin and his shoulder-length hair. He was America's No. 1 literary seed, at the top of a hierarchy that was, one suspects, largely meaningless to him'.[3] Wallace's aloof disregard for fame cemented the categorical definition of his *genius*, while Foer's extremely sudden literary and popular success at the age of twenty-five led him to be variously lauded or vilified. While John Updike gave a glowing review of Foer's novel *Extremely Loud and Incredibly Close* in *The New Yorker*,[4] the *New York Press* expressed its disdain for the author by dubbing him one of the 'most loathsome New Yorkers' in the city, a 'vile' author and 'eager-to-please fraud' who has received 'unearned comparisons to geniuses like Burgess and Joyce'.[5] From awe-inspiring exultation to angry opprobrium, the discourse of genius continues to invite divisive commentary in the literary field.

Public recognition often serves as a vital component of an author's purported *genius*, with much debate focusing on the writer's 'celebrity' and attitude toward critical and commercial success.[6] The links between celebrity and genius are much older than the media-saturated literary field of the present, dating back to the eighteenth century when the concept of genius began to acquire its modern connotations. The word derived from the Greco-Romans, for whom *genius* initially signified 'the tutelary spirit or attendant spirit allotted to every person at his birth, to govern his fortunes and determine his character'; later, the term began to express the more general notions of a 'prevalent feeling, opinion, sentiment, or taste' as well as a 'distinctive character, or spirit'.[7] In this sense, genius can be seen to represent the value-neutral 'feeling' of the times (epitomised by the concept of *Zeitgeist*) as well as the 'distinctive' character of a nation itself.[8]

Eighteenth-century usage of *genius* reveals considerable se-mantic variety, with the conception of the *genius* as a prodigiously gifted individual appearing with greater frequency only in the last quarter of the century.[9] In philosophical works in particular, *genius* was a polysemous term that was often employed to characterise indi-viduals' relationships with the nations in which they lived. For in-stance, Montesquieu described *genius* in the following manner: 'The manners and mental characteristics of different people, guided by the influence of the same court and the same capital, I call the genius of a nation'.[10] For Montesquieu, the 'influence' of 'court and capital' shapes people's thoughts and behaviours, which in turn express the particular *genius* of their nation.

Scottish philosopher John Millar came to a similar conclusion in his work *The Origin of the Distinction of Ranks* (1771), where he writes that nations 'have been so habituated to the peculiar manners of [the] age, as to retain a strong tincture of those peculiarities, through every subsequent revolution', adding that 'the character and genius of a nation may perhaps be considered as nearly the same'.[11] The process of building the nation's *genius* begins in infancy within Millar's system; he cites David Hume's essay 'Of National Characters' in sup-port of his contention, claiming that '"whatever it be that forms the manners of one generation, the next must imbibe a deeper tincture of the same dye; men being more susceptible of all impressions during infancy, and retaining these impressions as long as they remain in the world"'.[12] Thus, through the direct method of 'saturation', the nation is reproduced by each generation of its citizens.

The idea that such *genius* best expresses the nation's essential character became a rallying cry for nationalists early in the eighteenth century, particularly in Scotland. In the first book of *Sketches of the History of Man* (1774), Scottish philosopher Henry Home, Lord Kames assessed the state of the nation after the Union of the Crowns in 1603. This act, which removed the King and the Court from Edinburgh to London, was a literal and symbolic blow for the Scottish people; he writes, 'The union of the two crowns had introduced despotism into Scotland, which sunk the genius of the people, and rendered them heartless and indolent'.[13] In this state of deep depression, the Scots – their *genius* sunk – merely subsisted, exhibiting little optimism for their future as an independent nation.

A hundred years later, in a tract entitled *True Scots Genius, Reviving* (1704), William Forbes offers hope for the Scottish *genius*, depicted as wavering in a state of anxiety that was induced by lethargic Scots who have neglected their duty to the nation:

The Soul, the mighty Genius, with regret,
Seem'd to give way and yeild [sic] t'approaching Fate,
And moving so few members of the Nation
Seem'd landed in a state of Separation;
As fainting People sometimes have been layd
In Coffings [sic] and in Graves, reputed Dead.[14]

In Forbes's scenario, the 'mighy Genius' in a 'state of separation' is the 'soul' of Scotland itself, for whose salvation corpse-like Scots must be reanimated.

In a fit of divine inspiration, the Scottish genius is 'revived' with patriotic fervour, leading Forbes to offer a future glimpse of a free nation:

Old Caledonia had Transfus'd the Soul,
The Genius now Revived in the whole;
This noble Genius did soon inspire,
Each worthy breast with Freedoms large desire,
And rais'd their Souls to that Exalted Pitch,
Which the old Scottish Hero's once did reach.[15]

Reviving 'Old Caledonia' is Forbes's exhortation to his fellow Scots, whom he hopes will be 'inspired' by their country's 'noble Genius' to act the parts of the 'old Scottish heroes'. Coupling genius with nationalism became a key strategy for those who sought (especially in eighteenth-century Scotland) to preserve the distinctive character of their nation.

After the Union of 1707, Scots would find this an increasingly difficult process, requiring the work of nationally-minded writers who sought to preserve the essential *genius* of Scotland. For Kames, this Union (unlike that of 1603) gradually 'revived' Scotland much differently than Forbes's imagining. Kames writes,

Enmity wore away gradually, and the eyes of the Scots were opened to the advantages of their present condition: the national spirit was roused to emulate and to excel: talents were exerted, hitherto latent; and Scotland, at present, makes a figure in arts and sciences, above what it ever made while an independent kingdom.[16]

Kames underscores the fruits of Scottish participation in the Union, seeing it as a vital opportunity for the Scottish *genius* to excel in the arts and sciences. Where Forbes had issued his *cri de coeur* prior to the Act of Union in a desperate attempt to 'revive' his nation's moribund *genius*, Kames writes with the benefit of seventy-years' hindsight from Edinburgh, a city (in James Buchan's phrase) 'crowded with genius'.[17]

Both writers sought to explain and justify the *genius* of Scotland to its citizens, members of a nation whose very identity was in a process of ongoing change. The socio-political intonation of *genius* found its most indelible exponent much later in the century, when Robert Burns emerged from the Scottish countryside in a burst of literary celebrity not unlike that seen in the present day. His *genius* would be seen to express not only his undeniable gifts as a writer but also the 'distinctive spirit' of the nation, embodied by Burns himself. Resolute, proud, and 'heroic', Burns would 'revive' the 'mighty Genius' of Scotland by preserving its native literature against the forces of British assimilation (perhaps best embodied by figures like Lord Kames himself). This expressly-imagined yet pervasively influential view of Burns is the subject of this book; in particular, his representation as the 'genius of Scotland' will be explored from his first public recognition as such in 1786 until the death of James Hogg, deemed his 'only worthy successor', in 1835.

2. Robert Burns as the Genius of the Nation

Few figures in Scottish history have been put into national service as dramatically as Robert Burns, whose influence since his death in 1796 has been constant in Scottish culture. As Marilyn Butler has observed, 'Burns is the first of our cultural nationalists, through his brilliantly-imagined construction of modern Scotland'.[18] Burns's biography and body of works have been frequently used to support the perception of 'essential' national differences between Scotland and England. For instance, Liam Connell has suggested that 'the concept of Scottish literature is deeply marked by the belief in an essential division between English and Scottish culture'.[19] Similarly, Robert Crawford has examined both the 'Scottish invention' and the 'devolution' of 'English literature' in order to assess the distinctly 'Scottish' qualities of the latter.[20] Connell argues that 'the emergence of Scottish literature as a discursively coherent category was roughly contemporaneous with the emergence of a political Scottish nationalism' (256).

In this light, Burns has often quite literally been the face of this movement, witnessed vividly in the Scottish National Party's use of Burnsian iconography.[21] Burns's continuing national relevance resides mainly in the uses that his image has been made to serve, particularly across the political spectrum and in the commercial marketplace.[22] Claiming kinship with Burns is an intensely political process, requiring one to stake out territory and defend boundaries. One reason for such political ambiguity is the fact that for varying reasons, Burns never publicly announced a definite political position.[23] Because of this, there has been a burgeoning industry in promoting (and appropriating) Burns as an advocate of often wildly divergent political and/or cultural platforms since the early nineteenth century. He has at times been championed as both an advocate for Scottish independence and a supporter of the Union.[24]

The national identity that Burns embodies continues to be seen as resolutely *not* English, where his role as a Scottish national figure is defined through negation. Connell has claimed that 'England's dominance over Scotland is understood almost exclusively in cultural terms – as the exportation of English culture, exemplified by linguistic standardization' (262). In the face of such cultural imperialism, Burns – particularly as master of Scots poetry – stands as a heroic figure resisting the tide of assimilation and cultural obsolescence, acting as the 'genius of the nation' who would 'revive' the 'soul' of Scotland from the brink of the grave.

How exactly did this come to be? The primary goal of this book is to determine the means and methods that led to Burns's cultural and national valorisation, a process of veneration and consecration that continues into the present. In order to determine this, one must consider, in Butler's words, 'why an apparently local writer using a provincial idiolect at once found a receptive audience, and why the conditions were right for him to become a *national*, that is a Scottish, poet'. [25] Finding an answer invites detailed study of the literary field in eighteenth-century Scotland, with close attention to the process of 'cultural production' that valorised and elevated Burns to serve as the 'genius of the nation'.

3. Cultural Production and Legitimacy in the Literary Field

The concept of 'cultural production' in the literary field involves recognising the various agents concerned in the 'making' of authors, from editors and critics to readers and authors themselves. In the work of Pierre Bourdieu, the concept of 'habitus' denotes the process wherein principles of 'judgement' and 'classification' govern the process of culture's production and consumption:

The habitus is both the generative principle of objectively classifiable judgements and the system of classification [...] of these practices. It is in the relationship between the two capacities which define the habitus, the capacity to produce classifiable practices and works, and the capacity to differentiate and appreciate these practices and products. [26]

The process of 'classification, differentiation, and appreciation' operates within the literary field and 'produces' cultural capital as an object of authors' aspiration as well as the primary means of their evaluation.

The habitus expresses these relations, particularly as they expose the structure of the literary field. Bourdieu writes,

All positions depend, in their very existence [...] on their actual and potential situation in the structure of the field – that is to say, in the structure and distribution of those kinds of capital (or of power) whose possession governs the obtaining of specific profits (such as literary prestige) put into play in the field. [27]

Cultural capital underpins the field's structure, revealing the forces used to evaluate and classify literary production. As Robert Moore observes, the process of classification at the heart of cultural capital extends not only to literary works but also to their writers and readers:

Cultural capital is presented as reflecting the intrinsic value of art works in themselves ('essentialism') and the capacity for certain gifted individuals (those with 'distinction') to recognise and appreciate those essential qualities.[28]

This latter point is worth emphasising, for Bourdieu argues that 'a work of art has meaning and interest only for someone who possesses the cultural competence, that is, the code, into which it is encoded'. Gaining access to this 'code' is an inherently social act, delimited by mitigating factors of class and education. Indeed, Bourdieu underscores 'the very close relationship linking cultural practices [...] to educational capital (measured by qualifications) and, secondarily, to social origin'.[29] The relevance of class to the production and consumption of culture is paramount, for it acts as a primary delimiting factor in gaining (or being denied) access to cultural capital.

Throughout his analysis of cultural production, Bourdieu repeatedly emphasises the forces at work in the literary field, stating that it 'is a force-field acting on all those who enter it' as well as 'a field of competitive struggles which tend to conserve or transform this force-field' (233). He further claims that the field 'is the site of struggles between holders of different powers (or kinds of capital)' (215). In such a field of literary production, accruing cultural capital involves the acquisition of a body of knowledge that structures the field itself and serves as the 'force-field' that defines its boundaries. Indeed, the production of 'literature' depends upon the nature of an already constituted literary object/text that is recognised and 'decoded' by knowledgeable readers and writers.

In order for would-be producers to pass safely through this 'force-field' into the field of literary production, they must possess 'mastery'. Bourdieu states that

To the extent that the field closes in on itself, a practical mastery of the specific attainments of the whole history of the genre which are objectified in past works and recorded, codified and canonised by the whole corpus of professionals of conservation and celebration [...] becomes part of the conditions of entry into the field. (242)

This can be a daunting prospect for authors seeking to enter the literary field; as previously noted, authors' social and cultural backgrounds precondition their potential to be accepted as producers with sufficient 'cultural capital'. This speaks to what Bourdieu describes in *Distinction* as 'the aristocracy of culture', where issues of 'taste' become 'one of the most vital stakes in the struggles fought in the field of the dominant class and the field of cultural production'.[30]

As Michael Grenfell notes, authors are very aware of these mitigating factors which influence the reception of their literary efforts, for writers 'construct their work in relation to the possibilities available within the field and the position they occupy within it. They have interests in preserving or transforming the field through their work according to their perceived position "in the game"'.[31] Understanding 'the game' is vital for authors' success, which is measured by their 'mastery' of the field as well as their striving for recognition. In this scenario, authors may believe that they have a high degree of agency in the literary field; Bourdieu describes this as the authors' wish for 'autonomy', the ability to control their product. He observes that 'the pure intention of the artist is that of a producer who aims to be autonomous, that is, entirely the master of his product'.[32]

Such desires on the author's part, however, are as much pure fantasy as 'pure intention', for the reception of their work depends upon a network of various audiences whose consumption of texts is governed by the structure of the literary field. It is as significant an element in the communicative role of the literary field as production itself, requiring audiences who have the cultural competence necessary to understand the 'code': 'Consumption is [...] a stage in the process of communication, that is, an act of deciphering, decoding, which presupposes practical or explicit mastery of a cipher or code'.[33] Thus, the literary field presupposes mastery on the part of writers and readers, whose access to the 'code' is conditioned by social and cultural factors tied to class identities.

This social component of consumption requires specific attention to historical factors which 'create' consumers capable of 'appreciating' authors' texts. Class and education once more regulate access to the 'code'; as Bourdieu notes, 'The relative weight of home background and of formal education (the effectiveness and duration of which are closely dependent on social origin) varies according to the extent to which the different cultural practices are recognised and taught by the educational system'.[34] Moore notes that such factors are implicated in the construction of habitus as an operational concept, stating that 'the formation of habitus takes place initially within the family, the domestic habitus, but, for Bourdieu, the most important agency is education where capital assumes an institutionalised form'.[35]

Social and 'institutional' factors governing access to education condition the generative properties of the habitus, for it is (in Bourdieu's words) 'a structured structure: the principle of division into logical classes which organises the perception of the social world is itself the product of internalization of the division into social classes'. Because of the historicised nature of this 'principle of division', authorship and consumption rely on ever-changing criteria that reflect social differentiation through class. Bourdieu writes that 'art and cultural consumption are predisposed, consciously and deliberately or not, to fulfil a social function of legitimating social differences'.[36] The act of 'legitimation' directly influences the evaluation of literary production in the field, tending to discriminate texts upon the basis of their relationship to 'high' or 'low' culture (which is itself conditioned by such mitigating factors as class and place).

Bourdieu highlights these socio-economic conditions that directly affect the process of consumption, writing that

In cultural consumption, the main opposition, by overall capital value, is between the practices designated by their rarity as distinguished, those of the fractions richest in both economic and cultural capital, and the practices socially identified as vulgar because they are both easy and common, those of the fractions poorest in both these respects. In the intermediate position are the practices which are perceived as pretentious, because of the manifest discrepancy between ambition and possibilities. (176)

Within this network of socio-economic 'possibilities', the concept of 'distinction' is employed as a key criterion of value; it can even be used to indicate literary success *contra* commercial success. Patricia Thomson notes that 'each social field has a "distinction" [...] or quality – for example, between elite avant-garde and populist forms in literature'.[37]

Within the literary field, 'distinction' serves to discriminate authors' productions vis-à-vis their 'temporality', which is assessed by the works' degree of success in gaining popular versus critical success. Bourdieu states that 'according to the criterion of temporal success measured by the indices of commercial success [...] pre-eminence belongs to artists [...] who are known and recognised by the "general public"' (217). However, key markers of 'distinction' (such as *genius*) individuate an author's product by distinguishing its value as a index of cultural capital acquired through 'mastery', making it an object of value irrespective of temporality. As with theories of *genius*, authors with 'distinction' gain recognition for socio-cultural factors in addition to the reception of their literary productions.

Like their works, authors are 'culturally produced' by the nature of the literary field itself, a process which influences the nature of their texts' consumption. Such approaches to authorship mediate the reception of authors' 'creative projects'. Bourdieu claims that

> Positive or negative sanctions, success or failure, encouragements or warnings, conse-
> cration or exclusion [...] are effectively one set of the major mediations through
> which the incessant redefinition of the 'creative project' is shaped, with failure en-
> couraging reconversion or retreat from the field, and consecration reinforcing and
> liberating initial ambitions. (260)

The concept of 'consecration' has a strong correlation with the notion of an author's 'distinction' in the literary field, for the act of 'consecrating' authors and their texts depends explicitly upon the current standards of value used to define cultural capital. As with economic capital, cultural capital is a product of labour, an investment by authors seeking to gain recognition.

Bourdieu emphasises the expenditure of time and effort necessary for the acquisition of cultural capital: 'The accumulation of cultural capital [...] presupposes a process of embodiment, incorporation, which insofar as it implies a labor of inculcation and assimilation, costs time, time which must be invested personally by the investor'.[38] For these reasons, 'consecration' serves as both a point of initiation and discrimination as well as a boundary actively patrolled. Like the process of entering the literary field, seeking recognition and 'consecration' is a process fraught with continual conflict, described by Bourdieu as 'an endless struggle for a power of consecration which can no longer be acquired or consecrated except in and through the struggle itself' (230). In order to achieve such 'consecration', authors must distinguish themselves as much as their works, which is a part of a 'very particular process of production' that Bourdieu represents as 'the social creation of the "creator" as fetish' (231).

Achieving 'consecration' as fetishised 'creator' is the ultimate marker of success in the literary field, and it is closely guarded by those who seek to maintain their authority to define authorship itself. For Bourdieu, the power of definition tends to conserve the status of those who are 'established' in the field. He writes, 'The struggles over definition (or classification) have boundaries at stake [...] and, therefore, hierarchies. To define boundaries, defend them and control entries is to defend the established order in the field' (225). The most powerful boundary in the literary field is that which defines the author as legitimate(d) producer, one whose works and status as 'creator' can be 'consecrated'.

Policing this border can be regarded as *the* primary struggle within the field of cultural production, which (as Bourdieu stresses) is 'the site of struggles which, through the imposition of the dominant definition of the writer, aim to delimit the population of those who possess the right to participate in the struggle over the definition of the writer' (224). Negotiating such struggles can dramatically impact a writer's ultimate place in the literary field. Nick Crossley suggests that the struggle for 'distinction' in the literary field is ultimately a struggle for an author's definition as such:

'Distinction' is simply that clusters of individuals in social space each develop social peculiarities which mark them out from one another. They have distinct cultures – hence 'distinction'. However, these differences can become a focus of symbolic struggles (struggles for distinction) in which members of those clusters seek to establish both the superiority of their peculiarities and an official sanction for them.[39]

The central criterion for such definitions of the author is 'legitimacy'. In fact, 'legitimacy' might seem to be the final product of the negotiation between authors and 'producers of meaning' like readers and critics in the literary field.

However, it is only those with 'the monopoly of literary legitimacy' who control the definitions of 'legitimate' writers. Bourdieu describes this group as those who have 'the monopoly of the power to say with authority who are authorised to call themselves writers; or, to put it another way, it is the monopoly of the power to *consecrate* producers and products'.[40] The use of 'consecration' to authorise cultural production invests those 'with authority' with significant power in the literary field. In order to be 'consecrated', authors must work within the defined parameters of the literary field while seeking at the same time to individuate their work by means of stylistic and/or linguistic choices. Bourdieu aptly suggests that for such aspiring authors, '"making one's mark", initiating a new epoch, means winning recognition, in both senses, of one's difference from other producers'.[41] At the same time, one cannot be too different from competing producers, for this may lead authors to produce works that cannot be evaluated by existing criteria and standards in the literary field.

These then are the stakes involved in gaining recognition and achieving 'consecration' as an author in a literary field comprised of endless definitional struggles. Even 'newcomers' to the field cannot avoid engaging in these struggles, for (as Michael Grenfell observes) they have an 'interest' they cannot suppress: 'Newcomers into the artistic field have the most interest in a denial of interest [...] since only this claim can legitimise their own sense of the value of their art in itself'. Thus, in ironic fashion, 'disavowal of interest is itself a symbolic assertion of interest'.[42] Such is the Gordian knot of literary production.

4. Constructing Burns's Reputation as the Genius of Scotland

Robert Burns was able to 'make his mark' as a 'newcomer' in the early stages of his career, when visible markers of his difference (particularly his status as a 'heaven-taught ploughman') individuated his works from those of other Scottish and British poets.[43] For writers like Burns coming from the labouring class, such distinguishing markers can literally serve as the primary means of making an author's reputation. In *The Politics of Literary Reputation*, John Rodden explains 'how patterns of interpersonal and institutional relations [can] transform a writer into a literary figure'.[44] Noting that 'one index to a culture is the figures it exalts', Rodden examines 'the processes by which writers' images and identities are formed and literary reputations are gained, lost, consolidated, revised, and deformed' throughout history (4). As in Bourdieu's envisioning of the literary field as a 'site of struggles', literary reputation in Rodden's view is also an active process, one that is mediated and constructed by various agents with competing interests.

Such a view of literary reputation involves the collusion of 'critical' and 'popular' influences, both of which interact in the process of transforming authors into literary celebrities. The notion of *genius* plays a central role in such negotiations, offering a ready-made conceptualization of an author's difference from competitors in terms of criteria like talent and originality. The degree to which authors continue to retain influence after death depends upon the use and usefulness of their 'body of work', for (as Rodden claims) 'literary transfiguration is [...] a process with a large institutional component. Occasionally the process bears some marks of a *consciously coordinated effort* among several of the industry's spheres to "manufacture a reputation"' (9). This last point underscores the interconnections between agents in the literary field and those in popular culture, who work in tandem to construct literary reputation by using similar criteria for evaluation and selection.

Noting that 'the typically unscholarly questions of heroes and hero worship hover at the border of any study of the making of a literary figure' (10), Rodden argues that 'reputation-building is not only a matter of reader identification but also reader projection' (400). This has long been a feature of literary history, particularly in the province of biography. Rodden notes that 'such a focus upon a writer as a heroic character in his society was frequent, though often wholly uncritical, in nineteenth-century biography' (10). This process is plainly evident when surveying the history of Burns's reputation, where his 'consecration' as a 'hero' in the nineteenth century frequently came at the expense of the truth of his actual biography. His 'consecration' yields considerable evidence of censorship, misrepresentation, and outright falsity.[45] As Rodden notes, 'the search for the usable past easily becomes the quarry for the abusable past' (400).

For Burns, his posthumous reputation was constructed from such a quarry, where the competing interests of those in the literary field as well as those in popular culture sought to remake the poet into a suitable national figure whose *genius* expressed the 'soul' of Scotland.[46] Indeed, vying for control of Burns's legacy has been the task of many specialised communities, who have proffered competing images of the poet and his relationship to the Scottish nation. Groups such as Burns clubs, Freemasons, scholars, politicians, and fellow poets have perceived and represented Burns in often expressly imagined ways in order to meet each community's particular needs.[47] This has led to the understandable confusion one experiences when trying to assess Burns as a historical figure rather than as a composite of frequently contradictory characterisations advanced by various special interest groups.

However, despite this scenario, Burns's role as a national icon has long been paramount in his literary reception, especially regarding his role in 'preserving' Scottish vernacular culture and traditions. Arash Abizadeh states that the nationalist function of 'shared vernacular culture', consisting of 'dialects, customs, and traditions', acts as 'the cement that holds the nation together'.[48] In particular, Burns's role as 'genius of the nation' has been tied to his purported recuperation/restoration of Scottish vernacular culture in danger of British assimilation, best typified by his use of Scots dialect.[49] 'Authentic' Scottish identity in this formulation has a resolutely class-based dimension, for 'vernacular culture' serves as a by-word for the Scottish rural 'folk' of which Burns was a typical representative ('ploughman') as well as an anomaly ('heaven-taught').

His work and image expressed 'dialects, customs and traditions' that formed ethnic bonds for national identification; the notion of the land as nation (and nation as land) is a powerful bond invoked by Burns's image and works.[50] Constructing his national reputation has repeatedly involved integrating the poet within a circumscribed notion of Scottish national identity, one that has greatly depended upon the role of language to unify a shared national culture. Burns's key significance in this respect has been derived from his usage of Scots, a factor that has linked him with expressions of Scottish national sentiment from the nineteenth century to the present.[51] In literary circles, Burns has long been credited with promoting and sustaining the Scots 'vernacular revival', while in political terms his advocacy of Scots has served as a rallying point for Scottish nationalists.

In fact, the example of Scotland in relation to theories of nationalism has proved to be a particularly instructive one. Due to its historical status as a voluntarily incorporated nation, Scotland has traditionally been viewed through the case study model; its nationalist status has been famously assessed as 'failed nationalism' or 'non-national nationalism'.[52] Scotland's confused relation to nationalism has even led some observers to proffer a diagnosis of 'cultural schizophrenia' due to the country's push-pull tension between cultural assimilation and preservation.[53] In particular, the critical orthodoxy surrounding eighteenth-century Scotland's presumably 'schizophrenic' culture has had an extremely long shelf-life in literary and cultural histories.[54] The linking of national identity with Scots usage was a key feature of many nationalist theories in the eighteenth century, with persistent debates over cultural and linguistic matters. Noting that 'the idea of a dialect had little use before nation-states started establishing official ways of speaking and writing', Michael Billig argues that 'differences between languages and dialect, then, became hotly contested political issues'.[55] This is clearly the case when confronting Burns's role as a Scots poet, who 'preserves' Scottish national culture by not only his subject matter but its means of expression in dialect.

Throughout eighteenth-century Scotland, the topic of language – especially the promotion of English usage over Scots – was a source of continual debate, ranging from the enthusiastic advocacy of Scots seen in James Watson's *Choice Collection of Comic and Serious Scots Poems* (1706-1711) to James Beattie's prescriptive tract entitled *Scotticisms Arranged in Alphabetical Order, Designed to Correct Improprieties of Speech and Writing* (1787). In each case, national identity was either preserved or transformed based upon language usage; as in Forbes's *True Scots Genius*, Watson sees the task of poets (and editors) as reviving the 'spirit' of Scotland, while Beattie envisions a future when Scots can no longer be recognised as such because of their linguistic 'improvement'.[56] In this debate, the promotion of Scots as a distinct language rather than a dialect had an explicitly nationalist rationale, for (as Billig observes) dialect is 'a term which almost invariably carries a pejorative meaning' and is 'frequently a language which did not succeed politically' (32). Because of this negative perception of dialect, its usage invites a clear political endorsement of its role in promoting nationalism. Billig states that 'nationalist movements, seeking to form separate states, will seek to convert dialect into language. The power of writing down a way of speaking should not be underestimated: it provides material evidence for the claim that a separate language exists' (34).

For such nationalist movements, poetry proves to be of vital importance, and more than any other poet of the period, Burns has served for many fellow Scots as the quintessentially 'authentic' Scot.[57] Burns's relationship to Scottish national identity exemplifies the nationalist potential of poetry that Benedict Anderson represents as a valuable tool for constructing and sustaining the 'imagined community' of the nation. According to Anderson, a means of linking the disparate groups that form an imagined national community is a

pragmatic necessity 'because the members of even the smallest nation
will never know most of their fellow-members, meet them, or even
hear of them, yet in the minds of each lives the image of their com-
munion'. In eighteenth-century Scotland, for example, the role of lit-
erature in creating an 'image of communion' for citizens was central,
due especially to increased levels of literacy and greater access to
reading materials.[58] In his larger discussion of the relation of language
use to nationalism, Anderson isolates poetry and song as linguistic
bridges for a 'special kind of contemporaneous community' that can
unify heterogeneous populations in a nation.[59] Other theorists of
nationalism have also underscored the apparently 'magical' properties
of poetry that allow it to suture core differences in the nation.[60]

    This focus on the phenomenal properties of poetry, however,
presents a rather uncomplicated reception model that links artists and
national audiences in a rather too straightforward fashion.[61] This
qualification is worth noting when turning to Burns and Scotland, for
both share a tangled nationalist legacy. Perhaps more than any other
Scottish historical figure, Burns has been frequently (and often
willfully) misunderstood by members of his nation. The need for
Burns to serve as a unifying national figure since the early nineteenth
century has resulted in a series of often mutually exclusive images of
the poet.[62] As Abizadeh remarks, 'any nation that lacks an overarching
myth of shared descent must emulate shared ethnicity by creating
some sort of myth of origin to do the job'.[63] In this operation, Burns
has fit the bill for generations of Scots who have sought to consolidate
their national identity by means of a distinctly 'Scottish' myth of
origin, particularly that supplied by the poet's vernacular works and
'folk' image.

    Envisioning Robert Burns as a 'cultural production' allows one a
much more constructive vantage point from which to survey and
assess his living and posthumous reputations and their role in unifying
the nation. What Rodden remarks of George Orwell can be equally
applied to Burns: 'The books alone cannot fully account for his
cultural influence or inspirational power' (8). Like Orwell, Robert
Burns is preceded and surrounded by a powerful reputation that exerts
considerable cultural influence. This reputation has largely been a
posthumous construction, often promoted by groups with warring
interests and specific needs and expectations for the poet to fulfill.
That the image of Burns produced by these groups distorts the reality

of his actual life is unsurprising, for the very nature of reputation-building derives from the purposeful selection and omission of key details from the subject's life or work. Conceiving of Burns as a 'cultural production' highlights the dynamic interplay of forces that have struggled to gain ascendancy and 'authorise' Burns's reputation as the 'genius of Scotland'.[64]

5. The Cultural Production of Robert Burns

This book examines how Burns has been literally used by cultural producers and consumers in Scotland. In particular, Burns's role as the 'genius of the nation' will be explored, with close attention to the social and cultural factors that governed his reception in late eighteenth- and early nineteenth-century Scotland. I begin with the clamor and confusion surrounding his sudden popularity in 1786 that followed the publication of his Kilmarnock edition; it was then that his persona as a 'heaven-taught ploughman' engendered an abiding perception of the poet as a *genius* of prodigious gifts and little education. Over the intervening years, especially after his death in 1796, Burns became a central figure in Scottish popular culture as well as in the literary field.

The roles ascribed to Burns by a variety of audiences will be analysed in depth; of particular note will be his attempts to be re-garded as a 'Scotch Bard' rather than 'heaven-taught ploughman'. This was a deliberate process of self-construction that Burns wished (and failed) to control during his lifetime. The attempts of Burns's self-designated 'brother poets' to attain similar recognition in the lit-erary field will also be discussed in relation to the persona of national *genius* assumed by Burns. As will be shown, such endeavours on the part of fellow labouring-class poets often proved to be futile and mis-guided, as Burns grew increasingly aloof from members of his own class as he sought to redefine himself as a 'Scotch Bard'.

This transformative process continued after his death, adding new inflections in his multiple personæ that attested to the poet's perceived character flaws. Such flaws (most notably, those involving his conduct with women) began to be ascribed to the 'failings of genius', witnessed in much nineteenth-century discussion of the poet. The figure of Burns grew more and more mythic for such audiences, leading elements of his biography to become subject to censorship and obfuscation.

Burns's inheritance for practicing Scottish poets in the early nineteenth century proved to be complex and unstable, as a concluding examination of James Hogg (the 'Ettrick Shepherd') will attest. I argue that Hogg's desire to be regarded as Burns's 'only worthy successor' was met with difficulty and frustration throughout his career, revealing that assuming his great predecessor's mantle was a perilous professional enterprise.

As a whole, the book seeks to assess the 'cultural production' of Burns during the first fifty years following his death, in order to evaluate and interpret the various permutations of the poet's iconic identity as the 'genius of Scotland'.

----

[1] See for example Harold Bloom, *Genius: A Mosaic of One Hundred Exemplary Creative Minds* (New York: Warner Books, 2002).

[2] For Foer, see Joyce Wadler, 'Public Lives: Seeking Grandfather's Savior, and Life's Purpose', *New York Times*, 24 April 2002 <http://www.nytimes.com/2002/04/24/nyregion/public-lives-seeking-grandfather-s-savior-and-life-s-purpose.html> [accessed 7 January 2014]; for Wallace, see Lev Grossman, 'Death of a Genius', *Time*, 18 September 2008, p. 56. For an ironist's appropriation of the concept, see Dave Eggers, *A Heartbreaking Work of Staggering Genius* (New York: Vintage, 2001).

[3] p. 56. For more on Wallace's counter-cultural persona and its relationship to his *genius*, see Troy Patterson, 'Infinitely Sad: David Foster Wallace, Self-Absorbed Genius', *Slate*, 15 September 2008 <http://www.slate.com/articles/news_and_politics/obit/2008/09/ infinitely_sad.html> [accessed 7 January 2014]; and D. T. Max, *Every Love Story is a Ghost Story: A Life of David Foster Wallace* (New York: Viking, 2012).

[4] See John Updike, 'Mixed Messages: "Extremely Loud and Incredibly Close"', *New Yorker*, 14 March 2005. <http://www.newyorker.com/archive/2005/03/14/050314crbo_books1> [accessed 7 January 2014].

[5] Harry Siegel, 'Extremely Cloying and Incredibly False', *New York Press*, 20 April 2005, <http://nypress.com/extremely-cloying-incredibly-false> [accessed 7 January 2014], para. 6 of 33; Matt Taibbi and others, '50 Most Loathsome New Yorkers — 2003', *New York Press*, 25 March 2003 <http://www.fineorsuperfine.com/newyorkpress5.html> [accessed 7 January 2014], para. 50 of 54.

---

[6] For a detailed discussion of the relationship of literary *genius* and celebrity, see Gillian Higgins, 'Celebrity, Politics and the Rhetoric of Genius' in Tom Mole, ed., *Romanticism and Celebrity Culture* (Cambridge: Cambridge University Press, 2009). See also Higgins's book on the subject, *Romantic Genius and the Literary Magazine: Biography, Celebrity and Politics* (London: Routledge, 2005).

[7] See *OED*, *genius*, defs 3b and 3d. See def. 1a for the term's usage in 'classical pagan belief'.

[8] See *OED*, def. 3b. *OED* credits Matthew Arnold for first using 'Zeitgeist' in a letter from 1848.

[9] See *OED*, def. 5. The earliest citation for this definition is from Henry Fielding's *Tom Jones* (1749); other eighteenth-century citations include William Sharpe's *A Dissertation upon Genius* (1755), Joseph Warton's *An Essay on the Genius and Writings of Pope* (1782), and Hugh Blair's *Lectures on Rhetoric and Belles-Lettres* (1783).

[10] Montesquieu, Charles-Louis de Secondat, Baron of la Brède and of, *My Thoughts*, ed. and trans. by Henry C. Clark (Indianapolis: Liberty Fund, 2012), p. 138.

[11] *Origin* (2006: 85).

[12] Ibid., p. 85, n. 1.

[13] *Sketches* (2007: 104), Vol I.

[14] p. 4. T. M. Devine identifies the author of *The True Scots Genius* as 'William Forbes of Disblair', author also of *A Pill for Pork-Eaters; or, A Scots Lancet for an English Swelling*. See T. M. Devine, *Scotland and the Union 1707-2007* (Edinburgh: Edinburgh University Press, 2008), p. 53, n. 30.

[15] William Forbes of Disblair, *A Pill for Pork-Eaters; or, A Scots Lancet for an English Swelling* (Edinburgh: Watson, 1705), p. 8.

[16] *Sketches* (2007: 104), Vol I.

[17] See Buchan, James, *Crowded with Genius, The Scottish Enlightenment: Edinburgh's Moment of the Mind* (New York: Harper Collins, 2003).

[18] Butler, Marilyn, 'Burns and Politics', in Robert Crawford, ed., *Robert Burns and Cultural Authority* (Iowa City: University of Iowa Press, 1997), pp. 86-112, 111.

[19] Liam Connell, 'Scottish Nationalism and the Colonial Vision of Scotland', *Interventions: International Journal of Postcolonial Studies*, 6.2 (2004), 252-63, 256. Further references to this article are given after quotations in the text. See also Connell's 'Modes of Marginality: Scottish Literature and the Uses of Postcolonial Theory', *Comparative Studies of South Asia, Africa, and the Middle East*, 23.1-2 (2003), 41-53.

[20] Robert Crawford's influence in contemporary Scottish Studies has been widespread; see for example his edited collection, *The Scottish Invention of*

English Literature (Cambridge: Cambridge University Press, 1998), as well as his two works of critical/literary history, *Devolving English Literature*, 2nd edn (Edinburgh: Edinburgh University Press, 2001) and *Scotland's Books: A History of Scottish Literature* (Oxford: Oxford University Press, 2009).

[21] See Andrew Noble, 'Burns and Scottish Nationalism' in Kenneth Simpson, ed., *Burns Now* (Edinburgh: Canongate, 2003).

[22] For discussion of the varying popular and commercial uses of Burns's image, see Andrews, 'Venders, Purchasers, Admirers: Burnsian "Men of Action" from the Nineteenth to the Twenty-First Century', *Scottish Literary Review*, 2.1 (2010), 97-115.

[23] See Butler (1997), p. 95. For discussions of Burns's politics, see also Colin Kidd, 'Burns and Politics' in Gerard Carruthers, ed., *The Edinburgh Companion to Robert Burns* (Edinburgh: Edinburgh University Press, 2009), pp. 61-73; Liam McIlvanney, *Burns the Radical: Poetry and Politics in Late Eighteenth-Century Scotland* (East Linton: Tuckwell, 2002), pp. 1-14; and Jeffrey Skoblow, 'Resisting the Powers of Calculation: A Bard's Politics', in Carol McGuirk, ed., *Critical Essays on Robert Burns* (London: Prentice Hall; New York: G.K. Hall, 1998), pp. 17-31.

[24] For discussion of this element of Burns's image, see Nigel Leask, *Robert Burns and Pastoral: Poetry and Improvement in Late Eighteenth-Century Scotland* (Oxford: Oxford University Press, 2010), pp. 1-3; Murray Pittock, '"A Long Farewell to All My Greatness": The History of the Reputation of Robert Burns', in Murray Pittock, ed., *Robert Burns and Global Culture* (Lewisburg: Bucknell University Press, 2011), pp. 25-46; and Gerard Carruthers, *Robert Burns*, pp. 43-61.

[25] Butler (1997: 103).

[26] *Distinction* (1984: 70).

[27] Pierre Bourdieu, *The Rules of Art: Genesis and Structure of the Literary Field*, trans. Susan Emanuel (Stanford: Stanford University Press, 1991), p. 231. Further references to this edition are given after quotations in the text.

[28] Robert Moore, 'Capital', in Michael Grenfell, ed., *Pierre Bourdieu: Key Concepts* (Durham: Acumen, 2011), pp. 103-04. For a more extensive discussion of the concept, see Guillory, *Cultural Capital*.

[29] Pierre Bourdieu, *Distinction: A Social Critique of the Judgement of Taste*, trans. by Richard Nice (Cambridge: Harvard University Press, 1984), pp. 2, 13.

[30] *Distinction* (1984: 11).

[31] Grenfell (2011: 160).

[32] *Distinction* (1984: 3).

[33] Ibid., p. 2.

[34] Ibid., p. 1.

[35] Moore (2011: 105).

---

[36] *Distinction* (1984: 170, 7).

[37] Patricia Thomson, in Grenfell (2011: 71).

[38] Pierre Bourdieu, 'The Forms of Capital' in Hugh Lauder and others, eds., *Education, Globalisation, and Social Change* (Oxford: Oxford University Press, 2006), p. 107.

[39] Nick Crossley, in Grenfell (2011: 96).

[40] Pierre Bourdieu, *The Field of Cultural Production: Essays on Art and Literature*, ed. by Randal Johnson (New York: Columbia University Press, 1993), p. 42. Emphasis mine. Bourdieu's use of the 'sacred' as a marker of legitimacy is particularly relevant when considering Burns's reputation in the nineteenth century.

[41] Johnson (1993: 60).

[42] Grenfell (2011: 160).

[43] For a discussion of Burns's 'distinctiveness' at the early stages of his career, see Leask, *Robert Burns and Pastoral*, pp. 1-14 and Pittock, *Scottish and Irish Romanticism*, pp. 144-65.

[44] p. 3. Further references to this edition are given after quotations in the text. For a discussion of literary reputation in the context of eighteenth-century Scottish verse, see Rhona Brown, *Robert Fergusson and the Scottish Periodical Press* (Farnham: Ashgate, 2012).

[45] See for example J. DeLancey Ferguson, 'They Censored Burns', *Scotland's Magazine*, 51 (1955), 38-40.

[46] See A.M. Kinghorn, 'The Literary and Historical Origins of the Burns Myth', *Dalhousie Review* 39 (1959), 76-85. See also Raymond Bentman, 'Robert Burns's Declining Fame', *Studies in Romanticism*, 2 (1975), pp.217-52.

[47] See Andrews, *Literary Nationalism in Eighteenth-Century Scottish Club Poetry* (Lewiston: Mellen, 2004), pp. 215-338 for discussion of Burns's nationalist relationship to various Scottish clubs in the eighteenth century.

[48] Arash Abizadeh, 'Liberal Nationalist versus Postnational Social Integration: On the Nation's Ethno-Cultural Particularity and "Concreteness"', *Nations and Nationalism*, 10.3 (2004), 231-50p. 234.

[49] For more on the relation of Burns's language usage to Scottish national identity, see Andrews, '"Almost the Same, but Not Quite": English Poetry by Eighteenth-Century Scots', *Eighteenth Century: Theory and* Interpretation, 47.1 (2006), 59-79; Robert Crawford, *Devolving English Literature*, 2nd edn (Edinburgh: Edinburgh University Press), pp. 88-110; and Alan Riach, 'MacDiarmid's Burns', in Robert Crawford, ed., *Robert Burns and Cultural Authority* (Iowa City: University of Iowa Press, 1997), pp. 198-215.

[50] As early as 1822, Hew Ainslie wrote a paradigmatic account linking land and poet, entitled *A Pilgrimage to the Land of Burns* (Deptford: the author, 1822).

[51] See for instance Carnie, 'Hugh MacDiarmid, Robert Burns and the Burns Federation', *Studies in Scottish Literature*, 30 (1998), 261-76; and Christopher A. Whatley, 'Robert Burns, Memorialization, and the "Heart-beatings" of Victorian Scotland', in Murray Pittock , ed., *Robert Burns and Global Culture* (Lewisburg: Bucknell University Press, 2011), pp. 204-28.

[52] See for example McCrone, *Understanding Scotland: The Sociology of a Nation*, 2nd edn (New York: Routledge, 2001); and Tom Nairn, *The Break-Up of Britain Crisis and Neo-Nationalism* (London: NLB and Verso, 1981).

[53] The classic exposition of this theory remains David Daiches, *The Paradox of Scottish Culture: The Eighteenth-Century Experience* (London: Oxford University Press, 1964).

[54] For a succinct analysis of this trend in Scottish criticism, see Carruthers, 'Burns and the Scottish Critical Tradition', in Kenneth Simpson, ed., *Love and Liberty, Robert Burns: A Bicentenary Celebration* (East Linton: Tuckwell, 1997), pp. 239-47.

[55] p. 32. Further references to this edition are given after quotations in the text. For the relevance of this point to Scots, see Charles Jones, *A Language Suppressed: The Pronunciation of the Scots Language in the Eighteenth Century* (Edinburgh: Donald, 1995), and John Corbett, *Language and Scottish Literature* (Edinburgh: Edinburgh University Press, 1997).

[56] For more on Watson's *Choice Collection*, see Harriet Harvey Wood, 'Burns and Watson's *Choice Collection*', *Studies in Scottish Literature*, 30 (1998), 19-30; for analysis of the role of 'Scotticisms' in eighteenth-century Scotland, see James Basker, 'Scotticisms and the Problem of Cultural Identity in Eighteenth-Century Britain', in John Dwyer and Richard B. Sher, eds, *Sociability and Society in Eighteenth-Century Scotland* (Edinburgh: Edinburgh University Press, 1993), pp. 82-95.

[57] For contemporary evidence of Burns's continuing international appeal, see Alker and Nelson, 'Transatlanticism and Beyond: Robert Burns and the World Wide Web', in Sharon Alker, Leith Davis, and Holly Faith Nelson, eds, *Robert Burns and Transatlantic Culture* (Farnham: Ashgate, 2012), pp. 247-60.

[58] On literacy and reading in eighteenth-century Scotland, see Pittock, *A New History of Scotland*, pp. 235-36; Rosalind Mitchison, *A History of Scotland*, 2nd edn (London: Routledge, 1997), pp. 350-53; and Devine, *The Scottish Nation: A History, 1707-2007* (Edinburgh: Edinburgh University Press 2008), pp. 84-104.

[59] Benedict Anderson, *Imagined Communities: Reflections on the Origin and Spread of Nationalism* (London: Verso, 1991), pp. 6, 145.

[60] See for instance Christopher Harvie, *Scotland and Nationalism: Scottish Society and Politics, 1707 to the Present* (New York: Routledge, 1998), p. 7; Harvie employs the famous phrase of Andrew Fletcher of Saltoun to describe

the 'healing' properties of a nation's ballads ('If a man were permitted to make all the ballads, he need not care who should make the laws of a nation').

[61] For instance, none of these theorists suggests that poetry offers imagined national communities anything beyond the experience or sensation of unity, which may be limited in duration and scope. Nor do they account for the role that verse might play as propaganda for particular political parties and/or causes.

[62] See for example Finlay, 'The Burns Cult and Scottish Identity in the Nineteenth and Twentieth Centuries', in Kenneth Simpson, ed., *Love and Liberty, Robert Burns: A Bicentenary Celebration* (East Linton: Tuckwell, 1997), pp. 69-78; Pittock, '"A Long Farewell"'; Roy, 'Editing Robert Burns in the Nineteenth Century', in Kenneth Simpson, ed., *Burns Now* (Edinburgh: Canongate, 1994), pp. 129-49; and Johnny Rodger and Gerard Carruthers, *Fickle Man: Robert Burns in the 21st Century* (Dingwall: Sandstone, 2009), 'Introduction'.

[63] Abizadeh (2004) p. 237.

[64] For more on views of Burns as a 'poetic genius', see Thomas Crawford, 'Burns, Genius and Major Poetry'; see also Carruthers, 'Introduction'.

Chapter One

Ploughman, Minstrel, Bard: Poetic Personæ and the Rise of Genius Theory

1. The Personæ of the 'Heaven-Taught Ploughman' and the 'Scotch Bard'

Much of Robert Burns's early public recognition centered on his characterisation as a 'heaven-taught ploughman'. Perceived as unlearned and divinely inspired, the 'heaven-taught ploughman' presumably sprung naturally from the Scottish soil, speaking the language of everyday Scots and representing their simple experiences and desires in artless verse. A key feature of this persona was its class dimension, whereby the ploughman (decidedly gendered as male) existed as a labourer within a rural landscape in much the same fashion as a pastoral shepherd. However, its principal difference from pastoral tropes resided in the ploughman's *genius*, coded as 'heaven-taught'. This facet of the persona linked Burns with other famed labouring-class anomalies from the eighteenth century such as Stephen Duck (the 'Thresher Poet'), footman-turned-publisher Robert Dodsley, the bricklayer poet Henry Jones, and Ann Yearsley, the 'poetical milkwoman'. The ploughman, like the thresher or bricklayer, was an essential component of the label, qualifying 'heaven-taught' exceptionality as an interesting class aberration worthy of notice.

Unlike Theocritean idylls with their cast of lounging and loving shepherds and shepherdesses, the eighteenth-century variant strongly accented the labour that defined the poet's core identity. This cultural production, though not unique to Burns, proved to be life-long and ultimately distressing to the poet as he sought to redefine his public personæ. The 'heaven-taught ploughman' persona owed much to the publicity generated by early critics like Henry Mackenzie, whose review of Burns's 1786 Kilmarnock edition in the *Lounger* coined the expression.[1] Though not without reservations, Burns recognised the label's utility in attracting a sizable audience within (and without) Scotland. To the extent that he could (or desired to) control how he was perceived at this early stage in his career, Burns initially bought

in to ready-made labels like the 'heaven-taught ploughman' before
trying to refashion existing personæ like the minstrel and the bard. His
poetic aspirations from the beginning were grand indeed. One often
forgets Burns's immense confidence and brash desire for fame in
1786, when he began to see a future for himself in Scotland rather
than in the West Indies. Burns cannot be accused of timidity or false
modesty in these early years; he desired to be the voice of Scotland,
and he planned to use whatever advantages (of his own or others' in-
vention) to achieve that end.

He made few inroads challenging the 'heaven-taught ploughman'
persona in the first few years of his fame. In some respects, he had
publicly endorsed this representation in his preface to the 1787 Edin-
burgh edition, where he claims that 'the Poetical Genius of my
Country found me as the prophetic bard Elijah did Elisha – at the
plough; and threw her inspiring mantle over me'.[2] The appetite for
prodigious poets from the Scottish countryside was not yet whetted by
the hue and cry surrounding the Ossian controversy of the 1760s.
Even into the early nineteenth century, James Macpherson still had
defenders in his native country, who sought to validate Ossian's epic,
primitivist persona against all skeptics.[3] As will be shown, Burns
sought to restructure his poetic identity by assuming a different
persona – the 'Scotch Bard' – while still banking on the publicity
generated by his status as a 'heaven-taught ploughman'. This process
continued into the 1790s, after Burns had established his reputation
and was employing his creative energies collecting Scottish songs.

From quite early in his career, Burns wanted to be remembered
as a 'Scotch Bard', a wish he announced in an often-quoted letter to
correspondent Frances Dunlop: 'The appelation of, a Scotch Bard, is
by far my highest pride; to continue to deserve it is my most exalted
ambition – Scottish scenes, and Scottish story are the themes I could
wish to sing'.[4] However, as Robert Crawford notes, 'as soon as
[Burns] had established himself as 'bard', he began making fun of the
title'.[5] Nevertheless, the term appealed to Burns in a genuine way.
Crawford's biography offers some interesting possibilities for Burns's
choice of 'bard' to designate his poetic role and vocation: Burns bor-
rowed 'a particular word from Fergusson and started calling himself a
"bardie" […] an affectionate diminutive of "bard", a term familiar to
Burns from many sources, but most redolent of his enthusiasm for the
poems of Ossian' (154).

However, the term was not merely descriptive. Crawford states that for Burns, 'to be a bard was not just a pose; it required artistic finesse' (278). Being a bard also required a strong sense of purpose; although bards could be anonymous, their poetic role and function were decidedly public and unequivocally nationalist. To write as a bard involved fulfilling and enacting one's poetic duty of remembering and recording the nation's past. For Burns, achieving such goals would gratify his 'highest pride' and satisfy his 'most exalted ambition'. However, as with much else in his career and biography, his efforts at redefining his poetic persona would ultimately prove unsuccessful. Despite his best efforts, Burns's persona as an unlearned yet divinely taught labouring-class anomaly persisted during (and long after) his life, greatly influencing generations of readers and critics who would construe the poet's legacy with such limiting views of his *genius* squarely in mind.

2. The Cultural Legacy of James Beattie's *The Minstrel*

Among Burns's choices for poetic personæ, there were two distinct categories that had a strong Scottish inflection. The first was the minstrel, popularised by Scottish poet and philosopher James Beattie in his lengthy poem *The Minstrel; or the Progress of Genius* (1771/2). The second was the bard, a figure that Burns aspired to be from a very early stage; in his preface to the Kilmarnock edition, he refers to himself twice with this term, using it to oppose 'the public character of an Author'.[6] Burns's knowledge of the bardic persona derived not only from the works of Thomas Gray (a poet he greatly admired) but also the tradition of Scottish epic. Burns cited the importance in particular of Blind Harry's *Wallace*, which he read as a young man in the translation by William Hamilton of Gilbertfield. Burns also knew Beattie's poem very well, alluding to it in both his verse and correspondence.[7]

However, the figures of bard and minstrel were not synonymous during this period; while they retain a degree of similarity, they each performed different cultural functions. The *Oxford English Dictionary* defines 'minstrel' generically as 'a person employed by a patron to provide entertainment by singing, playing music, storytelling, juggling, etc'.[8] On the other hand, 'bard' is defined with specific reference to history and nationality as 'an ancient Celtic order of minstrel-poets, whose primary function appears to have been to compose and sing (usually to the harp) verses celebrating the achievements of chiefs and warriors'. Thus, although both minstrels and bards are invested with great communal significance, they perform for very different purposes, the minstrel for the pleasure of a specific audience and the bard for the preservation of national lore and legend. As Katie Trumpener notes, 'bardic performance binds the nation across time and social divides [...and] reanimates a national landscape', while 'the minstrel evokes the adventurous life of a strolling poet'.[9]

The distinction between minstrel entertainers and bardic chroniclers is essential, for it underscores the nationalist component of poetic personæ. Burns preserves this distinction in his use of the terms, overwhelmingly employing 'bard' over 'minstrel' in his poetic diction.[10] Indeed, in the literature of the eighteenth century, 'bard' has a decided edge as the preferred poetic term.[11] As will be shown, the figure of the minstrel could not express the depth and breadth of Burns's poetic ambitions. His selection of the bardic persona reveals his efforts at poetic self-construction, based upon his awareness of the limitations of both the minstrel and 'heaven-taught ploughman' personæ. Burns's desire to be seen as a 'Scotch Bard' needs to be regarded as a self-conscious choice with national implications.

In this respect, the influences of Allan Ramsay and Robert Fergusson upon Burns have been amply studied, particularly their roles as predecessors writing in Scots.[12] While their significance certainly cannot be overstated, the relevance of other poets, especially those writing in English, to Burns's poetic self-definition is equally important to recognise. Burns repeatedly referenced English-language poets, both Scottish and English, in his verse and letters and employed a wide range of allusions from their works as well. They run the gamut of British authors, including such notables as Pope, Gray, and William Shenstone, as well as Scottish poets like James Thomson and Robert Blair, among many others.[13] From this considerable pool of writers, James Beattie's influence upon Burns deserves further consideration.

In rather uncanny fashion, Burns and Beattie shared similar narrative paths to literary recognition. Both were great success stories in eighteenth-century Scotland, hailing from the provinces and achieving early, widespread fame for their poetry. While Beattie is now best remembered for his works of philosophy, his verse (especially *The Minstrel*) was enormously popular throughout the late eighteenth and nineteenth centuries.[14] Carol McGuirk has highlighted the importance of the connection between Burns and Beattie, stating that *The Minstrel* 'offers some fascinating parallels to Burns's career as a bard'.[15] However, despite its significance as both text and cultural figure, Burns had serious reservations about *The Minstrel* and sought to be regarded as a 'bard' in deliberate contradistinction to the minstrel persona.

In addition to the important matter of Burns's preference, it is worth considering some of the central reasons underpinning the eight-eenth-century cultural valuation of bards over minstrels. It may be, as Maureen McLane has argued, that 'compared to bards, minstrels were less obviously heroic or tragic; they lacked the grandeur of Macpher-son's Ossian, Gray's Welsh Suicide, or Blake's Ancient Bard'. She notes that when directly compared with bards' purposeful characteri-sation, 'minstrels are ambiguous figures'.[16] Such ambiguity most likely derived from contesting definitions and perceptions of min-strels, particularly regarding their role within their respective commu-nities. Beattie's source text for *The Minstrel*, Thomas Percy's 'An Es-say on the English Minstrels', claims that minstrels 'were an order of men in the middle ages, who united the arts of poetry and music, and sung verses to the harp of their own composing'.[17] In addition, Percy states that 'their skill was considered as something divine; their per-sons were deemed sacred; their attendance was solicited by kings; and they were every where loaded with honours and rewards' (xxiv). Their cultural valuation was so great that Percy claims 'the profession of oral itinerant Poet was held in the utmost reverence' (xxiv).

Percy's chief antagonist, Joseph Ritson, believed otherwise; as Kathryn Sutherland states, he was 'adamant that [...] the minstrel was never a figure of dignity'.[18] Regarding Percy's view of minstrels' sig-nificance within medieval communities, Ritson countered 'that a sin-gle province should, at that or any other time, contain [...] prodigious multitudes of itinerant minstrels, is an assertion as hypothetic and insupportable, as it is incredible and absurd'.[19] As Henry Burd claims, Ritson believed that English minstrels 'did not compose but only sang and played' existing songs. He further states that 'Ritson did not be-lieve the minstrels sufficient to account for minstrelsy', arguing that 'it was absurd to think of the minstrels as the authors of fabulous nar-

ratives several thousand lines in length'. Though he did not concede in
full to Ritson's counterarguments, Percy redefined the term minstrel
'to comply with Ritson's criticism'.[20]

Beattie was somewhere between these two extreme positions. He
accorded the minstrel the dignity that Ritson disavowed, but he was
unwilling to grant the figure the communal value envisioned by Percy.
Beattie was most interested in the minstrel as a creative individual; in
his construction of the minstrel, the figure sought not to entertain oth-
ers but to express the 'progress' of his own *genius*. This is made plain
in Beattie's preface to *The Minstrel*, where he writes that

The design was, to trace the progress of a Poetical Genius, born in a rude age, from
the first dawning of fancy and reason, till that period at which he may be supposed
capable of appearing in the world as a Minstrel, that is, as an itinerant Poet and Musi-
cian; – a character which, according to the notions of our forefathers, was not only
respectable, but sacred.[21]

The 'character' of such a 'Poetical Genius' is as much the subject of
the poem as is the minstrel's performance of verse and song.

Beattie further explained his conception of the minstrel's 'sacred'
character in a letter to John Gregory: 'The hint of the subject was
taken from Percy's "Essay on the English Minstrels". The first canto
is a description of a poetical visionary in a solitary country, who de-
rives most of his acquisitions in knowledge from his own observa-
tions'. This stage of the minstrel's development would be of much
interest to later Romantic poets, many of whom regarded *The Minstrel*
as a blueprint for their own explorations of self. Beattie further ex-
plained that 'in the second canto, I propose to introduce my Visionary
to a Hermit, who is to give him sundry instructions relating to arts,
literature, and human life'.[22] In terms of plot, this is the extent of *The
Minstrel* as it was written and published. Edwin, the titular minstrel,
encounters a hermit who discourages his poetic endeavours.

However, Beattie had plans for a third canto that would have
thrust Edwin into a warring, hostile world. In a letter to the poet
Thomas Blacklock, Beattie outlined this proposed third canto:

The poor swain acquiesces in [the hermit's] advice, and resolves to follow his father's
employment [as a shepherd]; when, on a sudden, the country is invaded by the Danes,
or English borderers, (I know not which,) and he is stript of all his little fortune, and
obliged by necessity to commence minstrel.[23]

This third canto was never written, however, and one is subsequently left with a fragmentary depiction of minstrelsy. As depicted by Beattie, the minstrel is 'itinerant', a trait that highlights his nomadic nature and defines his poetic status. If Edwin had indeed 'commenced' minstrelsy by 'necessity' in the unwritten third canto, he would have travelled and performed for his livelihood. Unlike the bardic persona, Beattie's minstrel would have been expressly linked to other types of entertainers and art forms that exist within the literary marketplace.

This is also the case in Percy's essay, where he remarks that 'the minstrels and harpers of the Anglo-Saxons' had 'talents [...] chiefly calculated to entertain and divert' (xxv). Such minstrels were capable (in Percy's words) of eliciting 'the most expressive of that popular mirth and jollity, that strong sensation of delight, which is felt by un-polished and simple minds' (xxvi). Thus, in the unwritten third canto, the 'rude age' into which Beattie's 'poetical Genius' has been thrust would have forced him to ply his poetic trade for the 'delight' of 'un-polished and simple minds'. This is hardly an inspiring scenario, one that perhaps speaks more to Beattie's own misgivings about poetry as a vocation rather than the historical veracity of minstrels.

That said, such an outcome is not found in *The Minstrel*; as Sutherland remarks, 'Edwin is not, during the course of the narrative as we have it, a minstrel by employment, but by temperament'.[24] In the first stanza of the poem, the speaker depicts this temperament as a kind of curse:

Ah! who can tell how hard it is to climb
The steep where Fame's proud temple shines afar;
Ah! who can tell how many a soul sublime
Has felt the influence of malignant star,
And waged with fortune an eternal war. (1.1)

Harassed by this 'malignant star', Edwin is compelled both to 'wage war' with fortune and climb the steep ascent to 'Fame's proud tem-ple'. Neither act is represented as a salubrious enterprise, both ap-pearing to denigrate the striving of 'sublime souls' who seek to gain recognition.

Nevertheless, Edwin is admonished to appreciate his gift. Perhaps he is addressing himself in these lines, or perhaps it is the author speaking to an earlier incarnation of his poetic self:

Know thine own worth, and reverence the lyre.
Wilt thou debase the heart which God refined?
No; let thy heaven-taught soul to heaven aspire,
To fancy, freedom, harmony, resign'd;
Ambition's groveling crew for ever left behind. (1.7)

These lines may have inspired Henry Mackenzie's description of Burns as a 'heaven-taught ploughman', but Edwin's 'heaven-taught soul' had several mid-century poetic predecessors: 'Beattie innovated within an earlier series of Spenserian poems concerned with aesthetic education'.[25] The most influential poem in this regard was Thomas Gray's 'Elegy Written in a Country Churchyard', which set precedent for a similarly distressed, aloof poet at odds with the world.

Like the funerary denouement of Gray's 'Elegy', Beattie's model of 'aesthetic education' offers little in the way of positive encouragement for would-be minstrels. The speaker can only advise Edwin to hope for the best, with no guarantee of happiness or success:

O Edwin! while thy heart is yet sincere,
Th'assaults of discontent and doubt repel:
Dark even at noontide is our mortal sphere;
But let us hope; to doubt is to rebel;
Let us exult in hope, that all shall be well. (1.47)

In addition to tendering such doubtful consolation, the poem suggests that pleasure itself may be a harmful delusion and that the only real happiness is actually unhappiness: 'Ah what is mirth but turbulence unholy, / When with the charm compared of heavenly melancholy!' (1.55). Given such sentiments, one can easily deduce why this poem attracted the attention of later poets like Wordsworth.[26]

The intensely personal nature of *The Minstrel* appealed to many readers, as Beattie acknowledged in a letter to Elizabeth Hay. He writes,

I find you are willing to suppose that in Edwin I have given only a picture of myself as I was in my younger days. I confess the supposition is not groundless. I have made him take pleasure in the scenes in which I took pleasure, and entertain sentiments similar to those of which, even in my early youth, I had repeated experience.

Beattie recounts such scenes from his childhood with embarrassment, further claiming that at the time, 'I did not understand my own feelings' and that 'I am ashamed to write so much on a subject so trifling as myself'.[27] For Burns and other readers, however, this may have been one of the key attractions of *The Minstrel*, for it offered aspiring poets a template for their own experimentation.

Despite its appeal for young writers, Beattie did not want readers to fully identify with Edwin – at least not with the version of Edwin represented in the first canto of *The Minstrel*. The second canto recounts Edwin's tutelage by the hermit, a disillusioned man whose sole consolation is the study of philosophy and history. The hermit instructs Edwin,

To those, whom Nature taught to think and feel,
Heroes, alas! are things of small concern;
Could History man's secret heart reveal,
And what imports a heaven-born mind to learn,
Her transcripts to explore what bosom would not yearn! (2.35)

The majority of Book Two aims to teach Edwin to enlarge his 'heaven-born mind' by learning those 'transcripts', fully described in Beattie's following footnote for stanza 46 as 'the influence of the Philosophick Spirit, in humanizing the mind, and preparing it for intellectual exertion and delicate pleasure: – in exploring, by the help of geometry, the system of the universe; – in banishing superstition; – – in promoting [...] moral and political science'.

Beattie's abiding principle appears to be that minstrelsy must be driven out or, better yet, tamed by the 'philosophic spirit' of enlightened education. Thus the hermit admonishes Edwin,

Hail sacred Polity, by Freedom rear'd!
Hail sacred Freedom, when by Law restrain'd!
Without you what were man? A groveling herd
In darkness, wretchedness, and want enchain'd. (2.44)

Such dismal conclusions about the fate of the 'uneducated man' did not affect the poem's major interest for Romantic poets, for even in its unfinished state, Beattie's *Minstrel* exercised a powerful cultural influence. The figure of the minstrel as a disaffected 'poetical genius' would appeal to many budding poets throughout the late eighteenth and early nineteenth centuries.

As a young man, Burns felt an intensely personal connection with Edwin, easily envisioning himself in the guise of Beattie's minstrel. Like his zeal for Henry Mackenzie's *The Man of Feeling*,

Burns's sentiments in favor of *The Minstrel* may seem a little excessive to later readers. Robert Crawford notes that 'Robert quoted with enthusiasm to Dugald Stewart lines from James Beattie's poem about the growth of a poet, *The Minstrel*' (138). Burns wrote a brief poem to Susan Logan that was enclosed with a gift of Beattie's *Poems*, claiming that 'I send you more than India boasts / In Edwin's simple tale' (and hoping that 'May, dear Maid, each Lover prove / An Edwin still to you').[28] Burns also acknowledges Beattie's influence in 'The Vision', where he writes that 'sweet harmonious BEATTIE sung / His "Minstrel lays"' (62, 171-72). Everard King suggests that 'Burns's preeminent role as the national bard of Scotland was realised to some extent by means of his imitation of Beatte's minstrel'.[29]

One should not be too swayed by the apparent extent of Beattie's influence on Burns. Although Burns may have been indebted to *The Minstrel* and the inspiring figure of Edwin, he did not share Beattie's views about poetry. The minstrel, as conceived and represented by Beattie, is a solitary individual, engaged in entertaining others out of necessity. In addition, Beattie's minstrel is in serious need of enlightenment that will disabuse him of the disposition (and desire) to express himself in verse. To Beattie, writing poetry was solely the work of imagination, having little bearing on one's actual existence. As he observed of Macpherson's *Ossian*, 'it is the poet's business, not to pourtray the characters as they really exist, (which is left to the historian,) but to represent them such as they might have existed'.[30] Indeed, in his 'Essay on Poetry and Music', Beattie attests that 'the end of poetry is, to PLEASE. Verses, if pleasing, may be poetical, though they convey little or no instruction; but verses, whose sole merit is, that they convey instruction, are not poetical'.[31] It is none too surprising then that Beattie's literary efforts trailed off once his more 'serious' endeavours in writing and teaching philosophy occupied his time.

3. Burns's 'Scottish Bard' Persona in 'The Vision'

It is my contention that Burns rejected the minstrel persona because his views diverged too greatly from Beattie's, especially the belief that poetry existed solely to 'please' readers. Although Burns recognised that his work could certainly 'please' readers, he had higher ambitions than simply gratifying this desire. For instance, in a letter to John Moore from 1787, Burns offered a deceptive self-assessment of his place in literary history:

> I know very well, the novelty of my character has by far the greatest share in the learned and polite notice I have lately got, and in a language where Pope and Churchill have raised the laugh, and Shenstone and Gray drawn the tear; where Thomson and Beattie have painted the landskip, and Littleton and Collins described the heart; I am not vain enough to hope for distinguished Poetic fame.[32]

While Burns acknowledges that the 'novelty of my character' has been a major element of his publicity (nicely coded as 'learned and polite notice'), his elaborate allusiveness belies his purportedly 'heaven-taught' character. This example is one of many where Burns reveals his extensive knowledge of mainstream British literature, which he exhibits with precise description of each poet's distinctive style.[33] In addition, his intertextual referencing allows him to individuate his own poetic practice, which he situates within a distinctly Scottish literary history. Despite his asseverations, it is clear that he is in fact 'vain enough to hope for distinguished Poetic fame'.

This technique is most apparent in 'The Vision', a lengthy poem that appeared midway through the Kilmarnock edition of *Poems* (1786). In an elaborate mock-historical manner, this work recounts Burns's seemingly humble placement within the continuum of Scottish national poets. As previously noted, the poem alludes to *The Minstrel* but decidedly emphasises Burns's identity as a bard. In choosing the vision as the literary frame of this poem, Burns was borrowing a well-worn rhetorical device much favored by nationally-minded poets. Indeed, the dream vision in the British tradition has supported prophetic utterance, political rant, and imaginative chronicle, often at one and the same time.[34]

In the context of Scottish verse, Allan Ramsay's 'The Vision' offered a compelling blueprint for Burns's poem with its explorations of the nation's past. In 1724, Ramsay published his second anthology of Scottish poems, *The Ever Green*. The collection garnered attention for its inclusion of a poem called 'The Vision'. Purportedly penned by a medieval poet dubbed only 'Ar. Scott', the poem is a fascinating pre-Ossian forgery in which Scotland's political present is measured up against its past.[35] Ramsay argued (in the guise of 'Ar. Scott') that the post-Union Scottish present needed to be re-envisioned by

comparison to an expressly-imagined, radically different Scottish
past.

Burns's 'Vision' is both simpler and subtler than Ramsay's.
Aptly described by McGuirk as 'the most eclectic of Burns's early
works' (37), 'The Vision' directly borrows from Macpherson's *Ossian*
by using 'duans'.[36] In Burns's self-styled 'digressive' poem, however,
one does not find poetic fragments detailing an epic national past;
rather the focus is on the visionary experience of a single individual, a
'Scotch bard'. As Robert Crawford notes in *The Bard*, 'in "The
Vision" Burns confirms his bardic status and enunciates what it might
mean' (192). Burns's bard complains that

I had spent my youthfu' prime,
An' done nae-thing,
But stringing blethers up in rhyme
For fools to sing. (62, 21-24)

His feelings about the value of his 'rhyme' are tonally ambivalent
(akin to similar passages in his 'Epistle to Davie, a Brother Poet'), but
his pessimism in 'The Vision' is short-lived.

He is soon visited by Coila, described as 'a tight, outlandish
Hizzie' (41) whom the speaker takes 'for some Scottish Muse' (51).
She admonishes the speaker for his self-pity and offers solace:

[No] longer mourn thy fate is hard,
Thus poorly low!
I come to give thee such reward,
As we bestow. (141-44)

In the second duan, Coila explains the system of spirits that governs
the unseen world. McGuirk notes that Burns's idea 'evidently draws,
though not comically, on Pope's system of presiding spirits in *The
Rape of the Lock*', where Burns's protagonist is guided by a lower
spirit who inspires rustic bards (39).

After identifying herself, Coila spends the last seventy-five plus
lines explaining how and why she has watched over the poem's
speaker, who is clearly meant to be Burns himself. Significantly, Coila
does not instruct Burns to wield arms in his nation's defense but ex-
horts him instead 'to pour in song, / To soothe thy flame' (185-86).
Within a lengthy encomium, Burns measures the achievement of his

poetic predecessor Beattie: 'Hence, sweet harmonious BEATTIE sung / His "Minstrel lays;"' (171-72). Crawford suggests that by 'linking himself to Beattie's Minstrel; bonding his poem to the work of Ossian; [and] having his muse hail him as "Bard"', Burns is signaling 'his ambition to be known as a bard or minstrel singing for his people' (192).

This seems accurate to an extent, but the subtlety of Burns's 'Vision' rests in its literal equation of Scottish nationalism with poetic achievement. Scottish history becomes the province not of minstrel entertainers but expressly bards, who serve as visionary figures tasked with interpreting Scottish history and translating its meaning for the present. Where other 'Vision' poems like Ramsay's rely on a literal rereading of the past as a blueprint for the present, Burns's focus is on the figurative future guaranteed by the past. To Coila, Burns's 'poetic destiny' as a bard must be achieved not for his own personal sake or gain but for his nation's. She explains to him that of her fellow spirits,

They Scotia's Race among them share;
Some fire the Sodger on to dare;
Some rouse the Patriot up to bare
Corruption's heart:
Some teach the Bard, a darling care,
The tuneful Art. (109-14)

Just as he had disclosed in his letter to Dunlop, Burns is confirmed in his poetic ambition to be considered a 'Scotch Bard', in this case tutored by a muse whose very purpose is to teach him 'the tuneful Art'.

In the poem's most famous lines, Coila unveils the duties of the Scottish bard, a figure whose 'bliss' (214) overmatches that of 'kings' (215). She entrusts Burns with the duty to 'preserve the dignity of Man, / With Soul erect' (219-20), further urging him to 'trust, the Universal Plan / Will all protect' (221-22). Burns took this directive seriously in the years following his initial bout of celebrity, and his song-collecting projects in the 1790s are in great respect his 'bardic' contribution to his nation. As will be shown, he faced many obstacles along the way, none more daunting than the early fame he achieved as a 'heaven-taught ploughman'. The notion of *genius* that informs this persona would resonate throughout Burns's reception history, due in large part to the term's varied and complex lineage in Scottish thought.

4. The Rise of Genius Theory in Eighteenth-Century Philosophy

As in so many other facets of his poetic career, Burns's ambitions were not matched by his early reception from British critics and readers. Among fellow Scots, Burns was frequently perceived as a prodigious anomaly, a poet of great genius whose gifts were of divine origin. While his efforts to be recognised as a 'Scotch Bard' met with some success later in his career, his early fame as a 'heaven-taught ploughman' did not enable him to become financially solvent upon his writing alone.[37] The process of achieving recognition with his self-defined bardic persona involved deliberate artistic choices that led him to abandon the type of poetry that had made him famous and concentrate his efforts on collecting Scottish songs. The aura of *genius* bedeviled his project from the start, for the concept was a singularly polysemous explanatory tool for critics of labouring-class verse.[38] Confronting the phenomenon of Burns as poet, in all the flashy display of his publicity, forced many of these critics to explore the possibilities of *genius* as a literary category of definition, one especially useful for accounting for class anomalies like Burns.

The class dimension complicated such applications of genius theory as Beattie's, who sought in *The Minstrel* to explain the 'progress of genius' without explicit reference to the figure's socio-cultural identity. For Beattie, the minstrel exhibits signs of genius that are first evidenced through poetic behaviors such as emotional responsiveness to landscape and other typical triggers. The 'progress' narrative leads the minstrel to privilege intellect over emotion, whereby self-definition as minstrel serves as a vital (though temporary) stage in the development of the figure's moral character. Hence Beattie's linking of minstrels to earlier stages of human progress, where their social roles as entertainers to the court fix them in historical time.[39] Beattie's view of *genius* as a historically discrete category was one of many competing views of the concept in the works of Enlightenment thinkers, whose perceptions and explanations sought to stabilise the conceptual ambiguity of genius as a definitional category.[40]

genius was readily applied throughout the eighteenth century to characterise the spirit of a people or an age, denoting its overall aptitude or feeling. In *Characteristicks of Men, Manners, Opinions, Times* (1711), Anthony Ashley Cooper, Third Earl of Shaftesbury describes the 'genius of the nation' that is illustrated by the works of early poets. He begins with a complaint about the present age, suitably contrasted with warrior-like poets of the past who had once stormed the 'vacant Field' of literary production:

One wou'd expect it of our Writers, that if they had real Ability, they shou'd draw the WORLD to them; and not meanly sute [sic] themselves to the WORLD, in its weak State. We may justly indeed make allowances for the Simplicity of those early Genius's of our Nation, who after so many barbarous Ages, when Letters lay yet in their Ruins, made bold Excursions into a vacant Field, to seize the Posts of Honour, and attain the Stations which were yet unpossess'd by the Wits of their own Country.[41]

The notion of writing as a form of martial combat is memorably drawn here, evoking the 'epic' battles of early bards to 'attain the Stations' of literary 'Honour'.

As he continues his invective against the literary field of his day, Shaftesbury introduces a key debate about poetic *genius* that would occupy the minds of many thinkers throughout the period. This involved the contrast between 'rules of art' and 'divine inspiration', where *genius* trumps craft and all its attendant artifice. He writes with some disdain that

There can be nothing more ridiculous than to hear our POETS, in their Prefaces, talk of Art and Structure; whilst in their Pieces they perform as ill as ever, and with as little regard to those profess'd Rules of Art, as the honest BARDS, their Predecessors, who had never heard of any such Rules. (I, 163)

Shaftesbury's view of 'honest BARDS' in this passage conforms to his contemporaries' perception of ancient verse as more 'genuine' than that of the moderns by being less rule-bound and formally unmediated.

However, Shaftesbury's argument develops unpredictably in *Characteristicks*, for by the third volume, he has changed his mind entirely. 'Rules of Art' have now become vital to the production of poetry, muddying the waters between 'inspired geniuses' and rule-bound pretenders. He claims that 'An English AUTHOR wou'd be all GENIUS' and 'wou'd reap the Fruits of Art; but without Study, Pains, or Application' (III, 159). Summoning the discourse of authenticity (which would be regularly invoked in later criticism of eighteenth-century labouring-class poetry), Shaftesbury debunks the 'English AUTHOR' who pretends to be a *genius*. Such a risible figure even hedges his bets, for Shaftesbury claims that this poet 'thinks it necessary, indeed, (lest his Learning shou'd be call'd in question) to show the World that he errs knowingly against the Rules of Art' (III, 159). 'Honest BARDS' are quite removed from this harangue against poets who seek to manufacture a persona (and forge a reputation) based on the ever-changing tastes that inform literary production.

Among Scottish thinkers, David Hume also used *genius* to describe various attributes of nations and their citizens. In his *History of England* (1754-62), Hume alludes to 'the barbarous and violent genius of the age' of Henry II's rule, a time when 'trial by battle [...] had become the general method for deciding all important controversies'.[42] In *Treatise of Human Nature* (1739-40), he employs the concept generically to characterise an individual's temperament: 'There are few persons, who are satisfy'd with their own character, or genius, or fortune, who are not desirous of shewing themselves to the world, and of acquiring the love and approbation of mankind'. This definition is modified further in the *Treatise*, where Hume compares learning and genius as 'pleasant and magnificent objects [...] adapted to pride and vanity'.[43] In other works, however, Hume highlights the exceptionality of the concept as it applies to gifted individuals and overrides his skepticism of genius as a source of vanity only.

For instance, in *Enquiry Concerning Human Understanding* (1748), Hume states that 'each adventurous genius will still leap at the arduous prize, and find himself stimulated, rather than discouraged, by the failures of his predecessors'.[44] The roots of genius theory as it was used to explain Robert Burns can be discerned in Hume's description of genius as 'a kind of magical faculty in the soul, which, tho' it always be most perfect in the greatest geniuses, and is properly what we call a genius, is however inexplicable by the utmost efforts of human understanding'.[45] In other works, Hume explored the peculiarly 'literary' dimension of genius. In his essay 'Of the Middle Stage of Life', he considers the place and utility of 'geniuses' in the remote past. He writes, 'Were we to distinguish the Ranks of Men by their Genius and Capacity more, than by their Virtue and Usefulness to the Public, great Philosophers wou'd certainly challenge the first Rank, and must be plac'd at the Top of human Kind'.[46]

Given his own status, Hume rates the 'genius and capacity' of poets just below that of 'great' philosophers: 'Great Poets may challenge the second Place; and this Species of Genius, tho' rare, is yet much more frequent than the former' (550). Indeed, in his essay 'Of Eloquence', he finds that poetic genius is worthy of recognition throughout history, especially for its role in promoting appreciation of 'correct' taste. He states,

It is seldom or never found, when a false taste in poetry or eloquence prevails among any people, that it has been preferred to a true, upon comparison and reflection. It commonly prevails merely from the ignorance of the true, and from the want of perfect models, to lead men into a juster apprehension, and more refined relish of those productions of genius. When these appear, they soon unite all suffrages in their favour, and, by their natural and powerful charms, gain over, even the most prejudiced, to the love and admiration of them. (107)

In this model, poetry performs aesthetic and moral functions by providing readers knowledge of the 'true' as well as 'refined relish' for 'productions of genius'.

He further characterises *genius* in this essay by claiming that one can recognise 'true genius' easily due to its inherently 'superior' nature: 'Whenever the true genius arises, he draws to him the attention of every one, and immediately appears superior to his rival' (107). He distinguishes the lineaments of *genius* in greater depth in his essay 'The Rise of Arts and Sciences', where he writes that 'a noble emulation is the source of every excellence. Admiration and modesty naturally extinguish this emulation. And no one is so liable to an excess of admiration and modesty, as a truly great genius' (135). Hume's notion of *genius* as spurring emulation by an 'excess of admiration and modesty' coincides with the thinking of literary critics and philosophers throughout the century, where it eventually takes on overtones of excessive passion (and later for Burns, excessive 'immorality' and 'irreligion').

In his essay 'The Stoic', Hume follows Shaftesbury's lead in arguing the merits of 'rules of art' that should regulate the productions of *genius*. If not, he argues, the 'richest genius' will produce 'poisons'. He writes, 'The richest genius, like the most fertile soil, when uncultivated, shoots up the rankest weeds; and instead of vines and olives for the pleasure and use of man, produces, to its slothful owner, the most abundant crop of poisons' (148). In his essay 'The Rise of Arts and Sciences', Hume further speculates about the need to 'cultivate' the 'natural genius of mankind', which he finds in need of 'patterns' and 'objects of imitation' that will guide its development:

If the natural genius of mankind be the same in all ages, and in almost all countries, (as seems to be the truth) it must very much forward and cultivate this genius, to be possessed of patterns in every art, which may regulate the taste, and fix the objects of imitation. (135)

Much as Voltaire advised readers to 'cultivate our garden' at the end of *Candide* (1759), Hume tenders the similar suggestion for the maintenance of the 'richest genius', which is in constant need of 'cultivation' and 'regulation'.[47]

In one of his best-known essays, 'Of the Standard of Taste', Hume elaborates upon the 'cultivation' of genius required to meet and/or 'regulate' the 'standards' of taste by 'comprehending' the construction and purpose of 'productions of genius':

In all the nobler productions of genius, there is a mutual relation and correspondence of parts; nor can either the beauties or blemishes be perceived by him, whose thought is not capacious enough to comprehend all those parts, and compare them with each other, in order to perceive the consistence and uniformity of the whole. Every work of art has also a certain end or purpose, for which it is calculated; and is to be deemed more or less perfect, as it is more or less fitted to attain this end. (240)

Like Shaftesbury, Hume ultimately values artworks that conform to 'rules of art' (which emphasise the 'consistence and uniformity of the whole'). Only through such conformity can an artwork be evaluated and found 'more or less perfect'.

Such artworks are expressly functional, designed to 'attain' a specific end that must be readily comprehended by authors as well as readers. This necessarily stresses a specific type of poetic persona, one in which an author must demonstrate clear knowledge and application of current standards of taste. In so doing, such poets perform a valuable social function. In his essay 'Of the Immortality of the Soul', Hume praises the role of 'poets and heroes' who should also be 'rewarded' for their 'virtue'. He writes, 'According to human sentiments, sense, courage, good manners, industry, prudence, genius, &c. are essential parts of personal merit. Shall we therefore erect an Elysium for poets and heroes, like that of antient mythology? Why confine rewards to one species of virtue?' (594).

Such rhetorical questioning found its counterpart in the works of other Scottish philosophers, who also repeatedly queried the definitions and goals of *genius* in the literary field. Like Hume, Adam Smith explored the variability of genius in his philosophical writings. One of

Burns's acknowledged influences – particularly *The Theory of Moral Sentiments* (1759) – Smith examined the concept of genius as it relates to class and economy in *The Wealth of Nations* (1776). Comparing the difference in genius between a philosopher and a porter, Smith writes, 'By nature a philosopher is not in genius and disposition half so different from a street porter, as is a mastiff from a shepherd's dog'.[48] Smith continues his analogy of class difference and genius by describing the lack of 'usefulness' between various species of dogs:

Those different tribes of animals, however, though all of the same species, are of scarce any use to one another. The strength of the mastiff is not, in the least, supported either by the swiftness of the greyhound, or by the sagacity of the spaniel, or by the docility of the shepherd's dog. The effects of those different geniuses and talents, for want of the power or disposition to barter and exchange, cannot be brought into a common stock, and do not in the least contribute to the better accommodation and conveniency of the species. (30)

Putting aside the fanciful notion of dogs engaging in 'barter and exchange', it is worthwhile examining the conclusion of this intriguing analogy contrasting the respective 'geniuses' of humans and canines.

In Smith's view, the world of dogs has no interdependence among species: 'Each animal is obliged to support and defend itself, separately and independently, and derives no sort of advantage from that variety of talents with which nature has distinguished his fellows' (30). Among canines, it is a 'dog eat dog' world, but humans are another animal altogether. Smith writes,

Among men, on the contrary, the most dissimilar geniuses are of use to one another; the different produces of their respective talents, but the general disposition to truck, barter, and exchange, being brought, as it were, into a common stock, where every man may purchase whatever part of the produce of other men's talents he has occasion for. (30)

In this formulation, *genius* is commensurate with one's class identity, which is a social property of the self. It is valued, however, only so far as it contributes to the interdependence of the species by fulfilling its specific role in the economy.

Comparing the philosopher to the porter once more, Smith observes that 'no two persons can be more different in their genius, but there does not seem to have been any originall difference betwixt them'. He describes their upbringing, finding no essential distinction

between them beyond their future social occupations. He concludes
that 'the difference of employment occasions the difference of gen-
ius'.[49] This maxim became a central tenet of his teaching and writing,
finding frequent expression in his lectures. Smith's perception of
genius in this example evokes Hume's notion of genius as a 'magical
faculty' but is more focused upon the concept as a marker of a per-
son's inclination or temper.

Smith expands upon this view of genius to include national ty-
pology, stating for example in his *Essays on Philosophical Subjects*
that 'imagination, genius, and invention seem to be the talents of the
English'. After describing the genius of Spenser, Shakespeare, and
Milton, he claims that 'in the eminent French writers, such sallies of
genius are more rarely to be met with'. He extends his praise of
English writers to include that of fellow Scots such as William
Hamilton of Bangour, for whom he wrote a preface for *Poems on Sev-
eral Occasions* (1748). He writes, 'It is hoped, that the many beauties
of language and sentiment which appear in this little volume, and the
fine genius the author every where discovers, will make it acceptable
to every reader of taste'.[50] The literary application of *genius* in this
example connotes textual properties rather than the author's character,
linking the concept to other aesthetic categories like 'sublimity' of
style.[51]

The use of genius as a key criterion of literary taste was an im-
portant feature of the literary criticism of Henry Home, Lord Kames,
in which he sought to lay the groundwork for a systematic approach to
the subject. He offered a detailed definition of the concept in the first
volume of his influential *Elements of Criticism* (1762), contrasting it
with 'delicacy of taste'. He writes:

Genius is allied to a warm and inflammable constitution, delicacy of taste to calmness
and sedateness. Hence it is common to find genius in one who is a prey to every
passion; but seldom delicacy of taste. Upon a man possessed of that blessing, the
moral duties, no less than the fine arts, make a deep impression, and counterbalance
every irregular desire: at the same time, a temper calm and sedate is not easily moved,
even by a strong temptation.[52]

Kames's description of the attributes of genius – a 'warm and
inflammable constitution' that is 'prey to every passion' – found
currency among many later critics, who often applied these criteria in
their analysis of poets like Burns.

For Kames, *genius* is more of a liability than an asset; its tendency to promote excessive behavior makes it especially worrisome. Art has the possibility to counteract the negative influence of *genius*, provided that the artwork is properly produced and consumed. In his discussion of art's imitative quality in *Essays on the Principles of Morality and Natural Religion* (1751), Kames states that 'nothing contributes so much to improve the mind and confirm it in virtue, as being continually employed in surveying the actions of others, entering into the concerns of the virtuous'. For this reason, Kames finds great utility in literature's capacity to create emotive possibilities in readers that they were unlikely to experience in their actual lives. The ability to imitate such scenes of virtue is a central facet of a writer's *genius*, for Kames argues that 'in compositions where liberty is allowed of fiction, it must be want of genius, if the mind be not sufficiently exercised'.[53]

Genius in this model of literary production resides in the writer's talent in provoking readers' empathetic responses to fiction, a key tenet of Smith's *Theory of Moral Sentiments* as well. However, Kames does find that an 'author of genius' can only produce works of quality if that author is selective and rational. Concerning 'transgressive' fiction, he writes that 'fictions that transgress the bounds of nature, seldom have a good effect; they may inflame the imagination for a moment, but will not be relished by any person of a correct taste' (II, 660). He concedes that 'they may be of some use to the lower rank of writers; but an author of genius has much finer materials of Nature's production, for elevating his subject, and making it interesting' (II, 660). Thus, though inspired by the raw 'materials of Nature's production', the 'author of genius' must still carefully employ them in order to craft works which 'have a good effect' on readers.

Along with its need for a moral component, Kames argues that genius can have a deeply inhibiting influence as it relates to literary tradition and other branches of knowledge. As 'emulation' had served a 'noble' purpose for the arts in Hume's model, it does so for Kames as well. There is a crucial difference in their philosophies, though, and that is the role that the *genius* performs in stimulating others to pursue 'perfection'. In *Sketches of the History of Man* (1774), Kames writes, 'As the progress of arts and sciences toward perfection is greatly promoted by emulation, nothing is more fatal to an art or science than to remove that spur, as where some extraordinary genius appears who soars above rivalship'.[54] The 'extraordinary genius' may define the standard of taste for Hume, but for Kames, this 'fatal' figure prevents others from emulating by 'removing the spur' of rivalry. In fact, he argues that Isaac Newton was just such a 'fatal' figure, preventing the emulation of other budding scientists due to his overwhelming *genius*.

Following this same logic and echoing the familiar eighteenth-century debate of Ancients and Moderns, Kames also claims that blind adherence to classical models results in inferior literary productions: 'Rude ages exhibit the triumph of authority over reason [...]. In later times, happily reason hath gained the ascendant: men now assert their native privilege of thinking for themselves' (I, 17). This 'new' privilege is exerted in the refusal of 'modern' men to follow the dictates of classical authority, for he finds that Homer and Virgil, 'however eminent for genius', are not owed 'blind obedience to their arbitrary will' (I, 18). The contours of genius theory as applied to Burns are to be found in Kames's agonistic model of literary production. For Kames and later Scottish thinkers, genius is an innate capacity of creative people whose responsibility it is to apply their artistic talent to the needs of contemporary readers. In this theory, genius has strong associations with morality and improvement, which were major areas of interest for Scottish Enlightenment thinkers.

Adam Ferguson further developed the ideas found in the work of Smith and Kames in his discussion of genius in *An Essay on the History of Civil Society* (1767), a work that begins to blur the boundaries separating the artistic genius and a nation's distinct genius as a people. Ferguson employs Smith's analogy of labourers and thinkers to describe his view of genius:

> Every mechanic is a great man with the learner, and the humble admirer, in his particular calling; and we can, perhaps, with more assurance pronounce what it is that should make a man happy and amiable, than what should make his abilities respected, and his genius admired.[55]

Despite this confusion of purposes, Ferguson finds that genius truly resides in the esteem that commands the attention and respect of others; he writes, 'To be admired and respected, is to have an ascendant among men. The talents that most directly procure that ascendant, are those which operate on mankind, penetrate their views, prevent their wishes, or frustrate their designs' (41).

As in Kames's agonistic model, genius is experienced as a powerful force of influence upon other writers and readers; the source of this influence is paradoxically enough the prior cultural approbation accrued by the writer's talents. Ferguson sees this process as the imposition of 'superior' talent, which is the sole criterion of value: 'The superior capacity leads with a superior energy, where every individual would go, and shews the hesitating and irresolute a clear passage to the attainment of their ends' (41). In his discussion of 'intellectual powers', Ferguson claims that 'men are to be estimated, not from what they know, but what they are able to perform' (43). He further states that such actions are to be witnessed 'even in literature' where writers are 'to be estimated from the works of their genius, not to the extent of their knowledge' (43).

Ferguson distinguishes this element of genius by claiming that 'liberal endowments bestowed on learned societies, and the leisure with which they were furnished for study, are not the likeliest means to excite the exertions of genius' (267). In Ferguson's theory, genius survives in a vacuum, existing without the support of others who would bestow 'liberal endowments' to ensure the 'exertions of genius'. Those with genius have 'superior intellectual powers' which direct the production of their works, without the need or pressure of exterior influence. As in Burns's case, genius is also to be met in uncommon people who exhibit it regardless of their lack of knowledge. Thus, more pointedly than Kames, Ferguson delineates the cultural production of genius with reference to personal identity but refutes its obligations to existing literary standards and practices.

Though lesser known than such luminaries as Hume and Smith, John Millar contributed to the discourse of genius in a markedly materialist fashion. In his *Letters of Sidney, on Inequality of Property* (1796), Millar examines the influence that lack of education has upon the production of genius in the labouring classes. Contra Ferguson, he finds that education is vital to the nurture of genius among the poor; he writes, 'The poor are deprived of every thing which can bear the name of education. Their parents are continually employed in providing the mere necessaries of life, and are themselves most deplorably ignorant'. Millar finds this lack of education to be most grievous, arguing that 'of all grievances, this total ignorance is the greatest; it degrades the mind, it smothers the lurking seeds of genius, it is a fertile source of all the vices'.[56] Such sentiments are echoed in much later arguments about the relationship between genius and poverty, most notably in Virginia Woolf's *A Room of One's Own* (1929).

Millar does not find the role of labour itself to be remunerative to the labourer, either materially or spiritually: 'A certain degree of labour is good for a man; but that degree which prevents him from informing himself of his interests, of his rights, and of his duties, is the most intolerable and destructive of all calamities'. In addition, he states that only through increased access to education will genius arise among the poor and disenfranchised; it appears not as an aberration among simple people but as a necessary byproduct of education itself. Millar claims that 'the more general liberal education became, there would be the greater probability of the discovery of genius'.[57] Taking sentiments directly from Thomas Gray's 'Elegy Written in a Country Churchyard', Millar suggests that only by educating the 'mute inglorious Miltons' of the poor will their *genius* be discovered.[58]

In fact, Millar argues that following his directives would necessarily enhance the stature of the nation itself. He writes,

The nation, becoming more opulent, would be enabled to execute greater public works; the wonders of art, no longer shut up in private repositories, to which few can procure admittance, would exist for the instruction and amusement of the people; discernment, feeling, taste, would be more generally diffused, and genius would find a full and noble recompense in universal, just, and merited admiration.[59]

Millar's radical democratising of genius would find few adherents in eighteenth-century Scotland, however, where the discourse of genius became increasingly defined by means of aesthetic (rather than sociopolitical) categories. Such definitional strategies would become the primary vehicle for Burns's initial reception by his Scottish readers and critics.

5.   Theories of 'Poetic Genius' in Eighteenth-Century Literary Criticism

The influence of Hugh Blair upon eighteenth-century readers and writers in Scotland was profound and long-lasting; the publication of his *Lectures upon Rhetoric and Belles-Lettres* (1783) reinforced Blair's teaching of generations of young Scots in the university context. His interest in genius as an element of literary production derived from his immersion in rhetoric, and his lectures reveal an understanding of literature as a communicative process mediated by rhetorical topoi.[60] Like Ferguson and Millar, Blair regards education as a vital step in the process of acquiring (and demonstrating) genius, and he also sees it as dependent upon historical contexts for its fullest expression. However, Blair offers a curious elaboration of the concept of genius in a lecture on the ancients and moderns, where he finds that genius attained through 'modern' education is decidedly inferior to that of the uneducated (or under-educated) ancients.

Blair writes that 'if the advancing age of the world bring along with it more science and more refinement, there belong [...] to its earlier periods, more vigour, more fire, more enthusiasm of genius'.[61] Claiming that the moderns exhibit 'more art and correctness, but feebler exertions of genius', Blair explores the forms of education available to the ancients and gauges their possible influence upon creative expressions of genius: 'It is proper to observe, that there were some circumstances in ancient times very favourable to those uncommon efforts of genius which were then exerted' (208). The reason for such 'uncommon' appearances of genius was historical contingency; he observes that 'learning was a much more rare and singular attainment in the earlier ages, than it is at present' (208).

As seen in Millar's deliberations on the socio-economic dimension of genius, Blair examines the social incentive driving the ancients' pursuit of knowledge and display of genius: 'Fewer had the means and opportunities of distinguishing themselves; but such as did distinguish themselves, were sure of acquiring that fame, and even veneration, which is of all rewards, the greatest incentive to genius' (208). Pursuit of recognition is thus valorised by Blair, who finds that literary fame (and 'even veneration') was incentive enough to motivate productions of genius among the ancients. However, one might ask if this same motive operates for the moderns, especially those (like Burns) without access to extensive learning.

Blair's answer is ambiguous. He argues that while access to education offers more opportunities for writers of potential genius to gain recognition, it also produces what he describes as a 'mediocrity of genius'. He writes,

We write much more supinely, and at our ease, than the Ancients. To excel, is become a much less considerable object. Less effort, less exertion is required, because we have many more assistances than they. Printing has rendered all books common, and

easy to be had. Education for any of the learned professions can be carried on without
much trouble. Hence a mediocrity of genius is spread over all; but to rise above that,
and to overtop the crowd, is given to few. (209)

In such a model of literary production, the concept of genius denotes
exceptional difference (displayed primarily in emotive expressiveness)
from 'mere' technical/formal mastery of literary discourse.

Blair's blindness to the class dimension in the above passage is
striking, particularly given his valorisation of purportedly 'primitive'
and/or uneducated poets like Ossian (in whose defense Blair wrote a
'critical dissertation').[62] Assuming that all writers were like his stu-
dents – that is, financially capable of university education and having
access and time to read books – Blair denigrates their productions as
'mediocre'. There is a rich irony in this, for it is their usage of the
common modes and tropes of literary discourse (the very subject of
Blair's teaching and scholarship) which makes them 'mediocre'. The
genius who would 'rise above' such banality is the writer who
emerges from the 'primitive' wilderness of the nation. This figure,
inspired by the same 'vigour' and 'enthusiasm' as the ancients, is ca-
pable of 'overtopping the crowd' of mediocre genius.[63] It should come
as no surprise that Blair was one of Burns's early supporters, for the
'heaven-taught ploughman' fit this mold quite nicely and appeared
(initially at least) to exhibit appropriately aberrant, fiery genius.[64]

Alexander Gerard offered a more detailed stylistic analysis of
'poetic genius' than that found in Blair, although his views would gain
less currency. In *An Essay on Genius* (1774), Gerard largely focused
on the necessary mental powers displayed by poetic genius rather than
scrutinising its possessor's character or personality. Gerard argued
that 'genius implies such *comprehensiveness* of imagination as
enables a man, on every occasion, to call in the conceptions that are
necessary for executing the designs or compleating the works in which
he engages'.[65] Underscoring abilities like 'the power of association'
(43) and 'boundless fertility, that inexhaustible copiousness of
invention' (44), Gerard constructed his theory of poetic genius almost
exclusively upon the productions of such genius. In this respect, his
theory harkens back to predecessors like Shaftesbury and Kames,
where the principal focus resides on 'works of genius' rather than
writers identified as possessed of *genius*.

In fact, Gerard's analysis is strikingly formal. He claimed that
'regularity' was of central importance in a work of genius, for regu-

larity ensured that the design initiated by poetic invention would be revealed by the work's execution:

Genius implies *regularity*, as well as comprehensiveness of imagination. Regularity arises in a great measure from such a turn of imagination as enables the associating principles, not only to introduce proper ideas, but also to connect the design of the whole with every idea that is introduced. (46)

Therefore, in Gerard's theory of poetic genius, genius is 'incomplete' without the union of imagination and design. As Gerard states, 'To render genius *complete*, fertility and regularity of imagination must be united. Their union forms the boundless penetration which characterises true genius' (54). In the absence of 'regularity' and successful design, a poet 'who follows any association, however trivial or devious, that hits his fancy, may show a great deal of imagination without displaying any real genius' (49). Contra Blair, Gerard argues that the poet must have a complete working knowledge of mainstream literary discourse and be capable of constructing a rhetorically-sound literary production. Accomplishing such ends reveals true 'poetic genius' that is decidedly not 'mediocre'.

Other Scottish critics took a decidedly less formal approach to the theory of poetic genius, instead seeking to delineate the *genius* as a figure existing outside the strictures of mainstream literary discourse. In particular, the proto-Romantic figure of the genius as passionate outsider became increasingly the object of critical study in the work of William Duff, spurring elaborate inquiries into the nature of such a peculiar character.[66] More consistently than other types of writers, the poet was singled out for distinction, purportedly embodying the kind of genius that defied the shaping influences of history, education, and culture. In this respect, Duff was quite influential in promoting a view of *genius* that found the character of the poet to be of as much (if not more) interest than the poetry itself. His critical views contributed to the popularisation of poets like Burns, particularly the emphasis in Duff's work placed upon the 'singularity' of genius.

In his *Essay on Original Genius* (1767), Duff stressed the preponderance of 'irregularity' in the works of a poet of 'original genius'. Claiming that 'it is the prerogative of a great Genius to think and to write with ease, very rarely, if ever, experiencing a barrenness of Imagination', Duff argues that literary imitation cannot be accepted as a province of 'poetic genius'.[67] He writes, 'A moderate degree of praise is no doubt due to successful imitators; but an author of original Genius will not content himself with a mediocrity of reputation; conscious of the strength of his own talents, he disdains to imitate what perhaps he is qualified to excel' (131). Like Blair before him, Duff conceives of formal proficiency as merely the province of mediocrity. Little, if anything can be gleaned from literary imitation, for a poet must be so 'conscious of the strength of his talents' that he can look upon the works of other writers with considerable hauteur (indeed, 'disdain').

For Duff, poets must display their genius through 'NEW SENTIMENTS, as well as NEW IMAGES, on every subject on which he employs his talents' (149). The emphasis on novelty leads Duff to promote Pindaresque 'irregularity' in poetic practice: 'An irregular greatness of Imagination, implying unequal and disproportioned grandeur, is always discernible in the compositions of an original Genius, however elevated, and is therefore an universal characteristic of such a Genius' (166).[68] Because of his focus on imaginative originality in both expression and style, Duff insists that 'the efforts of Imagination, in Poetry at least, are impetuous, and attain their utmost perfection at once, even in the rudest form of social life' (262). This leads Duff to suggest that 'genius naturally shoots forth in the simplicity and tranquility of uncultivated life' (271).

The promotion of 'primitive life' as especially conducive to poetry is not peculiar to Duff; as previously noted, it can be found in the works of many Scottish thinkers from the period.[69] What distinguishes Duff's account, however, is the diminishing returns he assigns to 'post-primitive' poetry: he writes, 'In the earliest and most uncultivated periods of society, Poetry is by one great effort of nature, in one age, and by one individual, brought to the highest perfection to which human Genius is capable of advancing it' (264). 'Post-primitive' poets can only harness this originary creative power by disabusing themselves of the influence of 'Literature'. Duff remarks that 'a Poet of original Genius has very little occasion for the weak aid of Literature: he is self-taught' (281). The introduction of autodidacticism in Duff's theory of poetic *genius* would prove to be paramount in later theories that sought to account for the presence of genius in members of the labouring class.[70]

Duff strenuously argues against the need for 'an original poetic genius' to be educated, arguing that an 'effect of learning is, to

ENCUMBER and OVERLOAD the mind of an original Poetic Genius' (281). In Duff's theory, such education precludes the possibility for 'original' poetic compositions. In fact, the only way for a poetic genius to truly express original insight is to studiously avoid alluding to any prior writing to which he may have once been exposed. As Duff definitively puts it, 'a Poet who adopts images, who culls out incidents he has met with in the writings of other Authors, and who imitates characters which have been portrayed by other Poets [...] cannot surely with any propriety be considered as an Original' (276). In order to further analyse the nature of such an 'original', Duff examined the issue in another work three years later, this time focusing on the unique 'character' of a 'poetic genius'.

Writing in *Critical Observations on the Writings of the Most Celebrated Original Geniuses in Poetry* (1770), William Duff stated that

A man of Genius is really a kind of different being from the rest of his species. The bent of his disposition, the complexion of his temper, the general turn of his character, his passions and his pursuits are for the most part very dissimilar from those of the bulk of mankind.[71]

Where in his *Essay on Original Genius* Duff had analysed the component elements of 'original genius', he sought in *Critical Observations* to explore the character of 'original poetic geniuses' themselves in order to discern the sources of their distinction. He was especially interested in determining the 'Effects of Genius on the Temper and Character, and of the Advantages and Disadvantages attending the Possession of It' (338). Following the lead established by Edward Young in *Conjectures upon Original Composition* (1759), Duff concentrated his efforts on delimiting the character of the 'original poetic genius' in order to assess the benefits and drawbacks of such exceptionality.[72]

Not surprisingly, Duff found the 'original genius' to be a highly sensitive, passionate individual with a 'warm' temper: 'True Genius [...] naturally produces a warmth and sensibility of temper. It is in-deed incompatible with a cold, or phlegmatic constitution of mind. All its sensations, and all its affections are ardent, lively and exquisite' (341). Noting that 'this extreme sensibility is the effect of a vivacity and strength of fancy' (341), Duff outlines the constituent personality of an 'original poetic genius', a figure he represents as having both a 'cheerful and sanguine temper of mind' as well as 'a sublime, sooth-ing, and pensive melancholy' (345). As Duff continues in his cata-logue, poetic geniuses emerge as composites of various (often contra-dictory) personality traits like a 'humane, *compassionate* and devotional temper of mind' (350), 'a bashful timidity and diffidence' (354), 'a distant and dignified reserve' (355), and an 'Irresolution and Inconstancy of mind' (356).

For Duff, the 'original poetic genius' lived in the grip of strong feelings that were variously ardent, warm, exquisite, pensive, cheerful, melancholy, devotional or irresolute. In order to confirm whether being possessed of such genius were an advantage or disadvantage, Duff explores pragmatic concerns like the impact of a person's age and social class upon the life of an 'original genius'. Of particular note are the effects of the 'passion of love' upon 'the mind of a man of Genius' (342); Duff finds that 'a very great sensibility of the influence of female charms is upon the whole highly unfavourable to the exertions of youthful Genius' (343). Another disadvantage that Duff examines is the unhappy state of a genius born into poverty: 'If his fortune is narrow, or his situation dependent, he will [...] be exposed to a familiarity of treatment, which from persons of very inferior abilities, and very dissimilar tempers and modes of life, is peculiarly disgusting to an ingenious mind' (365).

Personal affronts aside, the poor genius finds himself continually confronted by assaults upon his character, attempts by 'the malicious part of mankind to reduce an aspiring Genius to their own level, baffled by its manifest and acknowledged superiority' (363-64). In addition to such insults, the original genius often discovers that 'it hath often been the lot of Genius to be without a protector, and without a patron' (365). Accordingly, Duff concedes that the disadvantages of genius may in fact outweigh its advantages, concluding that 'the life of a man of Genius, like that of a Christian, is for the most part a state of warfare' (363). Such remarks call to mind Bunyan's passage in *Pilgrim's Progress*, where he writes that 'tho' an host encamp against me, my heart shall not fear; tho' War should rise against me, in this will I be confident'.[73] Like Pilgrim reassuring himself of his strength in the face of war, Duff's *genius* must rise to the occasion and be prepared to fight in his own defense.

Duff's analysis of the temperament of the 'original poetic genius' signals a change in the aesthetic valorisation of this concept seen in the works of Hume, Smith, Kames, Ferguson, Millar, Gerard, and Blair. Like the later enshrinement of 'poetic genius' by Romantic writers, Duff locates the concept squarely in the self and its capacity to express powerful sentiments that others cannot experience. Such views anticipate Wordsworth's definition of the poet as 'a man endued with more lively sensibility, more enthusiasm and tenderness [...] than are supposed to be common among mankind'.[74]

6. Burns and the Persona of the 'Poetic Genius'

The pertinence of these theories of genius to the reception history of Robert Burns is manifold; in nearly all respects (and particularly in the instance of Duff's *Critical Observations*), the terminology and conceptualisation of genius finds common expression in the poet's early reviews. The suffering of the poetic genius depicted in Duff's account – especially the experiences of poverty and neglect by patrons – is echoed by critics of Burns who voiced much indignation at the plight of the 'heaven-taught ploughman'. As will be discussed in the next chapter, the rise of genius theory resulted in a perception of Burns that consistently misrepresented his talents as a poet. By not only allowing himself to be seen as a 'heaven-taught ploughman' but also acting the part with considerable panache, Burns found himself facing a critical and creative impasse once his fame had been established.

Achieving repute as a poetic genius in the mold of Duff and Blair was a short-lived affair, and Burns's publicity proved to be ultimately confining to his efforts to be recognised as a major British poet. As his novelty waned, Burns sought to dispense with the persona of the 'heaven-taught ploughman' in favour of the 'Scotch Bard'. In some respects, he succeeded in this effort, gaining further recognition later in his career for his work collecting Scottish songs. However, his success in this endeavour came at the expense of his own creative work as a practicing poet; the numerous epistles, satires, and monologues found in the Kilmarnock edition disappeared from his output. The more he worked to become a Scotch bard, the more he effaced himself as a 'poetic genius' writing solely by means of divine inspiration. As this process took place in the 1790s, Burns sought to redefine himself as the 'genius of the nation' rather than as a mere 'poetic genius'.

[1] For Mackenzie's review, see *Robert Burns: The Critical Heritage*, ed. by Donald A. Low (London: Routledge and Kegan Paul, 1974), pp. 67-70.

[2] Robert P. Irvine, ed., *Robert Burns: Selected Poems and Songs* (Oxford: Oxford University Press, 2013), p. 123.

[3] For example, the Highland Society released a report on the Ossian controversy in 1805; for more on Ossian's reception, see Howard Gaskill, ed., *Ossian Revisited* (Edinburgh: Edinburgh University Press, 1991).

[4] J. Delancey Ferguson and G. Ross Roy, eds., *The Letters of Robert Burns*, ed. Vol I (Oxford: Clarendon, 1985), p. 101.

[5] Robert Crawford, *The Bard: Robert Burns, a Biography* (Princeton: Princeton University Press, 2009), p. 3. Further references to this edition are given after quotations in the text.

[6] Irvine (2013: 3-4).

[7] Ferguson and Roy (1985: 62, 88), Vol I. Burns alluded to Beattie and The Minstrel in 'The Ordination', 'The Vision', 'Stanzas […] in the Manner of Beattie's Minstrel', 'To William Simson, Ochiltree', and 'To a Mountain Daisy'.

[8] *OED* also provides a more historically-concrete definition: 'a singer or musician of the medieval period, especially one who sings heroic or lyric poetry, providing musical accompaniment on a harp, lute, or other stringed instrument'.

[9] Katie Trumpener, *Bardic Nationalism: The Romantic Novel and the British Empire* (Princeton: Princeton University Press,1997), pp. xii, 118.

[10] J. B. Reid lists 45 instances of 'bard' in Burns's poetry and only five for 'minstrel'. See *A Complete Word and Phrase Concordance to the Poems and Songs of Robert Burns* (Glasgow: Kerr & Richardson, 1889).

[11] A quick search on Eighteenth-Century Collections Online (Gale's full-text eighteenth-century database) yields an impressive 1,344 hits for 'minstrel' but an overwhelming 22,802 hits for 'bard' (search conducted 17 May 2013).

[12] See Pittock, *Scottish and Irish Romanticism*, pp. 32-58, 120-43. See also Robert Crwaford, ed., *'Heaven-Taught Fergusson': Robert Burns's Favourite Scottish Poet* (East Linton: Tuckwell, 2003).

[13] See Sergeant and Stafford, eds., *Burns and Other Poets* (Edinburgh: Edinburgh University Press, 2012); Christopher Ricks, *Allusion to the Poets* (Oxford: Oxford University Press, 2002), pp. 43-82; and Corey Andrews, '"Almost the Same, but Not Quite": English Poetry by Eighteenth-Century Scots', *Eighteenth Century: Theory and Interpretation*, 47.1 (2006), 59-79.

[14] See David Hill Radcliffe, 'Completing James Beattie's The Minstrel', *Studies in Philology*, 100.4 (2003), 534-63.

[15] Carol McGuirk, *Robert Burns and the Sentimental Era* (Athens: University of Georgia Press, 1985), p. 144. Further references to this edition are given after quotations in the text.

[16] Maureen McLane, 'The Figure Minstrelsy Makes: Poetry and Historicity', *Critical Inquiry*, 29.3 (2003) pp. 429-52:433-34. See also McLane, *Balladeering, Minstrelsy, and the Making of British Romantic Poetry* (Cambridge: Cambridge University Press, 2011), and Newman, *Ballad Collection, Lyric, and the Canon: The Call of the Popular from the Restoration to the New Criticism* (Philadelphia: University of Pennsylvania Press, 2007).

[17] Thomas Percy, *Reliques of Ancient English Poetry*, ed. by J. V. Prichard, Vol I, (London: Bell, 1893), p. xxiii. Further references to this edition/volume are given after quotations in the text. For more on Percy's *Reliques*, see Nick Groom, *The Making of Percy's 'Reliques'* (Oxford: Oxford University Press, 1999).

[18] Kathryn Sutherland, 'The Native Poet: The Influence of Percy's Minstrel from Beattie to Wordsworth', *Review of English Studies*, 33.132 (1982), pp. 414-33: 417-18.

[19] p. 8.

[20] Henry Alfred Burd, 'Joseph Ritson: A Critical Biography' (unpublished doctoral dissertation: University of Illinois, 1915), pp. 152, 155, 153.

[21] p. xi. Hereafter cited in-text by book and stanza numbers.

[22] Margaret Forbes, *Beattie and his Friends* (Westminster: Constable, 1904), p. 56.

[23] Alexander Dyce, ed., *The Poetical Works of James Beattie, with a Memoir* (Boston: Osgood, 1871), p. xii.

[24] p. 425.

[25] David Hill Radcliffe, 'Completing James Beattie's *The Minstrel*', *Studies in Philology*, 100.4 (2003), pp. 534-63: 535. For other Spenserian poems of 'aesthetic education', see William Shenstone's *The School Mistress* (1742), James Thomson's *The Castle of Indolence* (1748), and Gilbert West's Education (1751).

[26] See Sutherland (1982: 430-33).

[27] Forbes (1904: 55).

[28] James Kinsley, ed., *The Poems and Songs of Robert Burns*, Vol I (Oxford: Clarendon, 1968), poem 139, ll. 7-8, pp. 11-12. Quotations from Burns's poetry refer to this edition/volume and will be cited in-text by poem and line numbers.

[29] p. 56.

[30] William Forbes, *An Account of the Life and Writings of James Beattie*, 2 vols (Edinburgh: Constable, 1806), Vol I, p. 60.

[31] Beattie (1777: 27).

[32] Ferguson and Delancey (1985: 88), Vol I.

[33] On Burns's use of allusion, see Ricks (2002: 43-82).

[34] See Nancy van Deusen, ed., *Dreams and Visions: An Interdisciplinary Enquiry* (Leiden: Brill, 2010).

[35] See Pittock, *Scottish and Irish Romanticism*, p. 44, and Newman, pp. 44-56.

[36] Burns defines 'duan' in a footnote as 'a term of Ossian's for the different divisions of a digressive Poem'.

[37] For Burns's ongoing financial difficulties, see Crawford (2009) p. 166.

[38] See Tim Burke, 'Labour, Education and Genius', in Johnny Rodger and Gerard Carruthers, eds, *Fickle Man: Robert Burns in the 21st Century* (Dingwall: Sandstone, 2009), pp. 13-24; and Andrews, 'The Genius of Scotland: Robert Burns and his Critics', *International Journal of Scottish Literature*, 6 (2010), pp. 1-16.

[39] This also relies on his use of Percy as a source text. See Groom (1999: 106-44).

[40] See Ronnie Young, 'James Beattie and the Progress of Genius in the Aberdeen Enlightenment', *Journal for Eighteenth-Century Studies*, 36.2 (2013), 245-61.

[41] Shaftesbury, Anthony Ashley Cooper, Third Earl of, *Characteristicks of Men, Manners, Opinions, Time*, ed. by Douglas den Uyl, 3 vols (Indianapolis: Liberty Fund, 2001), Vol I, 163. Hereafter cited in-text by volume and page numbers.

[42] *History* (1983: 359), Vol I.

[43] *Treatise* (1896: 331, 391).

[44] *Enquiry* (2007: 9).

[45] *Treatise* (1896: 24).

[46] David Hume, *Essays: Moral, Political, and Literary*, ed. by Eugene F. Miller (Indianapolis: Liberty Fund), p. 550. Other citations from Hume's essays refer to this edition and will be noted in-text by page numbers.

[47] Voltaire's phrase—il faut cultiver notre jardin—has various translations. For instance, 'it is necessary to cultivate our garden', 'let us take care of our garden', 'we must go and work in our garden', and/or 'we must cultivate our garden'. However rendered, though, the phrase invites readers (in the first person plural) to participate in the process of 'cultivation' as its primary moral injunction.

[48] Adam Smith, *Wealth of Nations*, ed. by R. H. Campbell and A. S. Skinner (1982), Vol I, p. 30. Further references to this edition/volume are given after quotations in the text.

[49] Adam Smith, *Lectures on Jurisprudence*, ed. by R. L. Meek, D. D. Raphael and P. GT. Stein (Indianapolis: Liberty Fund, 1982), p. 348.

[50] Adam Smith, *Essays on Philosophical Subjects*, ed. by W. P. D. Wightman and J. C. Bryce (Indianapolis: Liberty Fund), pp. 243, 244, 261.

[51] See Karl Axelsson, *The Sublime: Precursors and British Eighteenth-Century Conceptions* (Bern: Peter Lang, 2007).

[52] Henry Home, Lord Kames, *Elements of Criticism*, ed. by Peter Jones, 2 vols (Indianapolis: Liberty Fund, 2005), Vol I, p. 17. Hereafter cited in-text by volume and page numbers.

[53] Henry Home, Lord Kames, *Essays on the Principles of Morality and Natural Religion*, ed. by Mary Catherine Moran (Indianapolis: Liberty Fund, 2005), pp. 17-18.

[54] Henry Home, Lord Kames, *Sketches of the History of Man*, ed. by James A. Harris, 3 vols (Indianapolis: Liberty Fund, 2007), Vol I, p. 105.

[55] p. 41. Further references to this edition are given after quotations in the text.

[56] Millar (1796), 'Letter III. To the Editor of the Scots Chronicle'.

[57] Ibid., 'Letter III'.

[58] See *The Complete Poems of Thomas Gray: English, Latin, and Greek*, ed. by H. W. Starr and J. R. Hendrickson (Oxford: Clarendon, 1966), p. 39, l. 59.

[59] Millaer (1796), 'Letter XVIII. To the Editor of the Scots Chronicle'.

[60] See Liam McIlvanney, 'Hugh Blair, Robert Burns, and the Invention of Scottish Literature', *Eighteenth-Century Life*, 29.2 (2005), pp. 25-46.

[61] James Finlayson, ed., *The Works of Hugh Blair*, 5 vols (London: Cadell and Davies, 1820), p. V, 207. Further references to this edition/volume are given after quotations in the text.

[62] See Hugh Blair, *A Critical Dissertation on the Poems of Ossian the Son of Fingal* (London: Becket and De Hondt, 1763). See also Ronnie Young, 'Genius, Men and Manners: Burns and Eighteenth-Century Scottish Criticism', *Scottish Studies Review*, 9.2 (2008), p. 129-47.

[63] For more on the appeal of such 'primitivism', see E. H. Gombrich, *The Preference for the Primitive: Episodes in the History of Western Taste and Art* (London: Phaidon, 2002).

[64] In some respects, Blair's thoughts on genius resemble those expressed by Samuel Johnson in his *Lives of the Poets*, where the figure of Shakespeare (and to a lesser degree, Richard Savage) resembles Blair's 'primitive' genius. Despite his avowed skepticism of Macpherson's *Ossian*, Johnson favored the emotive expressiveness of genius embodied by Shakespeare, whose 'errors' in literary production he defended in his celebrated 'Preface'.

[65] Alexander Gerard, *An Essay on Genius* (London: Strahan and Cadell, 1774), p. 42. Further references to this edition are given after quotations in the text.

[66] See Marshall Brown, *Preromanticism* (Stanford: Stanford University Press, 1991).

[67] William Duff, *An Essay on Original Genius* (London: Dilly and Dilly, 1767), pp. 128-29. Further references to this edition are given after quotations in the text.

[68] For more on Pindar's influence upon eighteenth-century verse, see Dustin Griffin, *Patriotism and Poetry in Eighteenth-Century Britain* (Cambridge: Cambridge University Press, 2002), pp. 65-67.

[69] See Murray Pittock, *Inventing and Resisting Britain: Cultural Identities in Britain and Ireland, 1685-1789* (New York: St. Martins, 1997), pp. 156-59.

[70] See Julie Prandi, *The Poetry of the Self-Taught An Eighteenth-Century Phenomenon (New York: Peter Lang, 2008)*. See also Andrews, '"Work Poems": Assessing the Georgic Mode of Eighteenth-Century Working-Class Poetry', in Sandro Jung, ed., *Experiments in Genre in Eighteenth-Century Literature* (Ghent: Academic Scientific, 2011), pp. 105-33.

[71] William Duff, *Critical Observations on the Writings of the Most Celebrated Original Geniuses in Poetry* (London: Becket and Hondt, 1770), p. 339. Further references to this edition are given after quotations in the text.

[72] See Howard Weinbrot, *Britannia's Issue: The Rise of British Literature from Dryden to Ossian* (Cambridge: Cambridge University Press, 1993), p. 85.

[73] John Bunyan, *Pilgrim's Progress* (New York: Collier, 1909), p. 300.

[74] William Wordsworth, *Lyrical Ballads, with Pastoral and Other Poems*, 3rd edn, Vol I (London: Longman and Rees, 1802), p. xxviii.

Chapter Two

'Who are you Mr. Burns?': Admirers and Sceptics of the 'Heaven-taught Ploughman', 1786-1788

1. Ofellus or Othello: The Roots of Burns's Critical Reception

The earliest review of Burns's Kilmarnock edition appeared as an unsigned notice in the October 1786 issue of the literary miscellany *Edinburgh Magazine*. The reviewer (most likely James Sibbald, the magazine's publisher) begins with a sketch of the situation at hand; of the unknown author, he writes, 'When an author we know nothing of solicits our attention, we are but too apt to treat him with the same reluctant civility we show to a person who has come unbidden to our company'.[1] This gets nicely to the point: Burns, as an 'unbidden' stranger to the literary field, is most likely to be met with 'reluctant civility' by those like Sibbald who stake their claim as arbiters of taste. Their motivation in this regard is primarily an assertion of their ability to wield critical judgment in public forums; as Pierre Bourdieu claims, such workings operate throughout all negotiations of literary value, which take place within 'the field of power'.[2]

In order for strangers like Burns to gain notice (and therefore potential entry) in the literary field, their work must exhibit both competence and distinction. In this context, competence is defined as knowledge of mainstream literary practice, while distinction is seen as differentiating/individuating skills and talents.[3] The reviewer makes this quite clear in his assessment of Burns's verse, writing that 'talents and address will gradually diminish the distance of our behavior, and when the first unfavourable impression has worn off, the author may become a favorite, and the stranger a friend' (63). It is important to note here the emphasis that is placed upon 'talents' and 'address', both working in concert to distinguish the writing of the unknown poet. The reviewer's ultimate motivation may be the critical distinction to be gained by recognising the talent of such a poet, which links the work of reviewing to that of the discovery and promotion of gifted unknowns.

The reviewer ends his introduction with a curious statement, one which blends approbation and defensiveness: 'The poems we have just announced may probably have to struggle with the pride of learning and the partiality of indulgence; yet they are entitled to a particular indulgence' (63). This appeal will be absent in Burns's later reception history; indeed, after his sudden fame following the review of the Kilmarnock edition in the *Lounger*, few reviewers would feel the need to argue for their readers' 'indulgence' in reading Burns's poetry. Such uncertainty appears throughout the rest of the *Edinburgh Magazine* notice, however, especially when the reviewer seeks to explain his appreciation for a poet whom he perhaps wishes to promote as a 'favorite' and 'friend' in the literary field, both for the sake of the poet and the renown of the critic.

To explain the rationale for his 'particular indulgence', the reviewer offers a series of revealing questions, written from the perspective of a 'surly critic' interrogating the poet's 'qualifications'. He asks,

Who are you Mr. Burns? [...] At what university have you been educated? what languages do you understand? what authors have you particularly studied? whether has Aristotle or Horace directed your taste? who has praised your poems, and under whose patronage are they published? In short, what qualifications entitle you to instruct or entertain us? (63)

Listing such 'qualifications' is not entirely facetious on the reviewer's part. In fact, such qualifications (particularly those relating to education and facility with multiple languages) often serve as definitional criteria for recognition in the field of literary production.[4]

This relates specifically to the notion of 'competence' in the field; Bourdieu notes that 'a work of art has meaning and interest only for someone who possesses the cultural competence, that is, the code, into which it is encoded'.[5] Without this necessary knowledge of the 'code', an author cannot expect recognition by those (like the 'surly critic') who confer legitimacy. Considering Burns's response to the impertinent questioning of the 'surly critic', the reviewer imagines that 'perhaps poor honest Robert Burns would make no satisfactory answers' (63). The review's tone abruptly changes at this point, as the reviewer's 'indulgence' for the poet stalls before the critic's demands for 'qualifications'. If Burns had hoped for a vigorous defense of his 'competence' in this review, he must have been deeply disappointed.

Instead, the reviewer offers the following retort to the 'surly' critic by 'poor honest' Robert Burns. Ventriloquising the poet, the reviewer writes,

I am a poor country man; I was bred up at the school of Kilmarnock; I understand no languages but my own; I have studied Allan Ramsay and Ferguson [sic]. My poems have been praised at many a fire-side; and I ask no patronage for them, if they deserve none. I have not looked on mankind *through the spectacle of books*. An ounce of mother wit, you know, is worth a pound of clergy; and Homer and Ossian, for any thing that I have heard, could neither write nor read. (63-64)

This imagined response underscores several significant strains that would be repeatedly found in the reception history of Burns's life story and body of work. It is worth stressing that such biographical speculation appears in the very first critical response to Burns's published poetry. Indeed, during his lifetime and well after his death, Burns himself would be as much the focus of his criticism as his verse. His exceptionality – construed here as existing outside '*the spectacle of books*' – is closely tied to his identity as a 'poor country man'.[6]

In fact, the reviewer suggests that along with his provincial background, Burns's class status defies the standards imposed by 'surly' literary critics and provides an alternative model of legitimacy in the literary field. The key criterion in this critical judgment is not competence but distinction, evident in Burns's irrefutable 'poetic genius'. Like Homer and Ossian before him, Burns is 'a striking example of native genius bursting through the obscurity of poverty and the obstructions of laborious life' (64). Such distinction, directly opposed to competence acquired through education, is validated only as the expression of prodigious, unmediated *genius*. When compared to later criticism, the review's only anomaly appears in the statement that Burns is poetically inferior to both Ramsay and Fergusson: 'Those who view him with the severity of lettered criticism, and judge him by the fastidious rules of art, will discover that he has not the doric simplicity of Ramsay, nor the brilliant imagination of Ferguson [sic]' (64). This is the first (and only) early review that finds Burns to be 'inferior' to his predecessors in the 'Scots triumvirate', that sturdy explanatory tool that has long been credited with conceptualising the 'vernacular revival' of eighteenth-century Scottish verse.[7]

Despite his limitations, Burns is dignified at the review's ending with a direct comparison that (according to the reviewer's logic) the poet could not possibly understand. There is a Latin allusion to Horace's Ofellus, the wise peasant from whom the Roman poet sought advice in the *Satires* (Bk II, II) on the 'discourse of plain living'. H. R. Fairclough describes Offellus's appeal as a 'plain but shrewd countryman', noting that the peasant represented to Horace 'the simplicity and other sturdy qualities of the Apulian farmers'. In this guise, Ofellus is considered to be an especially fitting model for Burns, who is hailed by the same phrase Horace employed in the third line of the *Satire*: '*Rusticus abnormis sapiens, crassaque Minerva*'.[8] However, given the review's representation of Burns as a 'poor country man', such an allusion to the 'philosopher peasant' would have been lost on a poet who did not see 'through the spectacle of books'.[9] By such means, this review establishes parameters followed by many later critics, especially in the valorisation of Burns as a 'plain but shrewd' peasant; in addition, the use of 'national' criteria is established to evaluate his role as a distinctly 'Scottish' poet following Ramsay and Fergusson.

Burns appreciated this review, writing to Sibbald to thank him for 'the warmth with which you have befriended an obscure man, and young Author' (I, 78). He affirms Sibbald's representation of the 'poor country man', stating that 'so little am I acquainted with the Modes & Manners of the more publick and polished walks of life, that I often feel myself much embarrassed how to express the feelings of my heart, particularly Gratitude' (I, 77-78). Such deference is short-lived in Burns's letter, which promptly proffers a seven-line paraphrase of *Othello* in which the titular character eloquently denies his eloquence – 'Rude am I in speech, / And little blessed with the set, polish'd phrase' – before attesting that 'little can I grace my cause / In speaking of myself'.[10] Burns finishes his letter with Othello's *sotto voce*, claiming that 'I can only say, Sir, I feel the weight of the obligation, and wish I could express my sense of it' (I, 78). However, as previously noted, Burns would not have to wait long before his work gained further (and much more widespread) recognition through the auspices of Henry Mackenzie. As in his letter to Sibbald, Burns would prove to be much more Othello than Ofellus, much more capable of double-voiced irony and sly satire than his early critics would have believed possible.

This chapter will provide a survey of critical responses to Burns and his poetry from 1786-1788, in order to reveal and evaluate consistent patterns and issues in the early stages of his reception history. As will be shown, the primary critical approach to Burns and his work involved the application of *genius* theory. Indeed, the continuum of critical responses demonstrates the fluid nature of this concept as a literary criterion during the period. Burns's critics explored the application of multiple perceptions of genius, some which praised the poet's 'natural' facility for 'original' expression while others sifted his work for learned allusions that would discredit such 'natural' genius. Ronnie Young is certainly correct to assert that Burns's early reviews were 'a damaging blend of myth-building and moralising'.[11] This chapter will demonstrate that the process of 'myth-building and moralising' surrounding Burns began in earnest from the very beginning of his critical reception, particularly as critics assayed the poet's nationalist iconicity while attempting to assess the influence of his *genius* upon his literary reputation. In particular, such critics began to fuel the growing perception among Burns's fellow Scots that he was not only a literary *genius* but a national one as well, a designation that conveyed both honour and obligation. The cultural production of Burns was in full swing from the start.

2. The 'Divinity of Genius': Early Critical Admirers of the 'Heaven-Taught Ploughman

The most influential review of Burns's Kilmarnock edition, written by Henry Mackenzie and published in *The Lounger* (9 December 1786), appeared two months after the *Edinburgh Magazine* review. Unlike the relentless inquiry that marks the opening of that review, Mackenzie begins his assessment with an invocation of the concept of *genius* as a positive trait that invites the admiration of sentimental readers. Like Sibbald, he may have sought (and indeed gained) his own measure of recognition for heralding the arrival of a new Scottish *genius*. Mackenzie writes, 'To the feeling and the susceptible there is something wonderfully pleasing in the contemplation of genius, of that supereminent reach of mind by which some men are distinguished'.[12] Mackenzie's description of genius as a 'supereminent reach of mind' links the concept with sublime objects (glossed as

'great and stupendous natural objects') that also stimulate sentimental
audiences and 'fill the soul with wonder and delight' (385). In the
same manner as a sublime object like a storm at sea, Mackenzie repre-
sents Burns as a 'genius of no ordinary rank' (385), whose 'superemi-
nent reach of mind' will occasion much delightful contemplation for
readers of the poet's work.[13]

As in the review in the *Edinburgh Magazine*, Burns's strangeness
– stemming from his *genius*, as well as his class and provincial
identities – is the main source of the critical (and soon-to-be popular)
interest surrounding the poet. Mackenzie exploits these differentiating
factors early in his review, first by claiming that the 'divinity of gen-
ius [...] is best arrayed in the darkness of distant and remote periods'
(385). Following the theories of Hugh Blair and William Duff,
Mackenzie highlights the contemporary appeal of figures like Ossian,
whose 'distant and remote' voice captivated many Scottish and
English readers.[14] Mackenzie observes, however, that while 'it may be
true, that "in the olden time" genius had some advantages which
tended to its vigour and growth', nevertheless 'even in these degener-
ate days, it rises much oftener than it is observed' (385). Such is the
case with Burns, who has 'risen' from the 'distant and remote' past to
express his 'divinity of genius'. As with Sibbald, Mackenzie's moti-
vation here is fairly plain: introducing a poet of such *genius* confers
distinction on the critic who has discovered him. While James
Macpherson's 'discovery' of Ossian initiated one of the most conten-
tious debates in Scottish literary history, Mackenzie's recognition of
Burns established his own critical authority in *The Lounger* and per-
manently linked his name with the poet's.

The self-serving nature of this critical enterprise is also fairly
transparent; as Mackenzie rather slyly quips, 'there is [...] a natural,
and indeed a fortunate vanity in trying to redress the wrong which
genius is exposed to suffer' (385). Throughout his substantial review,
Mackenzie isolates specific character traits (based solely on inference
from the poems) that he believes are the primary sources of Burns's
genius. Of the poet's 'spirit', Mackenzie writes, '*Burns* possesses the
spirit as well as the fancy of a poet. That honest pride and independ-
ence of soul which are sometimes the muse's only dower, break forth
on every occasion in his work' (385). Analysing a good sampling of
verse in his review – including selections from 'The Vision',
'Despondency', 'Invocation to Ruin', 'Man was Made to Mourn',

'The Cotter's Saturday Night', 'To a Mouse', and 'To a Mountain Daisy' – Mackenzie claims that Burns's 'power of genius is not less admirable in tracing the manners, than in painting the passions, or in drawing the scenery of Nature' (388).

Though he qualifies the comparison, Mackenzie even suggests that Burns may have 'that intuitive glance with which a writer like Shakespeare discerns the characters of men' (388). However, unlike the Bard of Avon, Burns is found to be too obscure in his present state to appeal to an audience outside Scotland. Mackenzie introduces a key critical refrain at this point, arguing that Burns's usage of Scots not only makes his poetry too 'difficult' for English readers but also for those within his native country:

> Even in Scotland, the provincial dialect which Ramsay and he have used, is now read with a difficulty which greatly damps the pleasure of the reader; in England it cannot be read at all, without such a constant reference to a glossary, as nearly to destroy that pleasure. (386)

Of Burns's more accessible works, Mackenzie concedes that some 'are almost English' (386). The eruption of Burns's 'spirit' and 'fancy' in such 'almost English' poems speaks not only to his poetic skill but also to his character, especially the sources of his difference from others in his class and locale.

As noted in the first chapter, Mackenzie's review provided a phrase – 'the Heaven-taught ploughman' – that would follow Burns throughout his career.[15] The phrase appears in a sentence in which Mackenzie marveled at the poet's ability to understand and empathise with others: 'With what uncommon penetration and sagacity *this Heaven-taught ploughman*, from his humble and unlettered station, has looked upon men and manners' (388, emphasis mine). Mackenzie's reference may have been indebted to James Beattie's *The Minstrel*, where Edwin the minstrel is described as having a 'heaven-taught soul' (1.7). Regardless, Mackenzie's phrase stuck, becoming the *de facto* title that Burns endured throughout his career. As discussed in chapter 1, Burns recognised the utility of this label, occasionally acting the part in company with great facility. However, he also understood the limitations that such a label imposed on his writing and tried to furnish a different title – the 'Scotch Bard' – that would be more liberating and fulfilling for his poetic ambitions. He was not entirely successful in either endeavour, and it is to

Mackenzie's review that he owed both his fame and his frustrations as a practicing poet.

Mackenzie's reference to Burns's 'humble and unlettered station' coincides with the judgment of the reviewer in *Edinburgh Magazine* which underscored the poet's lack of 'competence' in the literary field. As in that review, Mackenzie's finds that Burns's 'distinction' resides in his difference from mainstream literary practitioners, as well as his difference from those in his own class and place. His *genius* makes him a true anomaly, unlike other competitors in the literary field. However, part of the poet's apparently liberating distinction had the potential to alienate and offend his more conservative readers; as early as Mackenzie's review, Burns had to be defended from charges of 'libertinism and irreligion' that might be evidenced in his satirical poems. In fact, in Burns's defense from such charges, Mackenzie (consummate lawyer that he was) asks readers to consider first the 'ignorance and fanaticism of the lower class of people in the country where these poems were written' (388). He further qualifies such 'fanaticism' among the 'lower class of people' as that which 'sets faith in opposition to good works' (388). Burns's distinction from such compeers resides in his ability to refute this 'fallacy': Mackenzie writes that 'a mind so enlightened as our Poet's could not but perceive' the 'dangerous' fanaticism of those in his class (388).

Mackenzie's defense of Burns's religious satires distinguishes the first wave of admirers from early skeptics, who would voice complaints about the poet's heterodox (and possibly irreligious) beliefs. Such criticism of Burns's 'irreligion' was based upon slender evidence, when considering the Kilmarnock edition alone; the most likely 'irreligious' works are 'The Holy Fair', 'To a Louse', and 'Address to the Deil', with perhaps 'The Lament, occasioned by the unfortunate issue of a friend's amour' thrown in for good measure. However, there are several relatively orthodox religious poems in the volume as well, most notably 'The Cottar's Saturday Night' and 'A Prayer in the Prospect of Death'. With such poems in mind, Mackenzie suggests that we 'look upon his lighter Muse, not as the enemy of religion' but rather as 'the champion of morality, and the friend of virtue' (388).

He notably ends his review with an injunction for readers (particularly Scots) to prevent this distinctive Scottish *genius* from emigrating to the West Indies by providing suitable emolument:

To repair the wrongs of suffering or neglected merit; to call forth genius from the obscurity in which it had pined indignant, and place it where it may profit or delight the world; these are the exertions which give to wealth an enviable superiority, to greatness and to patronage a laudable pride. (388)

Like William Duff before him, Mackenzie announces the need for patrons to support poor but 'worthy' poets such as Burns; in Mackenzie's case, this call for action is distinctly national in exhorting Scots to aid a deserving poet with *genius*, one who has been 'called forth from obscurity' from the countryside. Without such aid, Burns may abscond to the West Indies and be lost to Scotland altogether. This regrettable state of affairs may be redressed by the 'exertions' of the Scottish elite, who recognise the need to support indigenous talent like Burns – once, of course, they have been suitably informed by critics like Mackenzie, themselves only motivated by 'a natural, and indeed a fortunate vanity' to discover talent and achieve critical recognition. In fact, despite his contemporary renown as a novelist and critic, Mackenzie is still perhaps best-known for this review and the 'heaven-taught ploughman' label he devised for Burns.

A letter from 'Allan Ramsay' that appeared in the *Edinburgh Evening Courant* from 13 November 1786 articulates a similar critical judgment to that found in *The Lounger* review. Like Mackenzie, 'Ramsay' praises the arrival of a provincial 'rarity' who competes in the literary field for the honor of his country:

This part of the kingdom has not produced many poets, and therefore, when a rarity of the kind appears, it becomes the business of those whose fortune and situation enable them to promote the *cultivation of genius* to lend him assistance to such a laudable pursuit.[16]

This leads to the letter's main purpose, which is to deride those potential patrons in Ayr who have not yet stepped up to 'cultivate' Burns's *genius*. The current situation, according to 'Ramsay', is pitiful indeed, for he complains that no 'attempt [has] been made in his favour. His poems are read, his genius is applauded, and he is left to his fate. It is a reflection on the country and a disgrace to humanity' (65). Such high-toned rhetoric occasioned the indignant reply of Gavin Hamilton, who defended the honor of Ayrshire by noting the numerous subscribers to Burns's Kilmarnock edition.[17]

Nevertheless, as with Mackenzie's review, the letter by 'Ramsay' anticipates much future criticism of Burns. The poet is represented as

provincial yet exceptional, while the poetry is regarded as the work of
genius. 'Ramsay' admits that 'to this self-taught poet I am an entire
stranger', yet he argues that 'his productions have afforded me so
much pleasure that if this hint should raise an emulation in that county
to rescue from penury a genius which, if unprotected, will probably
sink into obscurity, I will most cheerfully contribute to it' (65-66).
Such impulses to provide charity for Burns mark the course of many
future responses that seek to legitimise the poet through the act (and
recognition) of patronage. In this respect, patronage not only confers a
degree of financial security for the poet, but also indicates the extent
to which his works have gained legitimacy in the literary field. Thus,
the investment made in the author speaks as much (if not more) to pa-
trons' legitimating role than to their 'charity'.[18]

Even from this early date, perceptions of Burns's indigent *genius*
served as key refrains in contemporary reviews of Burns's
Kilmarnock edition. In *The Monthly Review* 85 (December 1786),
James Anderson begins with the maxim, *Poeta nascitur, non fit*. This
phrase, which was first used in a commentary on Horace,[19] is applied
in order to understand Burns and his great talents: Anderson claims
that 'the humble bard, whose work now demands our attention, cannot
claim a place among [...] polished *versifiers*'.[20] In contrast to the
productions of 'polished versifiers', Burns's works 'seem to flow
without effort, from the native feelings of the heart' (71-72). As in
Mackenzie's review, Anderson also regards Burns's use of Scots as an
obstacle to the reader's enjoyment. He writes that many of the poems
'are written in some measure in an unknown tongue, which must
deprive most of our Readers of the pleasure they would otherwise
naturally create' (72).

While Burns's genius could be recognised and appreciated for its
vivacity and felicity of expression, readers like Anderson complained
that the poet's linguistic choices made his work too 'primitive'. The
sole qualifying component of poetic genius for Duff had been its utter
estrangement from other writing – in other words, its poetically
distinctive particularity which owes no debt to precursors:

A poet endued with a truly original Genius, will […] be under no necessity of drawing any of the materials of his composition from the Works of preceding Bards; since he has an unfailing resource in the exuberance of his own Imagination, which will furnish him with a redundance of all those materials, and particularly with an inexhaustible variety of new and splendid imagery, which must be regarded as one distinguishing mark of original poetic Genius.[21]

For Anderson, such instances of 'exuberant Imagination' do not appeal to a wide audience and prevent Burns's work from being properly understood and appreciated. In addition, because Burns's work also 'abound[s] with allusions to the modes of life, opinions, and ideas, of the people in a remoter corner of the country, which […] render many of the passages obscure, and consequently uninteresting', Anderson declares that his poetry 'can only be fully relished by the natives of that part of the country where it was produced' (72).

As an example of Burns's provincial appeal, Anderson discusses the poem 'Halloween', which he describes as 'a lively picture of the magical tricks that still are practised in the country at that season' (73). Anderson gives high praise to this production, likening it to Virgil's eighth *Eclogue* because 'it is a valuable relic, which […] will preserve the memory of these simple incantations long after they would otherwise have been lost' (73).[22] Despite the success of 'Halloween' (one of Burns's longest and densest Scots productions), Anderson proposes that Burns needs to increase his appeal to English readers. In fact, he advises that Burns should 'modernise the orthography a little, wherever the measure would permit, to render it less disgusting to our Readers south of the Tweed' (73).

This leads to a complaint that Anderson feels the need to articulate in depth. It concerns the key source of Burns's influences, which Anderson identifies as the 'ancient Scottish bards'. In his view, imitating such bards delegitimises the majority of Burns's verse: 'The modern ear will be somewhat disgusted with the measure of many of these pieces, which is faithfully copied from […] the ancient Scottish bards; but hath been, we think with good reason, laid aside by later Poets' (74). Anderson's critique runs counter to much prevailing critical opinion in Scotland at the time, which was still enamoured with 'primitivist' verse. It should be noted that Anderson was very much in the camp of Scottish improvers, having invented a two-horse plough without wheels called the Scotch plough. He also started his own periodical *The Bee*, to which mutual friend Thomas Blacklock

advised Burns to submit.[23] Given Anderson's following advice in his
review, though, it is understandable that Burns chose not to send any
verse to *The Bee*:

> If ever [Burns] should think of offering any thing more to the Public, we are of the
> opinion his performances would be more highly valued were they written in measures
> less antiquated. The few Songs, Odes, Dirges, &c. in this collection, are very poor in
> comparison of the other pieces. The Author's mind is not sufficiently stored with
> brilliant ideas to succeed in that line. (74)

The tenor and thrust of this critical interpretation expose the
overriding problems facing many of Burns's early critics, as they
sought to classify his work and reconcile his language usage with the
standards governing practice in the literary field.

In his discussion of 'habitus', Karl Maton notes that 'practice
results from relations between one's dispositions (habitus) and one's
position in a field (capital), within the current state of play of that
social arena (field)'.[24] For Anderson, Burns's *genius* alone cannot
reconcile the poet's 'disposition' with the 'position' available to him
in the field in its 'current state of play'. That 'state of play' demanded
that the poet employ a language common to critics, authors, and
readers. Despite Burns's desire to be recognised as a 'Scotch Bard',
critics like Anderson urged him to write 'in measures less antiquated'
in order to receive lasting distinction in the literary field. Unlike
previous critics, Anderson departs from the aesthetic conceptualisation
of Burns's *genius* by refusing to grant the poet unqualified praise. His
motivation may have been influenced by the desire to dissent from
prevailing critical opinion, epitomised by Mackenzie's review.
Though not an overt skeptic, Anderson was clearly not an admirer in
the vein of Sibbald, Mackenzie or 'Ramsay'. He ends his review with
an intriguing farming metaphor that Burns would have certainly
understood, if not appreciated. He writes, 'This collection may be
compared to a heap of wheat carelessly winnowed. Some grain of a
most excellent quality is mixed with a little chaff, and half ripened
corn' (74).

A year later, Anderson revisited Burns in a review of the Edin-
burgh edition of *Poems* (1787). With a degree of self-satisfaction, he
states, 'We are glad to find, by the numerous and respectable list of
subscribers prefixed to the volume before us, that this Bard of Nature
has no reason to complain that "a poet is not honoured in his own

country"'.[25] As if in response to the appeals of Mackenzie and 'Allan Ramsay' in their reviews, Anderson finds that Burns has now received suitable recognition in the literary field by his fellow Scots. This is evidenced most obviously by the appearance of the second edition of Burns's *Poems*, newly revised, expanded and published in the Scottish capital. Anderson seems content to merely highlight the obvious success achieved by a poet whom he initially found worthy but flawed in his appeal to readers without knowledge of Scots. Measured by the large number of subscribers to the second edition, as well as by the considerable reading public, Burns's success remains rather bewildering to Anderson. He writes with some surprise that 'it appears that he has been very liberally patronised by an indulgent Public; and we rejoice to see that he may now have it in his power to tune his oaten reed at his ease' (90). The ambivalence of critics like Anderson about Burns's fame is nicely rendered here, as the critic's diction captures his bemused perception of an 'indulgent Public' that has 'liberally patronised' the poet. Anderson seems to believe that like a pastoral shepherd, Burns can now 'tune his oaten reed at ease' without need of further assistance.[26] The poet's continuing financial difficulties during this period (particularly the suit for damages pursued by James Armour, his future father-in-law) tell a different story, belying the critical platitudes about patronage that were fast becoming a central element of his advance publicity.

Such views represent the apogee of Burns's fame in the late 1780s. With the publication of the Edinburgh edition in 1787, the 'heaven-taught ploughman' persona continued to be readily applied in most contemporary reviews. Burns's *genius* was still consistently linked with his class status, causing much speculative inquiry about the sources of such an apparent aberration among the labouring class. However, once the initial novelty had worn off, more attentive focus to the actual poems can be found in this next wave of reviews. In an unsigned notice in the *New Annual Register* from 1787, the reviewer begins with the by-now commonplace assertion that Burns's *Poems* are 'the productions of a man in a low station in life'.[27] After this requisite allusion, Burns's skill in writing 'serious' and 'humorous' poems is evaluated in order to determine his true affinity. The reviewer writes that many of the poems in the collection are 'elegant, simple, and pleasing' and further claims that 'those that are written in a more serious strain have much poetical merit; but the humorous and satirical pieces appear to have been most congenial to the author's feelings, and turn of mind' (75). This is an intriguing assertion, one which counters the beliefs of many of Burns's early associates like Hugh Blair, famously (or infamously) responsible for discouraging him from writing and/or publishing exuberant satires like 'The Jolly Beggars'.

For the reviewer from the *New Annual Register*, the 'heaven-taught ploughman' remained an appealing persona, for it could easily explain the poet's propensities; for example, he writes that Burns's poems 'of the descriptive kind contain faithful and pleasing delineations of the simplicity of manners, and engaging scenes to be found in a country life' (75). Such comments betray a lack of close attention to rural poems like 'The Holy Fair' and 'The Twa Dogs', which employ satire to puncture the pastoral idealism of 'country life'. This is a major critical oversight, for 'The Twa Dogs' was the inaugural poem in both the Kilmarnock and Edinburgh editions. Like Anderson's second review, the *New Annual Register* review provides ample commentary on the apparent fruits of Burns's success, concluding that 'upon the whole, we think our rural bard is justly entitled to the patronage and encouragement which have been liberally extended towards him' (75). While the reviewer begins to explore new terrain in this discussion of the newly famous 'rural bard', there is a rote rehearsal of critical conceits that would become quickly ossified in Burns's reception history.

An unsigned notice from the *Universal Magazine* (1787) reveals the obvious distortions at work in these early years of acclaim; in this case, such distortion resulted from the critic's compounding the poet's idealised 'heaven-taught ploughman' persona with a factual error about Burns's place of origin. Considering the Edinburgh edition, the reviewer writes that 'these Poems, the author of which is in the humble situation of a ploughman, in the Highlands of Scotland, possess uncommon excellence, whether we consider them as adorned with beautiful sentiments, picturesque imagery, or harmonious versification'.[28] The valorisation of the poet's 'uncommon excellence' is accomplished by vague praise of 'sentiments' and imagery, while the description of Burns as a ploughman in the Highlands displays a curious and striking ignorance of both Burns's biography and Scottish geography. Perhaps for this reviewer, Burns's Lowland rural identity melded with prevailing cultural attitudes about Scottish Highlanders and their presumably 'primitive' lives and locales. At any rate, the reviewer ends with a notice of Burns's newfound sophistication, noting the poet's dedication to the gentlemen of the Caledonian Hunt 'which is distinguished by a dignity and spirit worthy of bards in more exalted situations' (86).

Abiding perceptions of Burns's less 'exalted' situation, however, are witnessed in a letter by a 'Friend of Genius', published in a supplement of the *Universal Magazine* (1787). Hailing from Eton, the correspondent remarks upon the prior publication of two poems by Burns – 'A Winter Night' and 'Epistle to Davie' – in the *Universal Magazine*. His reason for writing is to provide the magazine's readers with more information about the poet: 'The two Poems which you inserted in your Magazine for May last, must have excited a Curiosity in your Readers to know something of the extraordinary Genius that produced them'.[29] To satiate their 'curiosity' about this 'extraordinary Genius' hailing from the Scottish provinces, the 'Friend of Genius' appends Mackenzie's *Lounger* review, thus perpetuating the already-existing publicity surrounding the 'heaven-taught ploughman'.

Two remaining reviews from 1787 are worth remarking upon for their generic, semi-plagiarised quality, as well as for their repetition of critical conceits and stereotypes about Burns. The first, an unsigned notice from *New Town and Country Magazine* (1787), reports that 'Robert Burns, we are informed, is a ploughman, but blessed by Nature with a powerful genius'. An unsigned notice from *General Magazine and Impartial Review* (1787), the second review echoes the first almost word for word, with some interesting variations: 'By general report we learn, that R. B. is a *plough-boy*, of small education, but blessed by nature with a powerful genius'.[30] Making Burns a 'plough-boy' perhaps suits the vogue for youthful and prodigious labouring-class poets initiated by Chatterton's reception in the 1770s, amplified here by the notion of the poet's 'small education'.

Both reviewers echo existing complaints about Burns's work in Scots, finding (in the words of the *New Town and Country Magazine* reviewer) that 'these poems being "chiefly in the Scottish dialect", it must necessarily confine their beauties to a small circle of readers' (87). Both concede that 'the author has given good specimens of his skill in English' (87), a judgment which is not found in many early reviews. The reviewer from *General Magazine and Impartial Review* finishes his brief discussion of the Edinburgh edition with a nod to the poet's success in acquiring patronage through subscription, another persistent refrain in the reception history. He writes, 'We are happy to observe prefixed to this collection of natural genius and strong sense, a list of subscribers, at once so numerous and respectable, as to do honour to the author's countrymen' (89).

As Anderson had alluded in his second review, the notion of patronage as an act of national 'honour' is promoted by this reviewer. In order for Burns to achieve distinction in the literary field, he needs for both his identity and his writing to be recognised as 'cultural capital' by critics and readers. In this sense, Burns may be seen to represent the 'embodiment' of cultural capital, which is 'incorporated within the corporality of the person as the principles of consciousness in predispositions and propensities'.[31] For Burns, such 'predispositions and propensities' refer explicitly to his socioeconomic identity, which is a critical element of the cultural capital he has acquired as a writer of *genius*. One might add here the category of national origin as well, for it is expressly Burns's shared national identity that binds him and his work to fellow Scots regardless of class status. Only by banking upon this shared component of his social identity will Burns be recognised as a competitor in the literary field, one whose work has gained substantial 'cultural capital' by virtue of the exceptionality of his *genius*. The only means for Burns to continue to write (and thus continue to express his 'poetic genius') is to secure the patronage of his fellow Scots, an act which validates both his writing and his person.

As the reviewer from *General Magazine and Impartial Review* concludes, patrons' 'bounty we trust will enable [Burns] to preserve that independence of mind, and to indulge himself in those flights of imagination which he appears to possess in an eminent degree, and which constitute the genuine poet of nature' (80). Such enthusiasm that the poet's *genius* would be 'indulged' with 'bounty' was not borne out by his later career, which was marked repeatedly by the failure of patrons to follow through on their promises to aid Burns with appointments and money.[32] The vista of unbridled success imagined by the poet's early critics was ultimately damaging to Burns as he sought to remain a serious competitor in the literary field, for it continued to depict his efforts as solely dependent upon the charity of patrons.

While his need for patronage was true to a certain extent, Burns repeatedly attempted to establish and maintain his independence as a writer with full creative and financial control over his works. As Bourdieu observes, 'The pure intention of the artist is that of a producer who aims to be autonomous, that is, entirely the master of his product'.[33] As his career continued, however, Burns would find his effort to be the 'master of his product' continually frustrated by such devices as the 'heaven-taught ploughman' persona. Indeed, this persona quickly became the dominant cultural production of the poet, one that was fostered and promoted by his critical admirers from the earliest point in his career.

3. 'The Applause of the Moment': The First Wave of Skeptics

Despite the tide of largely positive critical reviews, Burns had his skeptics from the very start. One of the earliest skeptical views of Burns and his advance publicity was published in *The English Review* (February 1787). Though its author has not been verified, it is believed to have been written by the controversial minister and poet John Logan.[34] Logan had helped in the publication in 1770 of a volume of poems by his former classmate Michael Bruce (who had died three years prior). After a difficult stint delivering lectures on 'universal history' in Edinburgh, Logan published his own collection of verse in 1781. However, he included poems in his volume that had appeared in Bruce's collection, including the celebrated 'Ode to the Cuckoo'. The Bruce family tried to prevent Logan from issuing a second edition including these poems, which he claimed to have authored rather than Bruce. The controversy continued throughout the 1780s, and Logan's supporters included Henry Mackenzie and Thomas Robertson, among others. At this time, Logan's personal problems were mounting as well, for he was an alcoholic and had fathered two illegitimate children.[35]

Despite his difficulties, Logan was an active critic with a formidable intellect; Adam Smith stated that his lectures were 'approved and even admired by some of the best and most impartial judges'.[36] Logan's review of Burns's poems appears at first glance to be little different from those of the admirers, including praise of the poet's distinctive *genius*. He writes, 'The mountains, the forests, and the streams are the living volumes that impregnate his fancy and kindle the fire of genius'.[37] Despite such marks of approbation, Logan was the first to openly question Burns's legitimacy, in particular his persona as the 'heaven-taught ploughman'. In fact, Logan seeks to debunk this persona by describing Burns as a '*natural*, though not a *legitimate*, son of the muses'; he further states that although, 'the Ayrshire ploughman [...] is by no means such a poetical prodigy as some of his malicious friends have represented, he has a genuine title to the attention of the public, as a natural, though not legitimate, son of the muses' (76). Walter Moffatt observes that 'just what this reviewer means by this last statement it is hard to say', also noting that perhaps Burns 'was not a legitimate son of the muses [...] because he had not acquired through the usual process of formal education the learning and artistic skill necessary to develop this talent'.[38]

I would counter that actually the opposite is the case: Logan calculates Burns's 'legitimacy' by *recognising* him as a fellow producer (and competitor). Following this interpretation, Logan judges Burns's productions according to existing standards of taste that apply to all competitors in the literary field. By using such criteria of evaluation, Logan claims that Burns is not an untaught, 'primitive genius' as attested by prior reviewers. In fact, Logan seems to regard such prior critical opinion quite cynically, seeing it as a fabrication introduced by reviewers primarily interested in gaining critical recognition. Logan sees such strategies as fundamentally dishonest, for they serve more to elevate reviewers (and diminish the poet's real talents) in a patently hypocritical fashion. This debunking spirit animates the rest of Logan's review, providing a bracing tonic to previous critical adulation of Burns as the 'heaven-taught ploughman'.

For instance, Logan is absolutely ruthless in its dismissal of the 'novelty' that elevates poets of Burns's class to the literary stage from time to time:

In an age that is satiated with literary pleasures nothing is so grateful to the public taste as novelty. This ingredient will give a gust to very indifferent fare and lend a flavor to the produce of the home-brewed vintage [...] From this propensity in human nature a musical child, a rhyming milkwoman, a learned pig,[39] or a Russian poet will 'strut their hour upon the stage', and gain the applause of the moment. From this cause, and this alone, Stephen Duck, the thresher, and many other *nameless* names have glittered and disappeared like those bubbles of the atmosphere which are called *falling* stars. (76)

The 'applause of the moment' that popularises 'nameless names' such as Duck and other novelties is seen here as a foolish absurdity, a mere transient 'bubble' of the atmosphere. Such passages tend to confirm Bourdieu's theory of the active 'struggles' that take place within the literary field, especially the active policing of borders that Logan engages in above.

The need to defend such boundaries derives from the porous nature of the literary field itself: Bourdieu writes, 'One of the most significant properties of the field of cultural production, explaining its extreme dispersion and the conflicts between rival principles of legitimacy, is the extreme permeability of its frontiers'.[40] However, Logan's central argument in his review is not that Burns has transgressed boundaries, but instead that he is a 'legitimate' player in the literary field. Unlike labouring-class anomalies like Duck, Burns is recognised by Logan as a fellow poet whose work displays considerable 'cultural and artistic competence'. Burns himself reveals such 'competence' by using mainstream poetic models and methods; concerning Burns's 'serious poems', Logan argues that 'we can trace imitations of almost every English author of celebrity' (76).

In a footnote to this passage, Logan expands upon the point and emphasises Burns's similitude with other practicing British poets. Instead of highlighting the poet's national, cultural, and class differences, Logan states that

Robert Burns, though he has been *represented* as an ordinary ploughman, was a farmer, or what they call a tenant in Scotland, and rented land which he cultivated with his own hands. He is better acquainted with the English poets than most English authors that have come under our review. (76-77)

This judgment is significant for several reasons; the first is its implicit granting of recognition to a fellow poet who has earned a place within the literary field. The second, overarching feature of this judgment is its desire to expose the artificial nature of the publicity Burns had received thus far.

To Logan, Burns may not be in the same class as a 'rhyming milkwoman' or 'learned pig', but he is *not* exceptional enough to be classified as a 'poetic genius'. Too much has been made of his difference (through *genius*) from practicing poets in Logan's view; in fact, it is precisely because of Burns's active participation in the literary field that he deserves critical recognition. Throughout his review,

Logan argues that Burns's status as a 'true and uncultivated genius' has been engineered by overenthusiastic reviewers with a taste for novelty in the literary field. In a letter to Henry Mackenzie (who had understandably expressed concern over Logan's review, given his own work promoting Burns), Logan explains the reasoning behind his review.[41] He tells Mackenzie that he has been 'misinformed with regard to the Critique it contains on the poems of Burns', stating that 'the article is not a very good one, but it is impartial, and I dare say Mr. Burns will be very pleased with the praise he has received' (78). However, he contends that 'I do not think [...] that [Burns] is so much an Original as has been represented, and indeed, I do not recollect a new image of nature in all his works' (79).

To support such claims, Logan offered the following explanation to Mackenzie:

I read his works under a considerable disadvantage. I received three letters from Edinburgh full of irrational and unbounded panegyric, representing him as a poetical phenomenon that owed nothing but to Nature and his own Genius. When I opened the book I found that he was as well acquainted with the English poets as I was, and I could point you out a hundred imitations. There is a kind of Imposture not infrequent among poets of conveying Modern ideas in a dialect of Antiquity. (79)

With this nod to the Ossian and Chatterton controversies as well as to the popularity of 'primitive' verse, Logan deflates the publicity that has taken hold of Burns and his poetry. With his explicit recognition of Burns as a fellow poet, though, Logan legitimises him in the literary field in a much different (and arguably more positive) fashion than that seen in other reviews' more populist endorsements. In fact, Logan is so confident in his debunking critical judgment that he claims in his letter to Mackenzie that 'when that rage and Mania which seizes Edinburgh at least once a year has subsided, I am confident that your own opinion will coincide with Mine' (79).

In his 'Rhyming Epistle to Mr. R— B—, Ayrshire' first published in the *Edinburgh Evening Courant* (23 June 1787) before its inclusion in *Poems in Scots and English* (1788), James Macaulay expressed similar doubts about Burns's authenticity at this early stage of his critical reception. Unlike verse epistles written by Burns's admirers, Macaulay's was written on his own initiative and published on his own behalf. An Edinburgh printer, Macaulay was among the first poet-critics to follow Logan's lead in questioning Burns's 'heaven-

taught ploughman' status.[42] Written in Scots, Macaulay's epistle of-
fers an urban deconstruction of the provincial poet's disguise, begin-
ning with a quote from Allan Ramsay that reads, 'Its education maks
the genius bright'.[43] This epigraph reveals the tenor of Macaulay's
critique, which also aims to expose the 'education' that nullifies
Burns's 'heaven-taught' persona.

After claiming that 'yestreen I read your buik / Frae end to end',
Macaulay confesses that 'I never like to mak a fraise / Or yet be lovich
o' my praise'.[44] Although the poem appears to be heading in the
direction of commendatory verse, Macaulay articulates serious doubts
about the *genius* in his midst. He is annoyed by Burns's presumptuous
relationship with the Muses:

You crack about the Nine,
An' how to you they've been sae kin',
By helping you the-day to shine
'Mang Scottish Worthies. (19-22)

To counter such audacious 'cracking', Macaulay goes on the offensive
by rebutting both the 'blast' of Burns's celebrity as well as the
authenticity of his status as a ploughman.

As Logan before him, Macaulay ventures that Burns is merely
assuming the persona of the 'heaven-taught ploughman' in order to
stoke the 'blast' of his publicity. Such self-aggrandising behavior
piques the urban printer:

Still for a' the blast that's made,
I doubt you are some sleekit blade,
That never handled shool or spade,
Or yet the pleugh,
Unless it were to hae it said –
An' that's enough. (25-30)

Having thus disabused the authenticity of Burns's status as a labourer,
Macaulay identifies another source of Burns's difference from 'real'
labouring-class poets: he refers to 'the scraps o' French an' Latin, /
That's flung athort your buik fu' thick in' (31-32). Due to such
allusive poetic practice, Burns is exposed: 'It's easy seen you've aft
been flitting / Frae school to school' (33-34).

The main point of Macaulay's epistle is clarified by extensive
interrogation of the poet, in which the factor of 'education' does not in

fact make Burns's *genius* bright but rather disqualifies him from such consideration. He asks the poet directly to respond to this charge:

I'm no for riving aff your brow,
The laurel folk may think you due;
But, gin a while you left the pleu'
To tend the College,
What need you smoor the thing that's true,
Wi' a' your knowledge? (37-42)

Thus, it is Burns's 'knowledge' that 'smoors' [smothers] the 'true' things about him, which would seem to be his class status; this background is true only if 'uncontaminated' by education. As Randal Johnson notes, 'schooling serves to reinforce, rather than diminish, social differences'.[45] In the coverage surrounding Burns, described as 'the prints – newspapers an' reviews' (43), Macaulay suggests that the poet's representation as the 'heaven-taught ploughman' is easily dismissed by an urban (and urbane) reader like himself.

As an Edinburgh printer, Macaulay uses his own authority in the literary field to demystify the cultural production of the 'heaven-taught ploughman'.[46] He flatly states that this persona will fail in Scotland's capital: 'That'll nae gae down / Wi' ilka chiel about this town' (49-50). Arbiters of poetic taste in the city cannot be fooled by such sham productions as that being foisted upon the public by Burns's eager critical admirers. Expounding on this country/city divide, Macaulay describes the state of the literary field in Edinburgh, which he insists is governed by rational principles rather than the foolish taste for novelty and difference:

In days o' yore, folk aft were fleec'd;
But miracles lang syne hae ceas'd
Among the gentry here, at least.
Wha ne'er can think
A bard direct frae Heav'n can feast,
An' write, an' *drink*. (55-60)

Feasting, writing, and drinking are actions that identify the poet as a mere mortal, a poet like any other poet. Summarising his case in the last stanza of his epistle, Macaulay exhorts Burns to 'ne'er try to put things out o' place' but instead to '*own your intellects*' as 'mony a ane, wi' honest face, / Has done afore' (92, 93, 95-96).

Macaulay's critique of Burns divests the poet of the promotional aura surrounding him in order to reinforce the governing standards of the literary field. As in Logan's review, Macaulay's poem seeks to force Burns to compete on the same playing field as other practicing poets rather than acting the part of the 'heaven-taught ploughmen'. Another contemporary poet found Burns to be an objectionable character in all respects. James Maxwell, author of *Animadversions on some Poets and Poetasters of the Present Age, Especially R—t B—s, and J—n L—k* (1788), supplies numerous 'animadversions' to support his case against the nefarious celebrity that Burns was enjoying. Known locally as 'the Paisley Poet', Maxwell was born in 1720 in Auchenback and worked a variety of jobs (weaver, packman, clerk, usher, schoolmaster, and stonebreaker) in England before receiving a charity in Paisley. He was widely published as a poet (often at his own expense) and seems to have resented Burns's popularity on a personal level. Calling himself a 'student of divine poetry', he attacked Burns and his friend John Lapraik for their purportedly immoral behavior and works.[47] In this respect, his criticism anticipates nineteenth-century concerns over Burns's purportedly 'immoral' life and 'irreligious' works.

Seeking to contrast the degraded taste of 'the present age' with that of the past, Maxwell situates Burns within a history of 'British' poets in order to precisely classify his crimes against readers and indeed, literature itself:

Of all British poets that yet have appear'd,
None e'er at things sacred so daringly sneer'd,
As he in the west, who but lately is sprung
From behind the plough-tails, and from raking of dung.
A champion for Satan, none like him before,
And his equal, pray God, we may never see more.[48]

Burns appears here as interloper and heretic in the literary market-place, his celebrity owing more to notoriety than to any pretense of poetic merit: 'He is to this land and this age a disgrace, / And mostly to those who his poems embrace' (4). Such readers must be morally polluted to enjoy Burns's verse, which Maxwell insists 'all sober people abhor'. He writes, 'His jargon gives rakes and vile harlots delight, / But all sober people abhor the vile sight' (4).[49]

Ceding no objections, Maxwell condemns those who seek to defend 'poetasters' like Burns and Lapraik:

But some say, 'Do justice, give Satan his due,
For ROB hath his virtues, although they be few:
A jolly companion at bottle and pot,
Tho' he be a drunkard, a rake and a sot:
And tho' he be wicked, he hath a good heart'. (4-5)

Such apologies fall on deaf ears, for there can be no excusing Burns in Maxwell's eyes. Unlike Logan and Macaulay, Maxwell does not comment on Burns's literary prowess, but instead focuses all of his energies on condemning the 'irreligion' at work in the poet's life style and writings. As the above quote also indicates, Maxwell is as angry (if not more) with Burns's readers as he is with the poet himself. The fact that Burns has gained and kept an audience fills Maxwell with splenetic rage: 'Let mankind beware how they favour that Bard, / Or surely with him they must have their reward' (8). Such critiques of Burns's 'immorality' do not resurface in force until after the poet's death, becoming a major bone of contention in his reception in the early nineteenth century. At this point in time, the majority of Burns's critics kept their attention focused on the persona of the 'heaven-taught ploughman', attempting to interpret and explain (whether through veneration or critique) the aura of *genius* surrounding the poet.

4. 'Brother' and 'Sister' Poets: Burns's First Wave of Poetic Admirers

Many more Scottish writers responded favourably in the late 1780s to the newly famous poet in their midst. Fellow poets frequently assayed Burns's importance for the future of Scottish poetry, as well as for their own futures as writers.[50] Several corresponded with the poet by means of verse epistles, often publishing the exchanges in their own collections of verse as Burns had done in his Kilmarnock and Edinburgh editions. In his 'Epistle to Davie', Burns had addressed 'Davie' Sillar as a 'brother poet'; he would soon discover that other poets viewed him in the same light, reaching out to him as a 'brother poet' in unsolicited verse. Such gestures were expressly calculated to help the authors gain recognition in the literary field, particularly those epistles penned by fellow labouring-class poets. Establishing kinship with Burns began to be perceived by such poets as the necessary first step to entering the literary marketplace as a 'legitimised' author.

To gain such entry, 'brother' (and 'sister') poets needed to find points of contact in order to claim kinship with Burns. Common class affiliation would most often be the default category for the exchange of verse epistles with Burns. Such efforts were based on the assumption that shared class status implied solidarity, with the underlying premise that Burns would aid 'brother' and 'sister' poets by recognising the value of their works in the literary field. This presents a rather different perception of Burns than that expressed by his critical admirers. To the extent that their reviews could (and did) enable Burns to gain recognition, the critics inhabited a dominant position in the literary field. Their representation of the poet as a 'heaven-taught ploughman' with 'native genius' served to convey their approbation as well as their authority, for it delimited Burns's appeal by providing a critical framework for interpreting and assessing his works.

However, a quite different scenario was in play when labouring-class poets tried to gain Burns's approval and aid in the literary field. In this case, Burns was invested with the authority to grant their works recognition and legitimacy through his own act of patronage. This form of patronage did not require a financial component necessarily, for its most decisive element was the symbolic (and sometimes literal) act of recognition. He could do this by several means, from simply writing a verse epistle in response to helping the would-be poet to find publication and patronage opportunities. Burns's celebrity as a Scottish labouring-class poet of *genius* drew many admirers from the Scottish countryside and the cities, each seeking to establish friendly kinship with him in order to gain their own share of literary fame. Surely, they must have thought, such a 'brother' poet – and fellow Scot – could be relied upon to aid a fellow farmer (or weaver, or milkwoman, or stonemason ...) in the business of literature.

So they hoped, but Burns proved to be singularly recalcitrant with such 'brother' and 'sister' poets. In a letter to his own patron Frances Dunlop from 4 March 1789, Burns expresses annoyance and disdain at the efforts of 'brother' and 'sister' poets who appealed to him. His rebuke of their efforts is exceedingly harsh: 'My success has encouraged such a shoal of ill-spawned monsters to crawl into public notice under the title of Scots Poets, that the very term, Scots Poetry, borders on the burlesque' (I, 382). It is difficult to reconcile the poet who made these statements with the same figure who wrote verse epistles to 'brother poets' in his early career, seeking to gain their acceptance and approval. That Burns would dehumanise fellow labouring-class poets once he had gained his own recognition speaks to changes in his character that are regrettable but perhaps understandable in light of the competitive nature of the literary marketplace.[51] Burns eventually spurned such admirers as he began to experience the vagaries of fame and his own litany of personal and professional disappointments.

One of his first poetic admirers was John Lapraik, an older provincial poet with whom Burns had initiated contact. The younger Burns found Lapraik to be a congenial figure, addressing three verse epistles to him that express no small measure of admiration for the elder poet. Lapraik replied to each epistle, eventually including them in his only volume of verse, entitled *Poems on Several Occasions* (1788), which was published by Burns's own printer John Wilson in Kilmarnock.[52] Lapraik's verse epistles offer an intriguingly ambiguous self-representation as Burns's 'brother' poet. Throughout his verse epistles (as well as in the preface to his volume), Lapraik repeatedly stresses his lack of education and describes his writing only as 'rhyming'. In this he resembles Burns's self-representation in his own verse epistles, including his epistles to Lapraik among others.[53]

Speaking of himself in the third person, Lapraik confesses in the preface that publishing his poetry 'proceeds not from motives of ostentation […] nor a desire of discovering to the world his Poetical abilities; neither does he find any violent inclination to wear the laurels of fame'.[54] If neither 'ostentation' nor a 'violent inclination' for fame motivates Lapraik, why did he seek to publish his verse? He explains that his 'disinclination' for recognition derives from a very practical consideration: 'The Author, alas! both from his circumstances and manner of life, being constantly engaged in labour or business, was denied the share of Education which is necessary to form the Gentleman and Poet' (3). At the time of the volume's publication, Lapraik was sixty years of age, working as an innkeeper and postmaster in Muirsmill. His life had been marked by much misfortune; he was born into a family of some stature in Muirkirk, inheriting

his father's estate which had been in the family for several genera-
tions. However, after the failure of the Ayr Bank in 1773, he lost the
property, was imprisoned for debt, and eventually found work as a
farmer.[55]

Given such experiences, it is little wonder that Lapraik found lit-
tle time or opportunity for the education 'necessary to form the
Gentleman and Poet'. Fulfilling such educational criteria is indeed
'necessary', for as Randal Johnson notes, authors must 'possess at
least the minimum amount of knowledge, or skill, or "talent" to be
accepted as a legitimate player' in the literary field (8). The 'minimum
amount' required is best expressed as 'artistic competence'. Johnson
remarks that

Artistic competence [...] is the result of a long process of inculcation which begins (or
not) in the family, often in conformity with its level of economic, academic, and
cultural capital, and is reinforced by the educational system. It also involves pro-
longed exposure to works of art. The understanding of a work of art thus depends
fully on the possession of the code into which it has been encoded, and this is neither
a natural nor a universally distributed capability. (23)

In this sense, Lapraik openly declares in the preface that he is 'artisti-
cally incompetent' in the literary field, self-consciously alerting read-
ers that he does not possess the necessary 'code' to be a legitimate
player.

He contrasts himself immediately with Burns[56], whom he sees as
a legitimate player indeed. Unlike many critical admirers of Burns
from this period, Lapraik views him as a writer with the necessary ar-
tistic and cultural competence to compete in the literary field. In this
respect, Lapraik feels that his 'rhyming' has little (if any) connection
with the accomplished verse of the younger poet:

My silly Muse,
That thou sae prais'd langsyne,
When she did scarce ken verse by prose,
Now dares to spread her wing. (35, 1-4)

Burns's example gives Lapraik's 'silly Muse' the temerity to 'spread
her wing'. Before he had known Burns, Lapraik confesses that he had
only written 'jingling worthless rhyme' (8). He now hopes to compete
in the same playing field with his young rival, though Lapraik seems
decidedly unenthused about his prospects.

Despite his misgivings, Lapraik decides to enter the literary mar-
ketplace. Burns's fame has inspired him to emulate his younger
'brother poet' in style and, hopefully, inspiration:

When I met a chiel like you,
Sae gi'en to mirth an' fun,
Wha lik'd to speel Parnassus' hill
An' drink at Helicon,
I'd aiblins catch a wee bit spark
O' his Poetic fire,
An' rhyme awa like ane half-mad,
Until my Muse did tire. (17-24)

The majority of Lapraik's epistle describes his efforts to 'rhyme awa
like ane half-mad', although the results are not satisfying. In
exasperation, he concludes his epistle by dismissing his own work as
'dull, insipid, thowless [ineffectual] rhyme, / And stupid, senseless
stuff' (31-32).[57] As if predicting his own dismal future as a poet,
Lapraik never published a volume of poetry again, nor did he receive
any aid (or further verse epistles) from Burns after 1788.

Another poetic admirer from this period was Janet Little, a 'sister
poet' connected with Burns through their mutual friend and patron
Frances Dunlop. Known as the 'Scotch Milkmaid', Little owed a large
measure of her public recognition to Burns's example. Like the col-
lections of Burns and Lapraik, Little's *Poetical Works* (1792) was also
printed in Ayr by John and Peter Wilson. However, despite the prom-
ising beginning of her poetic career, Little's work was largely ignored,
and she only started to receive serious critical attention in the twenti-
eth century.[58] In the same manner as her 'brother poets', Little felt a
strong kinship with Burns due to their shared class status, and she
sought to capitalise on this connection in her poetry written to or about
her famous 'brother poet'. For aspiring poets like Little, Burns's liter-
ary acclaim was a daunting precedent for their own emulation, fre-
quently leading them to express considerable doubts about their own
prospects for recognition.

Like Lapraik, Little was ambivalent about the nature of her
affiliation with her famous 'brother poet'. She may have hoped to gain
his favour as a fellow Scot from the labouring class by addressing him
first in verse, but she never received a reply. Gaining such approval
invited the possibility of further recognition in the literary field as well
as access to the 'power of consecration'. In *The Rules of Art*, Bourdieu

writes that 'the power of consecration [is] outside of the network of relations of exchange through which it is produced and circulates, that is, [it is] in a sort of central bank which would be the ultimate bond of all acts of credit'.[59] To the extent that Burns could (or wanted to) utilise his fame to promote the work of 'brother' and 'sister' poetslike Lapraik and Little, his 'power of consecration' relied on the 'credit' he had gained in the literary marketplace. This 'credit' was in turn bestowed upon Burns by his critics, who had 'consecrated' him as an exceptional 'poetic genius'.

Such 'consecration' was highly conditional, greatly relying on Burns's active participation in the 'heaven-taught ploughman' persona that was the ultimate guarantor of his credit in the literary field. In 'An Epistle to Mr. Robert Burns', Little analyses Burns's achievement in relative terms by assessing the preconditions that contributed to his literary fame. In addition, she situates Burns's achievements within the continuum of Scottish poetry, noting the influence of his poetic forebears:

Fairfa' the honest rustic swain,
The pride o' a' our Scottish plain;
Thou gi'es us joy to hear thy strain,
And notes sae sweet;
Old Ramsay's shade, reviv'd again,
In thee we greet.[60]

Using the language of pastoral, Little envisions Burns as an 'honest, rustic swain' whose artless simplicity harkens back to the poetry of Allan Ramsay, the key Scots poet of the early eighteenth century.[61]

She claims that Scottish readers of all ranks are eager to return to this simpler strain of national poetry: 'To hear thy song, all ranks desire; / Sae well thou strik'st the dormant lyre' (13-14). By awakening the 'dormant lyre', Burns has performed an expressly national duty in the manner of the 'Scotch Bard' whose title he had sought to earn. With this opening gambit, Little both valorises and delimits the scope and significance of Burns's poetry for the Scottish nation. His verse is primarily valued for being Scottish poetry, perhaps even more so on account of its own exceptional merits. Little makes this last point quite evident when she compares her literary skill with Burns's, to her own apparent disadvantage: 'In vain I blunt my feckless quill, / Your fame to raise' (39-40). Describing her 'quill' as 'feckless' is not an admission that she lacks literary talent as much as it is an assertion that labouring-class women poets like herself do not possess the cultural capital to praise with authority.[62]

The speaker's 'feckless quill' is further contrasted with the figure of Burns, who increasingly becomes held up for disbelief as well as admiration. Her bewilderment might be traced to one's sense of 'placement/investment' in the literary field, which Bourdieu suggests is 'one of the dispositions most closely linked to social and geographical origin'.[63] Although she feels an affiliation with the 'heaven-taught ploughman' through place and class, she senses that her efforts in verse will not be greeted with the same accolades as Burns's due to her lack of 'investment' in the literary field. As Lapraik had also expressed, Little understands that comparing herself directly with Burns may not be to her advantage, yet she will do so in order to further 'raise' the 'fame' of her 'brother poet'. In so doing, she hopes to gain his approval as well as increased 'investment' in the literary field.

As part of this promotional strategy, she depicts Burns as a 'plough-boy' in bitter contest with such paragons of English literature as Joseph Addison, Alexander Pope, and Samuel Johnson:

Did Addison or Pope but hear,
Or Sam, that critic most severe,
A plough-boy sing, wi' throat sae cleare,
They, in a rage,
Their works wad a' in pieces tear
An' curse your page. (43-48)

Marked by unusual violence, Little's imagined scenario highlights the competitive nature of the literary field which pits aspirants against established tastemakers. Burns's national identity is another marker of his difference in this passage, along with his class and age; vying with decidedly English (and in Johnson's case, Scottophobic) critics, the Scottish 'plough-boy' confounds their attacks with such 'cleare' singing that they destroy their own work.

While Little's scenario is deliberately exaggerated for effect, it does underscore an important element of the literary field, which is its social and national dimension. Bourdieu observes that 'there are rela-tionships between groups maintaining different, and even antagonistic, relations to culture, depending on the conditions in which they acquired their cultural capital and the markets in which they can derive most profit from it'.[64] By entering into a larger, more profitable market beyond Kilmarnock (and eventually far beyond Scotland), Burns has antagonised those groups in possession of considerable cultural capital, epitomised in this case by the formidable trio of Addison, Pope, and Johnson. In contrast to the heroic victory of the 'ploughboy' who leaves his English critics 'in a rage', Little describes her own efforts as destined to fail:

If I should strain my rupy throat,[65]
To raise thy praise wi' swelling note,
My rude, unpolish'd strokes wad blot
Thy brilliant shine,
An' ev'ry passage I would quote
Seems less sublime. (49-54)

However, as Margery McCulloch attests, Little's very poem itself stands as a vocal protest to such an admission: 'she has indeed praised him with skill and with an appreciative understanding of the features which make his poetry outstanding as well as the traditions which nurtured him'.[66]

Despite Little's overtures, however, Burns became increasingly reluctant to 'consecrate' 'brother' and 'sister' poets as his career advanced, finding their entreaties for recognition to be a source of continual irritation. Unlike his treatment of Lapraik, Burns dismissed Little's work altogether. This angered Frances Dunlop greatly, who wrote immediately to Burns after he criticised Little's poetry in her presence:

Methinks I hear you ask me with an air that made me feel as I had got a slap in the face, if you must read all the few lines I had pointed out to your notice in poor Jenny's book. How did I upbraid my own conceited folly at that instant that I had ever subjected one of mine to so haughty an imperious critic! I never liked so little in my life as at that moment the man whom at all others I delighted to honour [...] I then felt for Mrs Richmond [Janet Little], for you, and for myself, and not one of the sensations were such as I would wish to cherish in remembrance.[67]

Dunlop's diction in this passage is instructive, particularly her designation of Burns as a 'haughty, imperious critic'. In such encounters as that above, the negotiations working to exclude contenders (and maintain dominance) in the literary field are lived out in all their unpleasant machinations.

Not all of Burns's early poetic admirers expressed ambivalent feelings about their 'brother poet'. A verse tribute written in 1789 by Helen Craik, a poet living in Dumfries, is a more typical model of the commendatory verse written for Burns both during and after his lifetime. In this poem, Craik lauds the poet's 'native Genius' and its effect upon his fellow Scots: 'Here native Genius, gay, unique and strong, / Shines through each page, and marks the tuneful song'.[68] She further states that 'Rapt Admiration her warm tribute pays, / And Scotia proudly echoes all she says' (3-4). Craik offers unequivocal praise here, without qualifying Burns's *genius* or the 'warm tribute' owed to it by 'Scotia' itself. She further emphasises the poet's greatness, stating that 'bold Indpendence [...] illumes the theme / And claims a manly privilege to Fame' (5-6). That such fame is explicitly gendered does not seem to bother Craik, who does not assert her own identity as a poet in the tribute at all.

She concludes by exhorting Burns to appreciate his own great gifts as a poet: 'Vainly, O Burns! wou'd rank and riches shine, / Compar'd with in-born merit great as thine' (7-8). His 'in-born merit' is further magnified in the tribute's last two lines, where Craik advises that 'these Chance may take, as Chance has often given, / But Pow'rs like thine can only come from Heav'n' (9-10). To Craik, Burns's greatness resides not only in his 'in-born merit', a sense of individual worth that refuses the vain importuning of rank as merely the work of 'Chance', but is also the work of divinity. Echoing Mackenzie, Craik describes Burns's gifts as a 'Power' that 'Heaven' alone can bestow. This would become a common refrain in later tributes to Burns, for Craik's poem captures the spirit of Mackenzie's 'heaven-taught ploughman' representation in all its excessive and uncomplicated praise. Indeed, her portrayal suggests that the poet will remain a nationally-glorified figure (perhaps even an icon), despite the workings of 'Chance' in his future.

For his early critical and poetic admirers, Burns's *genius* guaranteed continued success, regardless of the influence of 'the power of consecration of producers and products'.[69] Once 'consecrated' as a 'native Genius', Burns could exert his own authority in the literary field, particularly among fellow Scots who increasingly viewed him with a mixture of awe, respect, and disbelief. As the critical admirers had contributed greatly to the emerging cultural production of the 'heaven-taught ploughman', so did poetic admirers who tried (often in vain) to gain both his respect and recognition in the literary field. As has been demonstrated, however, Burns was chary of such admirers and rarely offered any assistance beyond obligatory, perfunctory gestures. When confronted by early skeptics, Burns emerged unscathed, his persona and celebrity intact. As his fame grew, Burns himself grew increasingly isolated from other Scottish poets who hailed from his class and place and consciously sought to distance himself from such aspirants. Rather, he worked deliberately to consolidate his reputation and construct his own persona. This process – and Burns's ultimate failure in achieving his own self-definition as a 'Scotch Bard – will be the subject of the next chapter, which recounts the decline and fall of the 'heaven-taught ploughman'.

---

[1] Low (1974: 63). All citations of this review refer to this edition and will be given after quotations in the text.

[2] Pierre Bourdieu, *The Rules of Art: Genesis and Structure of the Literary Field*, trans. by Susan Emanuel (Stanford: Stanford University Press, 1996), p. 225.

[3] See Grenfell (2011: 160-61).

[4] For discussion of the constituent elements of literary recognition, see Pierre Bourdieu, *The Field of Cultural Production: Essays on Art and Literature*, ed. by Randal Johnson (New York: Columbia University Press, 1993), pp. 106-07.

[5] Bourdieu, Pierre, *Distinction: A Social Critique of the Judgement of Taste*, trans. by Richard Nice (Cambridge: Harvard University Press, 1984), p. 2.

[6] For a differing view of Burns at this stage in his career, see Nigel Leask, *Robert Burns and Pastoral* (Oxford: Oxford University Press, 2010) pp. 1-14.

[7] For discussion of this paradigm, see Rhona Brown, 'Allan Ramsay, Robert Fergusson and Robert Burns' in Sergeant and Stafford, eds. (2012: 23-38); and Kenneth Simpson, 'The Vernacular Enlightenment' in Johnny Rodger and Gerard Carruthers, eds, *Fickle Man: Robert Burns in the 21st Century* (Dingwall: Sandstone, 2009), pp. 91-103. For a contesting view, see R. D. S. Jack, 'Which Vernacular Revival? Burns and the Makars', *Studies in Scottish Literature*, 30 (1998), pp. 9-18.

[8] This translates as 'a peasant, a philosopher, unschooled and of rough mother-wit'. See Horace, *Satires, Epistles and Ars Poetica*, trans. by H. Rushton Fairclough, Loeb Classical Library, 194 (Cambridge: Harvard University Press, 1999), pp. 134, 136.

[9] It is intriguing to note here that Sibbald too was raised in the same class as Burns, working as a farm labourer in his youth before founding the *Edinburgh Magazine* in 1784. See *The Letters of Robert Burns*, ed. by Ferguson and Roy, II, 477-78. Letters referring to this edition will be cited by volume and page numbers in the text.

[10] These lines are paraphrased from *Othello*, III. 3.

[11] Young (2008: 129). For further discussion of the 'myth-building' surrounding Burns, see the entry on Burns in Gifford, Dunnigan, and MacGillivray, eds, *Scottish Literature in English and Scots* (Edinburgh: University of Edinburgh Press, 2002), pp. 46-169.

[12] Henry Mackenzie, ed., *The Lounger* (Edinburgh: Creech, 1785-87), p. 385. All in text citations refer to this edition.

[13] For more on the relationship of the discourse of sublimity to theories of genius, see Coleman, Patrick, *Anger, Gratitude, and the Enlightenment Writer* (Oxford: Oxford University Press, 2011).

[14] See for example *The Reception of Ossian in Europe*, ed. by Howard Gaskill (London: Thoemmes, 2004); and Fiona Stafford, *The Sublime Savage: A Study of James Macpherson and the Poems of Ossian* (Edinburgh: Edinburgh University Press, 1988).

[15] For more on this element of Burns's publicity, see Kenneth Simpson, 'Robert Burns: "Heaven-taught ploughman"?', in Kenneth Simpson, ed., *Burns Now* (Edinburgh: Canongate, 1994), pp. 70-91, Leask (2010) pp. 1-14.

[16] Low (1974: 65). Emphasis mine. The metaphor of 'cultivation' is a frequent refrain in discussions of Burns's *genius*. All in-text citations of this review refer to Low's edition.

[17] See Low (1974: 66) for Hamilton's response to 'Ramsay' in the *Edinburgh Evening Courant*.

[18] For more on this aspect of patronage, see Bourdieu, in Nice, ed., (1984) pp. 316-17.

[19] The phrase loosely translates as 'poets are born, not made'. For more on the history of the phrase and its links with Horace, see Ringler, 'Poeta Nascitur Non Fit: Some Notes on the History of an Aphorism'.

[20] Low (1974: 71). It is worth remarking that Anderson was given this review in lieu of other more regular poetry reviewers in *The Monthly Review* like John Langhorne. Anderson was 'an economist and student of "scientific farming" [who] wrote on agriculture in the *Monthly Review* for many years' (71). This background presumably made Anderson a more 'qualified' reviewer of Burns's poetry than the more seasoned Langhorne. All in-text citations of this review refer to Low's edition.

[21] Duff (1767: 148).

[22] Anderson even applauds Burns's use of extensive paratexts in the poem, noting that 'Halloween' is 'very properly accompanied with notes, explaining the circumstances to which the poem alludes' (73). For more on 'Halloween,' see Corey E. Andrews in 'Footnoted Folklore: Robert Burns's "Halloween"', in Patrick Scott and Kenneth Simpson, eds, *Robert Burns and Friends: Essays by W. Ormiston Roy Fellows Presented to G. Ross Roy* (Columbia: University of South Carolina Press, 2012), pp. 24-37.

[23] See John D. Ross, *Who's Who in Burns* (Stirling: Mackay, 1927), p. 16.

[24] See Karl Maton, 'Habitus', in Grenfell, ed. (2011: 49-68, 51).

[25] Low (1974: 90). All in-text citations of this review refer to Low's edition.

[26] Anderson's phrase ('tune his oaten reed') can also be found in Tasso's *Gerusalemme Liberata* (Bk 7) and Charles Churchill's 'The Prophecy of Famine' (1763).

[27] Low (1974: 75). All in-text citations of this review refer to Low's edition.

[28] Ibid., p. 86.

[29] Ibid., p. 87.

[30] Ibid., pp. 87, 88.

[31] Moore, in Grenfell, ed. (2011: 105).

[32] For a thorough treatment of Burns's varying fortunes throughout his career, see J. DeLancey Ferguson, *Pride and Passion: Robert Burns, 1759-1796* (New York: Oxford University Press, 1939), pp. 188-233.

[33] Bourdieu, in Nice, ed. (1984: 3).

[34] In his *Bibliography of Robert Burns* (Carbondale: Southern Illinois University Press, 1964).), J. W. Egerer states that this review is 'probably by Dr. John Moore' (4). He provides no support for this assertion, however. In 'Burns's Literary Reputation in England and Scotland, 1786-1834' (unpublished doctoral dissertation, Princeton University, 1941), Walter Moffatt points to a letter that Logan wrote to Henry Mackenzie on 28 February 1787 which appears to confirm his authorship of the review (32). He also notes, though, that the review has been attributed to Moore. In *The Critical Heritage* (1974), Low positively identifies the author as Logan (see pp. 17, 76). Given Moore's later relationship with Burns, it seems unlikely that he authored this review, while the evidence of the letter (printed in full in *The Critical Heritage*, pp. 78-79) suggests that Logan was its author. I side with Low in this attribution, but I cannot definitively establish Logan's authorship.

[35] See *DNB* for more on Logan's life during the 1780s. Current scholarship supports Bruce's authorship of the disputed poems.

[36] Qtd. in *DNB*, from *The Correspondence of Adam Smith*, ed. by Mossner and Ross, p. 290.

[37] Low (1974: 77). All in-text citations of this review refer to Low's edition.

[38] Moffatt (1941: 34).

[39] Logan's reference is not an idle one; in fact, there was a great deal of popular interest at the time in the spectacle of 'learned pigs'. For more on this intriguing fad, see Bob Malcolmson, and Stephanos Mastoris, *The English Pig: A History* (London: Hambledon, 1998), p. 17.

[40] Bourdieu, in Johnson ed. (1993: 43).

[41] This letter is reprinted in Low (1974: 78-79), from Thompson, pp. 226-27. All in-text citations refer to Low's edition.

[42] For more on Macaulay, see James Gibson, *The Bibliography of Robert Burns* (Kilmarnock: McKie, 1881; repr. New York: Kraus, 1969), p. 110.

[43] This quotation appears in scene four of 'The Gentle Shepherd', in Sir William's soliloquy before the fifteenth song.

[44] p. 193, ll. 1-2, 7-8. Hereafter cited in-text by line numbers.

[45] p. 23. Further references to this article are given after quotations in the text.

[46] See Richard Sher, *The Enlightenment and the Book* (Chicago: University of Chicago Press, 2006), for extended discussion of the Edinburgh book trade.

[47] For more on Maxwell, see *DNB* and Ross (1927: 207).

[48] p. 4. Hereafter cited in-text by page numbers.

[49] Maxwell was one of the most vocal and persistent of Burns's critics from early in his career; a major reason for his animosity is most likely due to his anger about Burns's great success. Although Maxwell was well-known locally as 'the Paisley Poet', he never received even a modicum of the fame that his rival achieved.

[50] For more on these poetic responses to Burns, see G. Ross Roy, '"The Mair They Talk, I'm Kend the Better": Poems about Robert Burns to 1859', in Kenneth Simpson, ed., *Love and Liberty, Robert Burns: A Bicentenary Celebration* (East Linton: Tuckwell, 1997), pp. 53-68.

[51] Burns's use of the term 'shoal' in his letter is worthy of notice. It appears in only one other place in his body of work, referring to 'shoals and nations' of lice in 'To a Louse' (*Poems and Songs*, I, 83, l. 16). In that poem, lice threaten to overwhelm the young lady, so perhaps Burns is imagining a similar fate from the 'shoals' of labouring-class poets assailing him.

[52] Lapraik departs from many Scottish labouring-class poets who published books of poetry after the great success of Burns's Kilmarnock edition; rather than name his volume *Poems, Chiefly in the Scottish Dialect* as many post-Burns poets did, Lapraik picks the more anonymous and generic *Poems on Several Occasions*.

[53] Burns refers to himself as a 'rhymer' in his first epistle to Lapraik, as well as in 'The Brigs of Ayr'. The practice of 'rhyme' or 'rhyming' appears in numerous poems and songs; Reid's *Concordance* lists forty instances. See *A Complete Word and Phrase Concordance to the Poems and Songs of Robert Burns*, ed. by J. B. Reid (Glasgow: Kerr & Richardson, 1889; repr. New York: Franklin, 1969).

[54] p. 1. Hereafter cited in-text by page and line numbers.

[55] See 'John Lapraik' in *DNB*, as well as Lindsay, pp. 209-10.

[56] Burns's preface to the Kilmarnock edition employs similar terminology as Lapraik's and may have served as a model for Lapraik's preface. Burns's preface, however, is much more sophisticated in its representation of the literary field; one senses that Lapraik's sentiments in his preface are entirely sincere.

[57] Interestingly, Burns used the word 'thowless' in his second epistle to Lapraik, where he describes 'Conscience' as a 'thowless jad'. The word can also mean 'inactive', 'lethargic', and/or 'having little initiative or capablity', as well as 'immoral' or 'dissolute'. See Mairi Robinson, ed., *The Concise Scots Dictionary* (Edinburgh: Chambers, 1997). All Scots definition refer to this edition.

[58] For critical discussion of Janet Little, see Bold, 'Janet Little "The Scotch Milkmaid" and "Peasant Poetry"'; Davis, 'Gender and Nation in the Work of Janet Little and Robert Burns'; Moira Ferguson, *Eighteenth-Century Women Poets*, pp. 91-110; Moira Ferguson, 'Janet Little and Robert Burns: An Alliance with Reservations'; Kord, pp. 216-39; and Landry, pp. 217-37.

[59] p. 230.

[60] p. 160, ll. 1-6. All further citations will be noted by line numbers in-text.

[61] For an intriguing discussion of this passage, see Carruthers, 'The Word on Burns', pp. 25-37 (p. 28).

[62] Moira Ferguson offers a contrary view, arguing that Little's 'commendatory tributes to Robert Burns enhance her own cultural standing' (*Eighteenth-Century Women Poets*, p. 91). Given the meager results of Little's commendatory verse, I find it difficult to maintain this stance. For a discussion of the pervasive influence of gender in commendatory verse, see Biester, 'Gender and Style in Seventeenth-Century Commendatory Verse'.

[63] *The Rules of Art*, p. 262.

[64] *Distinction*, p. 12.

[65] Little's word 'rupy' most likely refers to the Scots word, 'roupy,' which means coarse, rough, or husky.

[66] p. 141.

[67] Qtd. in *British Women Poets of the Romantic Era*, ed. by Feldman, p. 423. Dunlop's display of anger here is a rare instance in her correspondence with Burns and indicates her real disappointment with his treatment of Little, whom she warmly describes as 'one of her own'.

[68] *The Critical Heritage*, p. 94, ll. 1-2. All citations refer to this edition and will be noted by line numbers in the text.

[69] Bourdieu, *The Rules of Art*, p. 224

Chapter Three

'Ungrateful country! ill-requited Burns!': The Decline and Fall of the 'Heaven-taught Ploughman', 1788-1796

1. 'Mole-Hill Monuments': Scotland's 'Neglect' of Burns

Although Robert Burns achieved widespread acclaim as the 'heaven-taught ploughman' after the publication of his Kilmarnock edition of *Poems* (1786), his celebrity underwent major transformation until his death in 1796. Some of the changes were initiated by Burns himself, particularly those relating to his work collecting Scottish songs. To the extent that self-conscious choices on his part could influence the public perception of the 'heaven-taught ploughman', Burns proved resistant to the force of this stereotyped persona. However, the persona's influence was waning during these years, as a result of a number of factors over which the poet had no control. Chief among these was Burns's declining novelty as prodigious 'poetic genius', especially due to the fact that he was producing fewer poems during this period.[1] His self-appointment as a collector/editor of national song testifies to the poet's changing perception of his 'duty' as a 'Scotch Bard', coupled with his refusal to accept payment for this demanding, extensive work.[2]

In addition, Burns had revealed a side of his personality to the Edinburgh literati in the late 1780s that did not coincide with his 'heaven-taught ploughman' persona. Many commentators testified to the poet's 'hard' demeanour in public, as well as occasional bouts of social awkwardness. In a letter to James Currie that was published in Currie's edition of Burns's *Works*, Dugald Stewart described the poet's manners as 'simple, manly, and independent' and 'strongly expressive of conscious genius and worth'. However, he also observed that 'he had been accustomed to give law in the circle of his ordinary acquaintance, and his dread of anything approaching to meanness or servility, rendered his manner somewhat decided and hard'.[3] In a letter to the Rev. William Greenfield, Burns described the pressure he felt in such settings, where he was expected to conform to his advance publicity under the 'full glare of learned and polite observation'.[4] In addition, his propensity for abrasive topical satire (abundantly evident in the Kilmarnock edition) did not sit well with his urban audience of highly-educated elites, none of whom wished to be Burns's next target.

This inculcation process ended poorly for Burns, who retreated from the capital without the immediate patronage or employment that he (and many of his critical and poetic admirers) may have expected from the literati.[5] This situation created animosity that was repeatedly expressed by Burns's admirers throughout the 1790s. A by-product of his celebrity was the apparently ceaseless interest of others concerned on his behalf, whether he wanted their help or not. When those others were Scottish gentry, Burns took notice in the hope of future largesse.[6] Most often, however, his defenders were minor figures whose influence seldom extended beyond the publication of their (frequently poetic) support.[7] As noted in the previous chapter, Burns rarely took notice of such poets, tending to dismiss them out of hand as 'ill-spawned monsters'.[8]

A typical specimen of this sort was penned by James Graham in his *Poems, in English, Scotch, and Latin* (1794). His poem of support, entitled 'On Burns, the Scottish Poet', had been written three years prior but remained unpublished until its appearance in his volume of poems. Graham had been a Writer to the Signet since 1788, although he would later become an advocate in 1795 and eventually a curate in 1809. Like his career, Graham's poetry revealed a broad range of interests and influences, numbering not only Burns but also the pastoral in his *Rural Calendar* (1797) and Scottish history in *Wallace: A Tragedy* (1799) and *Mary Queen of Scots* (1801). Later in his career Graham became a vocal abolitionist, publishing his *Poems on the Abolition of the Slave Trade* in 1810.[9] However, when he composed 'On Burns, the Scottish Poet', Graham was certainly under the spell of his famous subject, whose fate was a source of both complaint and admonition.

Graham's indignant tribute sets the scene of Burns's neglect by his fellow Scots, who have allowed him to 'moil' with the common lot of labourers in his class:

The bard whose song still echoes in the vale,
The bard whose song each lovely tongue recites,
Is left to moil like men of common mould;
The song still charms us; but the bard's forgot.[10]

He likens Burns's fate to that of the 'thrush, sweet minstrel of the spring' overcome by winter, writing 'when stern Winter chills the leafless grove, / Shivering he's left to glean his scanty food' (7-8). Like Burns's hapless mouse, the thrush is confronted by the approach of 'stern Winter', made even worse by the threat of predation: 'Nor ever is the woodland path bestrewn, / Save with intent to lure him to the snare' (9-10). In Graham's scenario, Burns as 'sweet minstrel' is imperiled on all sides, forced to struggle for subsistence within a harsh and predatory world.

This leads Graham to vent his anger at Scotland itself, a country that has 'ungratefully' refused to nurture the talent of a 'poetic genius' like Burns:

Ungrateful country! ill-requited Burns!
Shall he who sung, in Scotia's Doric lays,
'The lowly train in life's sequester'd scene',
Remain neglected in the scene he paints,
And ask, perhaps in vain, 'for leave to toil'? (11-15)

Alluding to both 'The Cotter's Saturday Night' and 'Man was Made to Mourn', Graham depicts Burns as one of the 'lowly train' who begs only 'leave to toil' in order to stress the injustice of the poet's present condition.[11] While 'Man was Made to Mourn' has political overtones – particularly in its critique of 'the haughty lordling's pride' (I, 64, 20) – Graham's is focused only on the sufferings of the poet himself.

Like the 'poor, o'erlabored wight' (57) from 'Man was Made to Mourn', Burns barely ekes a living in such conditions and perhaps only wishes for 'death, the poor man's dearest friend' (81). Graham wonders if this is really to be the poet's lot, asking,

Shall he who sung far sweeter than the lark,
When upward springing from the daisy's side
To greet the purpling east,
Be driven from the fields cheer'd by his song? (16-19)

He ponders if 'being driven from the fields' will be the fate of the poet who 'with truth and yet with dignity / [...] rehears'd the annals of the poor' (20-21). Like the idealised speaker of Thomas Gray's 'Elegy Written in a Country Churchyard', Burns is represented as a figure whose knowledge of the 'annals of the poor' is matched only by his empathy for the 'mute inglorious Miltons' who have preceded him in many a country churchyard.[12]

Graham seeks to intervene and prevent the 'muting' of yet another 'Milton' by exhorting all Scots to support the worthy poet in their midst. He writes with passionate indignation, addressing patrons who venerate dead poets but neglect those living:

Ye patrons of the mighty dead, who strive
 T'immortalize immortal Thomson's name,
Rear not to angels mole-hill monuments,
While living merit owns no sheltering roof. (29-32)

The 'mighty dead' is epitomised here by James Thomson, whose popular and critical acclaim continued long after his death in 1748.[13] Burns himself wrote an 'Address to the Shade of Thomson' in 1791, the same year as Graham's tribute. In Burns's poem, Thomson is commemorated as the 'sweet Poet of the year' who is proudly (and tearfully) claimed by Scotland: 'Scotia, with exulting tear, / Proclaims that Thomson was her son' (II, 331, 17, 19-20).

Graham echoes this sentiment, praising patrons who have 'immortalised' a deserving national poet in Thomson, yet he chides them for honouring only the 'mighty dead'. Patronage as proof of national pride must be repeated in the present for living poets. Graham hectors his 'ungrateful country' for failing to provide 'ill-requited Burns' with a 'sheltering roof'. A 'mole-hill monument' is simply not enough, for the poet's material needs must be met (and exceeded) in order for him to continue to write. Graham ends his harangue with an appeal to the very poet Thomson, whom Graham imagines would redress Burns's suffering were he not among the 'mighty dead'. He writes that 'Thomson's gentle spirit' would rather see 'a mansion rais'd for his neglected Burns, / Than gorgeous mausoleums for himself' (33-35).

This conclusion plays the gambit for Burns's ardent defenders in the 1790s, employing an image – the poet as 'ill-requited', in need of his nation's patronage – that would be as persistently applied as was the 'heaven-taught ploughman' persona. Indeed, it would modify the latter and form a hybrid persona, one that was comprised of both 'poetic genius' and national bard. However, the bardic persona was not that championed by Burns himself, who sought increasingly to contribute his creative energies to Scottish song rather than Scottish verse. Spurred on by patriotism and empathy for a 'brother poet',[14] Graham expressed a powerful sentiment about the 'duty' of the Scottish nation to provide for a neglected 'poetic genius' like Burns.

Others would voice similar complaints throughout the 1790s, culminating in the wave of mournful yet angry elegies that followed the poet's death in 1796. Such a concentrated focus on Burns's life rather than his works is a common feature of this group of elegies, all of which reveal changing attitudes towards the poet's celebrity and the meaning of his legacy. As Pierre Bourdieu observes, 'What attracts and fascinates in the occupation of artist is not so much the art itself but the artist's lifestyle, the artist's life'.[15] This dictum applies particularly well to Burns's fame in the 1790s, when his tumultuous life story was increasingly being assessed by admirers like Graham who sought to intervene on the poet's behalf.

Despite his wishes, Burns's admirers represented him as a national figure whose work demanded Scottish adulation and patronage. This chapter examines the range of poetic responses to Burns during the 1790s, frequently composed by fellow Scots who sought to directly aid their 'brother poet' by arguing his case for patronage. The transformation that Burns's celebrity underwent throughout the 1790s will also be explored, particularly how his reputation began to change after his death in 1796. An array of elegies, widely varying in tone and purpose, will be examined in order to gauge how Scottish writers perceived their 'brother poet' once he had entered the ranks of the 'mighty dead'.

2. Burns's 'Power to Consecrate': The Second Wave of Poetic Admirers

By 1788, poems addressed to Burns continued to appear with regularity after the initial enthusiasm for the poet waned in the press.[16] This 'second wave' of verse began the process of reimagining Burns in a different persona, one no less inspired than the 'heaven-taught ploughman' but equally culturally produced. Reconfiguring the poet as a neglected victim of Scotland's indifference occurred gradually over the course of several years, and it was not a persona that Burns endorsed in his poetry or letters.[17] In fact, this persona had little correspondence with the actual events in his life during this period. By 1788, he had left Edinburgh with considerable profits from his Edinburgh edition (estimated at roughly £360) and taken a lease at Ellisland, a farm in Dumfriesshire. He was also commissioned as an exciseman that year, which he worked to supplement his income from the farm until he took on the post full-time in 1791.[18]

While Ellisland proved to be a risky financial venture, Burns was not as penurious and desperate as he was represented by his 'brother' and 'sister' poets. His life at this time was frequently difficult, to be sure; certainly the failure of the farm at Ellisland contributed to Burns's financial distress and led to the family's move to Dumfries.[19] However, other factors (such as his personal and/or political behavior) contributed more than the state of his finances to the troubles he experienced in the 1790s. Robert D. Thornton suggests that 'two of the subjects dearest to the heart of Robert Burns were Religion and Politics [...] the latter was to get him into boiling water with superiors in His Majesty's Excise'.[20] While his work for the Excise was frequently grueling, Burns began to experience a degree of financial and domestic security during this period in Dumfries, where he continued to enjoy renown as a national celebrity.

However, Burns's accrual of capital in the making and continuance of his celebrity was largely symbolic in these years following his initial discovery. Bourdieu's concept of 'symbolic capital' neatly captures the dynamic at work in this process; as Randal Johnson explains, 'Symbolic capital refers to a degree of accumulated prestige, celebrity, consecration or honour and is founded on a dialectic of knowledge (*connaissance*) and recognition (*reconnaissance*)'.[21] From 1788 and throughout the 1790s, Burns's recognition in the literary field was increasingly measured by means of the symbolic capital that his name came to represent, rather than the verse and song-collecting that he produced at the time.

This dialectical process underscores the competitive nature of the literary field, whereby celebrity serves to enhance reputation and bestow consecration on the producer. This process is integral to the making of reputation itself; Bourdieu states that reputations are made in 'the field of production, understood [...] as the site of the struggles for the monopoly of the power to consecrate'.[22] The 'power to consecrate' in this instance became progressively more associated with Burns himself; his status as a 'poetic genius' conferred authority upon his judgment of other Scottish poets from his class and place. To many aspiring Scottish poets, addressing a poem to Burns served to initiate them into the literary field. To the degree that a fraternal, convivial, and/or national relationship could be inferred in the verse, such poets hoped to bank on Burns's evolving reputation as a neglected 'poetic genius' whose favour they sought to both curry and cultivate. However, Burns was also taken to task for his apparent refusal to produce more poetry in the vein of his earlier work, leading fellow Scottish poets to imply that he was 'betraying' his responsibility to his audience and his country.

Constructing a poetic relationship with the 'heaven-taught ploughman' was not always an imaginative exercise. Established poets also reached out to Burns in verse, highlighting an already-existing friendship or seeking to create an affective bond. One of the earliest examples of this type of poem was composed by Thomas Blacklock, an Edinburgh poet who had already done Burns a great service by recommending his verse to Reverend George Lawrie in 1786. Thirty-eight years senior to Burns, Blacklock was born into the labouring class and lost his sight due to smallpox in his infancy; despite numerous obstacles, he published his first book of poetry in 1746. He went on to study divinity and philosophy at the University of Edinburgh, finding support for his work by David Hume in particular. By the 1780s, he had established himself in the Scottish capital and had turned his attention to Scottish poetry and song.[23]

When Blacklock wrote to Lawrie in 1786, his intention was to express his surprise and admiration for the new poet whose work Lawrie had offered for his perusal. Blacklock writes, 'Many instances have I seen of nature's force and beneficence, exerted under numerous and formidable disadvantages; but none equal to that, with which you have been kind enough to present me'.[24] Blacklock's affinity with Burns's 'numerous and formidable disadvantages' is telling, suggesting an affective link founded upon mutual class status. In addition, Blacklock finds that the young poet's verse cannot be 'too much admired', writing that 'there is a pathos and delicacy in his serious poems; a vein of wit and humour in those of a more festive turn, which cannot be too much admired, nor too warmly approved' (62). Indeed, he states that 'I think I shall never open the book without feeling my astonishment renewed and increased' (62).

Blacklock ended his letter to Lawrie with a very practical suggestion much to Burns's advantage; noting the difficulty readers in Edinburgh were having obtaining a copy of the Kilmarnock edition, he states that 'it were therefore much to be wished, for the sake of a young man, that a second edition, more numerous than the former, could immediately be printed' (62). Were his suggestion followed, Blacklock states that 'it appears certain that its intrinsic merit, and exertion of the author's friends, might give it a more universal circulation than any thing of the kind which has been published within my memory' (62). Blacklock's prescience was, of course, highly accurate. In fact, Burns credited Blacklock with convincing him to remain in Scotland rather than travel to the West Indies, writing in his famous autobiographical letter to John Moore that 'a letter from Dr. Blacklock overthrew all my schemes by rousing my poetic ambition'. He confesses that 'the Doctor belonged to a set of Critics for whose applause I had not even dared to hope'.[25]

Despite Blacklock's major contribution to his career, Burns never expressed his appreciation for the doctor in his verse. Rather, it was Blacklock who sought to commemorate their friendship with a poetic account, writing initially to Lawrie that 'it was my wish to have expressed my approbation in verse; but whether from declining life or a temporary depression of spirits, it is at present out of my power to accomplish that agreeable intention' (62). Three years later, Blacklock's spirits were sufficiently lifted for him to write a poetic epistle to Burns. Much had changed in Burns's life during that short time, including two stays in Edinburgh, a tour of the Highlands, the signing of the lease of the farm at Ellisland, and the beginning of his career in the Excise.[26] However, Blacklock writes as if the poet were still the same young man whose works had so 'astonished' him upon first reading.

Although Blacklock's poem bears the typical hallmarks of epistolary verse (particularly the rote rehearsal of one's fresh news), there is a clear purpose behind the elder poet's familial address to his successful young protégé. He writes,

Dear Burns, thou brother of my heart,
Both for thy virtues and thy art;
If art it may be called in thee,
Which Nature's bounty, large and free,
With pleasure on thy breast diffuses,
And warms thy soul with all the Muses.[27]

With the benefit of hindsight, hailing Burns's 'virtues' in 1789 was a dubious enterprise, but Blacklock's praise of the poet's 'art' reveals the continuing uncertainty that critics and readers felt about Burns. Blacklock is unsure if 'art it may be called in thee' (3), for the young poet's verse seems to express 'Nature's bounty' that is 'diffused' upon him; in fact, he avers that 'Tis Nature's voice distinctly felt, / Through thee, her organ, thus to melt' (11-12).

Such perceptions reinforce the view of Burns as 'heaven-taught ploughman' by insisting that the source of his 'poetic genius' is external. Blacklock gently reminds Burns of their former relationship – 'Whether to laugh with easy grace, / Thy numbers move the sage's face' (7-8) – before getting to the epistle's business end. After inquiring about the health of Burns's wife and children, Blacklock describes his current life:

> For me, with grief and sickness spent;
> Since I my journey homeward bent,
> Spirit's depress'd, no more I mourn,
> But vigour, life, and health, return. (21-24)

This new state of 'vigour, life, and health' has inspired him to appreciate his daily routines and avoid 'gloomy thoughts' (25); he vows to 'by turns my books and friends enjoy, / And thus my circling hours employ' (27-28). Blacklock was in fact nearing the end of his life, so these routine banalities have a touch of pathos that they might not otherwise convey.

The end of Blacklock's epistle expresses a wish that is otherwise buried in this congenial verse epistle. Blacklock writes that

> Happy, while yet these hours remain,
> If Burns could join the cheerful train;
> With wonted zeal, sincere and fervent,
> Salutes once more his humble servant. (29-32)

Though delivered in decidedly formulaic fashion, Blacklock's desire for Burns's company among 'the cheerful train' explicitly highlights the existing friendly relationship between them, one that Blacklock wants to continue if only in verse. His implicit recognition of Burns's new stature within the literary field attests to its competitive nature and always-shifting boundaries that define literary success among the established and the challengers. This state of play clearly differentiates producers in the field; Bourdieu notes that 'nothing divides cultural producers more clearly than the relationship they maintain with worldly or commercial success'.[28]

Poems written to Burns by anonymous or pseudonymous authors from this period have similarly symptomatic characteristics as those seen in Blacklock's epistle. Like the good doctor, these poets attempt to establish a fraternal connection with the 'heaven-taught ploughman' as a means of garnering his support and/or approbation. Often such poets produced highly imitative verse in Scots in order to initiate their poetic correspondence, a trait that is seen in most of the Scottish labouring-class poets who wrote after Burns.[29] In addition to entitling their collections with some variant of Burns's *Poems, Chiefly in the Scottish Dialect*,[30] this group of poets valorised his Scots verse above all other types of writing he was producing at the time. This is a distinctive feature that was not shared by other readers of Burns, who often praised his 'serious' poems (those in English) above those in the 'comic' (Scots) vein.[31] The anonymous poets from this period who wrote directly to Burns instead regarded his 'comic' vein as much richer than the 'serious', resulting in imitative epistles written in the by-then standard Habbie (soon to be 'Burns') stanza.

A typical example is an anonymous poem entitled 'Verses, written in Broad Scotch, and addressed to Robert Burns, the Air Shire Poet' that was published in the *Literary Magazine and British Review* (May 1789). It begins with a direct address that likens Burns to Allan Ramsay, in order to both underscore and imitate the Scots vernacular for which both poets were distinguished: 'Fair fa' you, Robie, canty callan, / Wha rhym'st amaist as weel as Allan'.[32] Burns's distinction as a Scots poet – beyond his stated ability to 'pleasest Highland lads and lawlan, / Wi your auld gab' (3-4) – resides in his *genius*, bestowed upon him (as in Blacklock's poem) by 'Nature'. The poet writes,

I've read your warks wie muckle glee,
Auld Lucky Nature there I see,
Has gi'en you genius like a bee,
To suck the flowers. (7-10)

This 'natural genius' makes Burns far superior to those writers who borrow inspiration from 'glib Horace', 'blin Homer', or Virgil (13-15).

Instead, the poet writes that 'a gude Scotch taste / Prefers your ain untutor'd lays' to the works of the ancient poets (16-17). The enduring representation of Burns as 'untutored' appears throughout, where his upbringing in the harsh Scottish landscape enables him to outperform competitors in the literary field: 'Ye was born whare hills are bleak, / And cauld winds bla' (21-22). To which the poet adds, 'tho' frae buiks nae helps ye seek, / Ye ding them a'' (23-24). After this obligatory praise, the anonymous poet spends several stanzas lamenting over the loss of pastoral idylls in which one could escape 'auld Time, that jinking slippery chiel' (62). This leads to a direct appeal to Burns, who presumably shares the speaker's disdain for 'auld Time'. Like the speaker, Burns must seize the day:

Let us the present hour then seize,
And reckon gain what the niest gies,
Its vain for what nane o' us sees,
Our heads to fash,
Or yet to let the warld teize
Us wi' its trash. (66-71)

An imagined convivial meeting concludes the poem, where the speaker would disdain the world's 'trash' together with Burns: 'We'd mak our hearts as light's a feather, / Wi' reaming jugs' (76-77).

As a whole, the poem demonstrates the increasing imitativeness of tributes during the period; it borrows liberally from Burns's own epistles to John Lapraik and David Sillar, as well as promotes a static perception of the poet as an 'untutored genius' inspired by 'Nature'. The familiarity with which the poet addresses Burns also speaks to the use that fellow Scots would make of his celebrity, believing that their shared nationality was sufficient occasion for familial and convivial closeness. Although the above poem is anonymous, it resembles several other tributes that were written to Burns during this time, many of which employ similar strategies to establish contact (and advantage) through association with their famous compatriot. As he would discover throughout the 1790s, Burns could not control this aspect of his fame which allowed Scots of all classes to address him as both an equal and a 'brother poet'.

Another tribute from this period, authored by 'K' and entitled 'To Robert Burns', appeared in the *Gazetteer and New Daily Advertiser* (14 August 1790). Unlike 'Verses Written in Broad

Scotch', this poem is entirely in English. In addition, it offers a quite
different appeal to the poet than that seen in the previous tribute. In
this poem, 'K' interrogates the 'heaven-taught ploughman', particu-
larly concerning his lack of new writing. The speaker begins with a
plaintive inquiry, one that perhaps other readers of Burns wanted to
ask:

Ah! wherefore dost thou drop thy sounding lyre?
That wont to set the bosom in a flame
That wont to fill my soul with noble fire,
And bade me still at high exertions aim.[33]

The competitive nature of the literary field plainly appears in this
complaint, where the speaker's exposure to Burns's 'sounding lyre'
fosters 'high exertions' wrought by the 'noble fire' of emulation.

Indeed, the speaker claims that 'thy verse each tender feeling has
inspir'd, / Taught ev'ry gen'rous sentiment to flow' (9-10). Owing
such a debt to Burns's inspiring example, he continues by further
stating that his verse 'taught whatso'er the barren mind requir'd, / And
with the love of science made it glow' (11-12). Burns's poetry has
saved the speaker from 'oblivion', for he attests that 'thy verses reach
my heart; and fair as day / I view the right, and from oblivion fly' (15-
16). Like Blacklock, 'K' perceives Burns as a 'brother of the heart', a
figure whose 'kind spirit' offers comfort, companionship, and inspira-
tion. However, the continuing silence of Burns's lyre depresses the
speaker, who can find no poetic sustenance in its stead: 'Not a line to
cheer the drooping soul, / Nor any song, soft-number'd, comes from
thee' (35-36). Coming not only from a fellow poet but also a reader in
the literary marketplace, 'K' reminds Burns of his obligation to his
readers, especially those who have formed an affective bond with the
'heaven-taught ploughman'.[34]

'K' ends his paean to literary productivity with a gentle appeal to
his 'brother poet', urging him to 'touch again thy easy moving string; /
Let the soft melody be heard around' (37-38). In order to further coax
his subject to write again, 'K' employs not-so-subtle flattery to ex-
press the demands of the reading nation upon their favourite poet:
'Sweet as the strain of Ossian canst thou sing; / Well canst thou charm
the bosom with the sound' (39-40). The reference to Ossian under-
scores Burns's status as a national bard, while the speaker also re-
marks (with a measure of hopefulness) upon the 'easy moving string'

of his fellow poet's lyre. This poem introduces a complaint that others would make against Burns in the 1790s, as he moved away from producing the types of poetry for which he became famous and turned his attention to song-collecting. This occasioned a reaction against Burns by those readers who expected their 'brother of my heart' to pick up his 'sounding lyre' once more. This demand coincides with what Bourdieu describes as 'the methodical attempt to distinguish the artist and the intellectual from other commoners by positing the unique products of "creative genius" against interchangeable products, utterly and completely reducible to their commodity value'.[35] It is worth remarking here that this demand is voiced by both Burns's readers and fellow poets, who work in concert to 'distinguish' him as a 'creative genius'. His own role in this process seems to be entirely secondary, as his reputation and celebrity are wielded against him to induce him to create the 'unique products' expected by his readers.

A poem that articulates a similar complaint, but with an entirely different tone, is 'To A' Scots Poets' written by 'Thomas Scotus' and published in the *Morning Chronicle* (6 September 1791). In this argumentative and angry poem, Scotus issues a challenge to all 'Scots Poets' that is both *cri de coeur* and spirited invective. He finds that 'in Scotland, now, thro' ilka neuk, / Grit grief an' sorrow ay shall leuk'.[36] Claiming that Apollo has abandoned the land that was 'anes the randevouse [sic] / O' mony's a hamely-cracking muse' (7-8), Scotus depicts an invasion of 'English fops' who have despoiled his country due to the absence of its national bards:

Now English fops may o'er you craw,
An' a' your kintry's bairns misca';
There's nane to punish them wha thraw
Reproaches on ye,
Synce a' your bards are een awa,
An' left you lonely. (13-18)

The neglect of Scotland's bards has resulted in the country's 'infestation', leaving it in a weakened state that makes it incapable of self-defense.

This sorry state is perpetuated from within as well, for Scotus argues that his fellow Scots have abandoned their own language and by extension, their country. He laments the passing of the time 'when our auld tongue by ilka ane / Was ay thought best' (19-20). Instead, he now discovers that his fellow Scots are speaking in other, foreign tongues:

Wi' gude braid Scots nane cane be faird,
Fouks now maun leave their native eard,
French, Dutch, an' German maun be lear'd,
An' tongues uncouth. (25-28)

This linguistic diversity has also infected the country's writers, who are in thrall to 'foreign' influences: 'Now English sangsters blaw the horn, / An' wi' their trash the land is storin'' (31-32).[37] In the face of this lamentable state of affairs, Scotus affirms that 'Scotland's sitting a' forlorn / Without a sang' (35-36).

One might rightly ask at this point where Burns figures into Scotus's representation of Scottish literature. When the poem was published in 1791, Burns was the most celebrated Scots poet of his day. However, at the half-way point of Scotus's poem, he has yet to be mentioned. We soon learn that the delay is for maximum rhetorical effect. After mentioning the losses of the incomparable Scots poets Allan Ramsay and Robert Fergusson – 'Rob Fergie, too, is likewise fallen, / That bonny sangster' (41-42) – Scotus recounts his first experience reading the verse of 'Ayrshire Rob': 'Wow but my heart great pleasure teuk, / Whan Ayrshire Rob sent out his buik' (43-44). Scotus's enthusiasm becomes mingled with anger over Burns's refusal to produce more Scots verse: 'Now he's taen'd in till his head, / To quit the sang an' aiten reed' (49-50). This decision occasions a stern rebuke from Scotus:

Trouth, Robby, ye've cause to dreid
Your kintry's anger:
Cou'd we get ane to fill your stead,
I'd mourn nae langer. (51-54)

Scotus's threat affirms the volatility of the literary marketplace, particularly when readers' needs are no longer being met by a favored author.

In this case, the notion that readers like Scotus could 'get ane to fill [Burns's] stead' relates to Bourdieu's concept of 'position-taking', which he describes as changing 'even when the position remains identical, whenever there is a change in the universe of options that are simultaneously offered for producers and consumers to choose from'.[38] Scotus reminds Burns that he is replaceable, were there any other Scottish bards available in the 'universe of options' available to readers and writers.

Accordingly, Scotus ends his screed against the state of Scottish literature in general (and Burns in particular) with a defiant call to arms:

Ye Scottish bards, whare'er ye be,
Now lift your pen fu' merrilee;
Stand furth, an' let your kintry see
Her ancient days. (61-64)

Tellingly, he does not admonish Burns to 'lift his pen'. By expanding the 'universe of options' wherein Burns has neglected his 'duty' as a Scottish bard, Scotus hopes to revive his country and help it repel foreign invaders and influences, with or without Burns's help. In his utopian scheme, Scotus affirms that 'Ilk Scotsman till the task wi' glee, / In's kintry's praise' (65-66).

Where Burns had received mild opprobrium from the pen of 'K', in this poem he is clouted with the blunt end of Scotus's vituperative rebuke. Burns's apparent abdication of his 'duty' as a Scottish bard reflects the dialectical process at work in the literary field, where an established author like Burns in the 1790s must continue to fend off competitors who seek to displace him. As Bourdieu observes, the nature of literary success involves a necessary process of displacement, for 'each author, school or work which "makes its mark" displaces the whole series of earlier authors, schools or works'.[39] Burns would find it more and more challenging during this period to maintain his position as an established author as others sought to displace him in order to 'make their mark'. Ironically enough, his work collecting Scottish songs – a project which he felt was his national 'duty' as a bard to do, without accepting payment or credit through authorship – would be the source of many readers' displeasure. Burns, it seems, could not be 'national' enough for this emerging audience.

3. 'Indignantly is Fled Thy Noble Spirit': Poetic Elegies in 1796

By the time Burns died in 1796, his reputation as a practicing Scots poet was in decline, for his creative energies from 1792 onward had been spent in writing and collecting songs for James Johnson's *Scots Musical Museum* and George Thomson's *Select Collection of Original Scottish Airs*. He had begun his work with Johnson in 1787, and *Scots Musical Museum* reached its fifth volume in December 1796 (five months after Burns's death). He began collaborating with Thomson in 1792 upon the *Select Collection*, for which Burns contributed not only songs but also occasional criticism.[40] During this time, William Creech (Burns's Edinburgh printer) reissued *Poems, Chiefly in the Scottish Dialect* in 1793; he owned the copyright and greatly expanded the edition to fill two volumes. However, Burns was not consulted during this process, for (as Carol McGuirk notes) he was 'absorbed in song-writing and work for the Excise'.[41] A notable exception to his concentrated focus on song at this time was the production of 'Tam O'Shanter' in 1790, written at behest of Captain Francis Grose for the second volume of his *Antiquities of Scotland* (1791). Despite the success of this poem, Burns did not compose another work in this vein in his lifetime.[42]

He may not have had adequate time for such pursuits. By 1794, Burns had been promoted to acting supervisor of the Excise, a post which required extensive travel throughout Dumfries. His family life also claimed much of his time and attention; the year 1794 brought a new child (James Glencairn Burns) into an already crowded household, while 1795 saw the loss of his three-year-old daughter Elizabeth. A year after becoming the acting supervisor, Burns became seriously ill and could no longer work; his death on 25 July 1796 – either from bacterial infection or endocarditis – was the culmination of nearly eight months of sickness.[43] Although Burns was quite productive throughout the 1790s (composing 323 works during the period by James Kinsley's account), the clear majority were songs written for *Scots Musical Museum* and the *Select Collection*.[44] Many of these songs were printed without Burns's signature, which was his express intention. In order to fulfill his ambition to be remembered as a 'Scotch Bard', he wrote or revised songs originating in Scottish folk culture and famously refused payment for his work.[45]

However, to a reader from the period, it must have seemed that Burns had vanished from the literary scene altogether. The poems which made him famous were no longer forthcoming from the 'heaven-taught ploughman'. In John Logan's caustic assessment, it appeared that Burns had 'strut his hour upon the stage' and disappeared with other novelties such as 'learned pigs' and 'rhyming milkwomen'.[46] After his death, however, his celebrity as a 'poetic genius' resurfaced, leading to a torrent of elegies from fond apologists who sought to derive a fitting moral from his life story. Many spoke of Burns's 'victimisation' by his country. Such elegists would ask the 'genius of Scotia' itself to 'mourn' its fallen son, lamenting the loss of a life that could have been spared had the nation performed the 'duty' it owed to its 'bard'. In a letter to the Reverend Mr. Edwards from 1796, William Roscoe reflected acerbically on Burns's recent death:

His example has fixed the value of high poetical attainments in Scotland, and they amount to the place of an exciseman, with a salary of fifty pounds per annum. Such has been the munificence of the Scotch peerage and the Scotch gentry to a man who has done more honour to his country than all the throat-cutters it ever had. May they never have another opportunity of insulting genius with paltry and insidious rewards![47]

Scotland's 'paltry and insidious rewards' for Burns – symbolised by a salary of 'fifty pounds per annum' – represent the nation's inexcusable treatment of a poet whose work 'fixed the value of high poetical attaintments'.

Others would agree with Roscoe that such 'insults' to *genius* amounted to a betrayal of Burns's talents and signified that Scotland's 'munificence' did not extend beyond the narrow interests of its peerage and gentry. In her poem 'To the Shade of Burns', Charlotte Smith voiced similarly pessimistic sentiments about Burns's opportunities for patronage during his life. She reiterates the difficulties faced by the 'heaven-taught ploughman', writing that

Even beneath the daily pressure, rude,
Of labouring Poverty, thy generous Blood
Fir'd with the Love of FREEDOM. – Not subdued
Wert Thou by thy low Fortune.[48]

Despite the energies he derived from his 'generous Blood' and 'Love of Freedom', Burns contended with a fundamentally unfair system of

patronage that rewarded 'parasites' over deserving poets of 'low For-
tune' like Burns: she writes that the time 'we live in, when the abject
Chime / Of echoing Parasite is best approv'd', was 'not for Thee!' (8-
9, 10).

Smith champions those like Burns who exist (for her at least) on
the peripheries of the literary field, lacking sufficient 'cultural capital'
to compete. Randal Johnson notes that the very notion of 'cultural
capital' implies such divisions between literary producers, whereby its
possession allows evaluative judgment to legitimise 'certain practices'
as 'naturally superior'. He writes, 'Cultural capital [...] participates in
the process of domination by legitimizing certain practices as "natu-
rally" superior to others and by making these practices seem superior
even to those who do not participate'. For this group of non-partici-
pants, Johnson argues that they 'are thus led, through a negative proc-
ess of inculcation, to see their own practices as inferior and to exclude
themselves from legitimate practices'.[49] Smith contends against such a
'negative process of inculcation' by valorising Burns's verse, in spite
of the purported indifference of the Scottish literary marketplace,
writing 'indignantly is fled / Thy noble Spirit' (10-11). She further
asserts that the 'shade' of Burns is 'no longer mov'd / By all the Ills
o'er which thine Heart has bled' (11-12). Burns regains his honour
and dignity upon his 'worthy' entry to the ranks of 'the illustrious
dead' (13), with whom he finally finds acceptance and appreciation.

Such spirited defenses of Burns as a poet 'wronged' by his
country appear with some regularity in other elegies from the period.
One such example, entitled 'Elegy on the Death of R. Burns the
Ayshire Plowman', appeared in the *Gentleman's Magazine* (August
1796). Penned by 'Ninfeild', the poem recounts the numerous
indignities suffered by Burns during his short, harsh life. Ninfeild
begins in winter, depicting Burns as a *genius* faced with 'frozen
Penury':

How oft shall Genius, mid the chilling cloud
Of frozen Penury, unheard complain;
Still unregarded speak its ills aloud,
And urge its modest merits, but in vain?[50]

Like Smith, Ninfeild believes that Burns has been mistreated and that
the complaints of *genius* were 'unheard'. However, he is much more
specific in detailing the (imagined) conditions of the poet's miserable

life. He writes with disbelief that 'the Bard, whose emulative lays / Shew ripen'd genius join'd to judgement chaste' had to 'pass in the turf-built roofless cot his days, / And pine unfed amid the dreary waste!' (5-6, 7-8). Though Burns's residence in the Wee Vennel tenement in Dumfries may have been cramped, it was hardly the 'roofless cot' imagined here by Ninfeild.[51]

This sentimental scenario of Burns's undignified suffering expands throughout the course of the elegy, allowing Ninfeild to represent the poet's fellow Scots as a 'pitiless', callous lot:

Over his urn let weeping Genius stand,
And mourn his fav'rite's sad untimely grave,
Point to th' instructive tale, with trembling hand,
Which tells a pitiless world refus'd to save. (41-44)

Burns's lack of productivity in the 1790s is explained as the influence of poverty, which 'damp'd the glowing ardour of his mind' (12). His fame alone could not save him, for 'Poverty diffus'd its sadd'ning gloom, / and Patronage deny'd its friendly ray' (19-20). Ninfeild suggests that Burns was only too aware of the injustice he faced as a *genius* whom the world 'forgot' after its first burst of applause: 'Oft would the sad, the just reflexion grieve, / "The world applauded – but the world forgot"' (22-24).

As with Roscoe and Smith, Ninfeild lays the blame squarely on Scotland's patrons, whose 'protecting gold' was withheld until beneficence was expressed too late: 'Had the warm sunshine of protecting gold / Beam'd its kind lustre on her hapless son', then the poet claims that 'to the world the sad tale were not told, / That Scotia pities only Burns undone' (25-26, 27-28). Thus 'undone' by his nation's neglect, Burns is added as 'a martyr to the lists of woe' (40) who will be long remembered by his indignant supporters. He writes that Scots will mourn for as long as 'Genius or Compassion chase their tears / For this thy hapless, thy neglected son' (55-56). Depicting Burns as a 'hapless' victim of his country's indifference reaches its crescendo at the elegy's conclusion, where the speaker expresses a blend of righteous anger and sentimental empathy:

Oft shall the pensive foot of Genius rest
Near the sad marble which his corpse inurns,
Oft shall Compassion heave her beating breast,
And sigh with pity at the name of Burns! (57-60)

Perhaps unwittingly, the speaker captures the transformation of
Burns's legacy and reputation at work in these early elegies, whereby
Burns the historical person becomes only a 'name' that lives on.
However, this name commands the same (if not more) respect and
attention for Scottish readers in the wake of the great poet's death.

Eight days after Burns's death, *The Telegraph* published an
anonymous elegy entitled 'Verses to the Memory of R. Burns' (29
July 1796); unlike the previous examples, there is little righteous an-
ger expressed about the poet's untimely death. Instead the author of
this elegy offers one of the first instances of sacralisation, written from
the vantage point of one purportedly close to the poet (yet still
anonymous). This act of consecration appears in the first stanza,
where the speaker declares, 'Let no unhallow'd hand approach the
bier, / Where low in death his sacred reliques lie'.[52] Representing
Burns's corpse as 'sacred reliques' accurately prefigures the nine-
teenth-century obsession with the poet's physical remains, which were
exhumed and subjected to phrenological measurement on at least two
separate occasions.[53] As the elegy proceeds, the portrayal of the living
Burns is uniformly positive. As the speaker states, 'BURNS, blest
with native vigour, struck the lyre: / Each heart assenting felt the
magic sound' (5-6).

Throughout this elegy, Burns is represented as a quite joyful
'heaven-taught ploughman', whose writing was primarily meant to
please his readers:

Alive to joy, while joy was on the wing;
To playful mirth, to humour void of art;
'Twas Nature's self that taught her bard to sing
The song of joy, pour'd genuine from the heart. (9-12)

The poet employs almost identical terminology to that employed in
the early critical reviews, with the depiction of Burns as 'artless' and
'genuine' due to his tutelage by 'Nature'. However, no mention is
made of 'frozen Penury' contributing to the poet's death as in previ-
ous elegies, nor are there patrons to blame. Instead the loss of Burns
occasions national mourning unmixed with recrimination: 'For Genius
gone let Scotia melt in tears: / Her darling son no more shall soothe
her woes' (13-14).

The sentimental tableau of the poet viewing his soon-to-be
widow and fatherless children presents the speaker with a perfect op-

portunity to describe Burns's last moments of anxiety and concern. The results are exceedingly pathetic, as Burns rehearses the grim prospects facing his family as he prepares to die:

His Jeanie's woes, his helpless babes forlorn,
The prospect dire of penury and want,
The insolent contempt, the haughty scorn,
The look disdainful, and the bitter taunt,
These, from th' unfeeling, never cease to fall
With all their weight upon the wretched head;
This well he knew: – the thought that heart appall'd
That smil'd in pain descending to the dead. (29-36)

The diction in this passage abounds with Burnsian keywords like 'haughty scorn' and 'look disdainful', tending to reinforce the poet's persona as a 'heaven-taught ploughman' whose fate is bound closely to his class status. His identity as 'ploughman' presumably guarantees his family a 'prospect dire of penury and want', although by the time of his death, Burns had not ploughed a field in many years. Despite this bleak prediction facing his family, Burns can still 'smile in pain' before finally departing to the land of 'the dead'.

The invective guiding the previous elegies is largely absent here, as the speaker substitutes national recrimination for an exclusive 'last words' scenario replete with attendant moralising: 'His last advice still rings upon my ear, / "These dying words, I now impart to you"' (39-40). The poet reviews his faults and presents his findings, offering an apothegm that would become *de rigeur* for Burns's nineteenth-century apologists:

In sprightly youth of syren vice beware:
Learn from my fate the helpless lot of man;
With caution learn to shun each gilded snare:
O'erlook my faults, and all my beauties scan. (41-44)

The plea to 'o'erlook my faults' would gain currency as Burns's posthumous reputation began to take shape, but at this early juncture, the speaker seems only to be assessing the 'helpless lot of man' with rather generic moral criteria.

The elegy ends with an 'epitaph' in the manner of Gray's 'Elegy', a favorite of Burns; as in Gray's poem, the 'epitaph' is set

apart from the body text and seeks to neatly capture the essence of its
subject. As if standing above Burns's grave, the speaker writes,

Consign'd to earth, here rests the lifeless clay,
Which once a vital spark from heav'n inspir'd;
The lamp of genius shone full bright its day,
Then left the world to mourn its light retir'd. (45-48)

Echoing Burnsian diction once more with the phrase 'a vital spark
from heav'n',[54] the speaker exhorts 'Scotia' to remember and
commemorate its departed *genius*: 'While changeful seasons mark the
rolling years, / Thy fame, O BURNS, let Scotia still retain' (51-52).
The consecration of Burns enacted in this elegy depends greatly upon
prior representations of the poet as 'heaven-taught ploughman',
employing similar strategies in order to 'retain' his 'fame' for the
nation.

The tide of elegies that followed this early effort suggests that
Scotia did not (and would not) forget the 'name' of Burns. An elegy
by E. Hyslop, entitled 'Verses to the Memory of Robert Burns' and
published in *The Star, Daily Evening Advertiser* (25 August 1796),
clearly articulates this national directive at work. The poet exhorts the
genius of the nation to mourn its bard, stating 'Genius of Scotia
mourn!' before 'the urn / Where BURNS lies dead'.[55] The use of
genius in this context implies both the characteristic 'spirit' of the
nation, as well as Burns's 'distinction' as a poet.[56] This connection
between Burns and Scotland becomes more tightly drawn as the elegy
continues, for Hyslop readily applies the term *genius* to the poet in his
unremittingly harsh national landscape:

Scotia! though cold thy clime, though hard thy soil,
Where Nature fosters life by brawny toil –
Yet Genius lives: thy hills and rocks inspire
The Muses' love, and force poetic fire. (7-10)

The mutual enrichment of *genius* and 'Scotia' is diminished by the
death of Burns, leading Hyslop to exclaim that 'weak grows that fire –
the Muses droop' and adding that 'Genius, unprop'd, begins to stoop –
/ Her Bard is gone' (11, 12-13).

The personification of 'Scotia' in this manner became a familiar
technique in the contemporary elegies to Burns, fitting the rhetorical
occasion for mourning and chastisement. Hyslop's elegy is a rather

simple affair, ending with the generally inoffensive call to action for Scots (and Scotia) to remember their 'Bard' and grant his *genius* continuing fame and 'matchless praise'. He writes,

Sweet Bard, adieu! Whilst Scotia bears a name,
Whilst Merit claims the laurel, Genius fame,
Thy name shall live: and though the world decays,
More vigorous still shall grow thy matchless praise. (17-20)

The posthumous reputation of the 'sweet Bard' was linked with invocations of national mourning as a process of consecration. Indeed, in Hyslop's vision, the work of mourning that Scotia must complete – even as 'the world decays' – guarantees that Burns's 'name shall live' beyond the grave.

An anonymous elegy entitled 'Written on a blank Leaf of Burns' Poems' offers a similarly reductive condensation of the poet's life and career. Published in the *Aberdeen Magazine* (October 1796), this poem finds Burns as man and poet wanting, however, and delivers a sterner judgment on both than the previous elegies. Indeed, his reputation was quickly assailed by those who sought to assess the overall significance of his life and work for Scotland. As would become common for nineteenth-century critics, editors, and readers, accounting for Burns's 'deficiencies' (especially those concerning his sexual conduct) required an apologia for the value of the writing.[57] It is important to note here that this process of accounting for the author's purportedly 'disreputable' character appears as early as this elegy, which was written only two months after Burns's death. Though criticism of Burns's purported 'irreligion' and 'immorality' was nascent in the early reviews, it was not until after his death that this aspect of his reputation became a pronounced element of the commentary (both poetic and critical) on the poet's life and legacy.

For the author of 'Written on a blank Leaf of Burns' Poems', expressions of praise for the dead poet are counterbalanced by disappointment with his conduct, evident from the very beginning of his career:

When first I heard thy simple strains,
O Burns, what music fill'd my ear!
Methought once more on Scotia's plains,
Another Ossian would appear.[58]

The speaker's anticipation for the arrival of 'another Ossian' becomes more insistent as he detects the poet's *genius* beneath the humble guise of the ploughman: 'Thro' rustic guise I trac'd the gleam / Of Genius, pure celestial light!' (5-6). As an elegy, this evaluation of Burns's character and reputation appears rather dilatory, but it soon becomes clear that the poet has much more to say about the 'gleam of Genius' that animated his subject's life and death.

In fact, the speaker is primarily interested in calculating the deleterious effects wrought by Burns's celebrity starting in the late 1780s. Despite the fact that ten years had passed from the publication of the Kilmarnock edition to Burns's death, the elegist is insistent on commemorating only his persona as the 'heaven-taught ploughman'. There is no disappointment over Burns's missed opportunities or obligations in the 1790s, a frequent refrain expressed by other poets during these years. Instead, for this elegist, Burns may as well have died in 1787 rather than 1796. He writes that 'I fondly hop'd the kindling frame, / Might yet with future lustre burn' before lamenting that 'now, alas! Death stops thy fame, / And bids the sons of Genius mourn' (9-10, 11-12). This self-appointed 'son of Genius' continues his account of the 'death' of the poet's 'fame' by speculating on the life that Burns might have led, had he been 'contented' with the 'Ploughman's joys alone':

O hadst thou, yet to fame unknown,
Contented with thy humble fate,
Admir'd the Ploughman's joys alone,
Nor sought to change that happy state;
On Ayr's green banks thou might'st have stray'd,
At solemn evening's pensive hour. (13-18)

The speaker begins to assign blame to the poet for rejecting this sylvan ideal, using Gray's 'Elegy' to reiterate the point that Burns willfully chose to complicate his life. He writes – 'In the calm scenes of rural life, / Thou might'st have liv'd obscurely blest' (21-22) – before adding the requisite allusion: 'Far from the "crowd's ignoble strife," / And sunk unnotic'd into rest' (23-24).[59]

His allusion to Gray's 'Elegy' runs counter to that poem's implicit recognition of the potential 'mute inglorious Miltons' in the graveyard. Here it is much better to be 'obscurely blest' and then forgotten. At this point, the elegist states plainly that it is Burns himself who is to blame for the difficulties that opened before him once his 'ambition' led him to pursue 'fame':

Soon ambitious views inspire
Thy soul to seek a Poet's name;
The breast that feels poetic fire,
Must ever feel – the love of Fame. (25-28)

Taking on a 'Poet's name' suggests that such a persona can negatively alter one's constituent identity, even that possessed by a possible 'Ossian' like Burns. The next step in the elegy's narrative follows the prescriptive formula of the eighteenth-century sentimental novel (or 'rake's progress'), whereby the uncorrupted rural lad heads 'to "fair Edina's lofty towers"' because 'Ambition led thy devious way' (29-30).[60] Once within the city limits, 'Fashion's gay fantastick powers, / Soon o'er thy reason gain'd the sway' (31-32).

Like the innocent bumpkin, Burns becomes gradually corrupted by the urban experience, leading him to no longer appreciate the simple rural joys of his younger life: 'The "banks of Ayr" can charm no more, / The Lark's gay song no longer please' (33-34). Instead, the poet is driven forward by the 'voice of praise', which is 'sweeter far, / And, ah! what scenes can vie with these' (35-36). This invariably leads to vice, as surely as Hogarth's Tom Rakewell was destined for debauchery the instant he stepped within London's city limits. This time-worn narrative gains a new wrinkle with the figure of Burns, an actual person whose life story was reframed to conform to the standards of the moralising elegist. For this author, it is important to underscore that Burns 'chose' the path of wrong, not only in following the lure of the 'poet's name' but also in committing numerous undisclosed indiscretions:

Deluded youth! – in search of praise,
To join the gay promiscuous throng,
To plunge in Error's guileful maze,
To know the right – and do the wrong! (37-40)

This last line neatly captures the elegy's overall purpose: Burns is judged *in absentia* by a 'court of equity' and found unequivocally guilty.[61]

For this elegist, it is enough to point out Burns's failings and move on. He writes, 'Let thy errors be forgot, / And still thy memory claim the tear' (41-42). As previously noted (and highlighted too by the apostrophe to Burns as a 'deluded youth'), the poet represents him as if he had only just achieved his celebrity before his death: 'Pity mourns the Poet's lot, / Who falls in early life's career' (43-44). The sum of Burns's life work – particularly the extensive, valuable song-writing and song-collecting he completed during the 1790s – is nowhere to be found in this elegy. He remains as full of promise as the speaker of Gray's 'Elegy', whose early death robs the world of 'a youth to fortune and to fame unknown'.[62] Like the tragic loss of this exceptional young man, Burns's death is treated as a case study for what might have been.

The finality of death is the occasion for the speaker's last thoughts:

May thy spirit rest in peace;
The cares of life with thee are o'er,
"Despondency" and pain shall cease,
And Pleasure's voice allure no more. (45-48)[63]

That this judgment was reached two months after the poet's death is worth restating, for it both clarifies and expresses the process through which Burns's posthumous reputation was to be transformed. Later editors, critics, poets, and readers would be much more explicit about what 'wrongs' Burns had willingly committed and (like the poet above) would use his own work against him.

4. Invoking the 'Muse of Caledon': Alexander Balfour's Elegy to the Memory of Robert Burns

Of the elegies written for Burns in 1796, Alexander Balfour's 'Elegy to the Memory of Robert Burns' is the longest at 200 lines. Published in the *Edinburgh Magazine or Literary Miscellany* (December 1796), Balfour's poem presents a thorough estimation of Burns's merits as a poet. Eight years younger than his subject, Balfour was also a labouring-class poet, having been raised in Monikie, Forfarshire and apprenticed as a weaver at an early age. However, Balfour outlived Burns by thirty-three years and gained renown as a novelist later in his career. Like his famous predecessor, Balfour's finances remained uncertain throughout his life; in 1796, he was working as a clerk for a merchant manufacturer in Arbroath and writing for the *Aberdeen Magazine*.[64] His elegy for Burns in many respects synthesises the dominant strains within the early tributes, expressing conceptualisations of the poet and his legacy that were fast becoming the standard elements of his emerging national iconicity. However, Balfour also provides some important variations in his elegy, especially those concerning Burns and his meaning for living Scottish poets.

One such difference is detectable in the poem's opening stanzas, where the speaker is represented not merely as an impressed spectator of Burns's great *genius* but as a poet himself, working in the same tradition as his predecessor. He writes:

The ling'ring sun's last parting beam
On mountain tops had died away,
And Night, the friend of Fancy's dream,
Stole o'er the fields in dusky grey.[65]

Within this gloomy natural setting, the speaker portrays himself as a solitary figure in the mode of Gray's 'Elegy', seeking repose and solace in the midst of the 'busy bustling throng' where 'I wander'd forth along the vale, / To list the widow'd blackbird's song' (6-7).

Beneath a 'sweetly sylvan shade' (10), the speaker falls victim to 'Morpheus' and experiences a vision which enthralls him in much the same fashion as Burns's speaker in his own 'Vision'.[66] He writes,

'Twas here my muse without control
Essay'd on flutt'ring wing to rise;
When listless langour seiz'd my soul,
And drowsy slumbers seal'd my eyes. (13-16)

The speaker describes the event in considerable detail, explaining the awe-inspiring approach of the Muse: 'A maid of matchless grace I saw, / Array'd in more than mortal pride' (23-24). Unlike Burns's sprightly Muse Coila in his 'Vision', Balfour's maid is gravely distressed: 'Pallid grief her cheek o'erspread' (28).

Her gloom infects the speaker and substantially darkens the remainder of the poem, which recounts her grief for the death of Burns. He writes,

On the daisied bank reclin'd,
She touch'd a harp for sadness strung:

The trembling strings – the murm'ring rill –
[...]
All join'd to swell the solemn scene. (31-33, 36)

The 'solemn scene' speaks to the future of Scottish poetry without
Burns, an absence which Balfour suggests cannot be filled with the
verse of living contenders. As in Burns's 'Vision', the encounter be-
tween poet and Muse is charged with emotion and freighted with
meaning for the Scottish nation. She prepares to instruct Balfour on
his present purpose, but her excessive sorrow for the loss of her bard
interrupts her design: 'To sorrow [she] gave unbounded sway' (38).

Empathy provokes Balfour to similar displays of distress – 'My
throbbing heart forgot to beat' (39) – before the Muse finally begins
her own elegy for a favorite son. She openly declares her identity as
'the muse of Caledon' and begins to list the 'sons' of Scotland whom
she has inspired:

I am the muse of Caledon',
From earliest ages aye admir'd;
Thro' her most distant corners known,
Oft has my voice her sons inspir'd. (41-44)

Among these sons numbers King James I, whom the Muse succored in
his captivity: 'I sooth'd his soul, with trouble prest, / When captive on
a foreign shore' (47-48). In addition she describes her role in prepar-
ing Scottish warriors for battle, perhaps alluding here to Wallace or
Bruce: '[I] Inspir'd his soul with martial glow, / And call'd his coun-
try's wrongs to mind' (51-52).

However, none of these heroic forebears compares with Burns,
whose loss to the Muse is immeasurable: 'Chief of all the tuneful
train, / Was BURNS, my last – my latest care' (57-58). Her 'care' of
the departed poet was maternal: 'I nurs'd him on his native plain'
(59). As Balfour expands his depiction of Burns's 'nursing', he under-
scores key elements in the 'heaven-taught ploughman' persona for
which the Muse herself was responsible, including his essential differ-
ence from others in 'peasant garb':

I hail'd his happy natal hour,
And o'er his infant cradle hung;
Ere Fancy's wild unbounded pow'r,
Or Reason's earliest bud was sprung.

I saw the young ideas rise
Successive, in his youthful mind;
Nor could the peasant's garb disguise
The kindling flame that lay confin'd. (61-68)

Balfour's Burnsian diction directly echoes 'The Vision', with its similar account of the poet's birth being attended by the Muse; unlike Burns's version, though, Balfour's Scottish Muse is not a lesser figure in the pantheon of Muses. Her place and role are sacrosanct, and her decision to shelter and feed Burns's 'kindling fame' is intended to prepare him for his future role as a national bard.

In Balfour's elegy, the young Burns is well-aware of this, spending valuable time in the company of the Muse to prepare for his eventual crowning as bard. The Muse recounts their period of apprenticeship: 'When the rural task was done, / We sought some wild sequester'd way' (75-76). She describes how she placed her 'darling child' in the Scottish landscape – 'On Coila's hills, or woodlands wild, / By Stinchar's banks, or Luggar's stream' (77-78) – to inspire him with love and appreciation of his native country.[67] Within this landscape, the poet is nurtured by 'Fancy', whose 'woodnotes wild' inspire him in the manner of Milton's 'L'Allegro': 'These haunts to him were blissful bow'rs, / Where all the soul was unconfin'd' (81-82). In such settings, 'Fancy cull'd her choicest flow'rs, / To warm her youthful Poet's mind' (83-84). Despite such promising beginnings, Burns had still to contend with poverty and 'mental Grief', both of which conspired to extinguish his effusive 'kindling flame'.

The Muse supplements the work of 'Fancy' with that of 'Nature', culminating in a 'heaven-taught' poet who can endure suffering and write 'heart-felt strains':

Nurs'd on the healthful happy plains,
Where Love's first blush from Virtue springs,
'Twas Nature taught the heart-felt strains,
That o'er the vassal'd cot he sings.
Keen Poverty with wither'd arms,
Compress'd him in her cold embrace;
And mental Grief's ungracious harms
Had furrow'd o'er his youthful face. (85-92)

Against such external (and internal) impediments, Burns used his verse to survive: 'Yet there, the dear delightful flame [...] Resistless fir'd his melting frame' (93, 95).

Describing him as 'a friend to mirth and foe to care, / Yet form'd to feel for worth opprest' (97-98), the Muse considers the future awaiting Burns's large family after his premature death, asking 'who shall thy sweet prattlers chear, / Now that a green-turf wraps thy head?' (103-04). This leads the Muse to briefly step outside the elegy proper, directly appealing to those Scots who have the means to aid the poet's family:

Ye souls, of sympathetic mind,
Whom smiling Plenty deigns to crown;
Yours be the task – their wounds to bind,
And make their sorrows all your own. (105-08)

After this impromptu address to potential benefactors, the Muse returns to her real subject, creating a template for Burns's posthumous reputation. For the Scottish Muse, Burns is everything a national bard could seek to be, representing the *genius* of the country effortlessly in his person and verse. He is guided by 'Nature' and 'Fancy', and he is uncorrupted by education and urban life. His loss is irreplaceable, leaving the Muse to mourn her poet without hope for another: 'This garland for my bard entwin'd, / No brow but his shall ever wear' (157-58). She will visit his body in the grave in continual remembrance – 'While dews descend upon his tomb, / So long the Muse shall love his name' (161-62) – and teach the living to sing his 'fame': 'Nor shall this wreath forget to bloom, / Till latest ages sing thy fame' (163-64).

She finishes her speech to her adherent Balfour with only a glimmer of hope for the future of Scottish poetry, despite the loss of such a singular poet in Burns. After admonishing would-be poets like Balfour to avoid 'seductive Pleasure's train' (168) and 'Luxury's lap' (173), she recreates the scene of Burns's upbringing in all its uncomplicated healthiness of 'jocund' labourers and 'village maidens':

The hedge-row'd plain, the flow'ry vale,
Where rosy Health delighted roves,
Where Labour tells his jocund tale,
And village maidens sing their loves,
'Tis there the Muse unfolds her charms,

From thence her sons should never stray –
Ye souls whom boundless Fancy warms,
Still keep this calm sequester'd way. (177-84)

Alluding to Gray's 'noiseless tenor of their way' from his 'Elegy',[68] Balfour's Muse seems at first to suggest that her present 'sons' should be content to live and die as 'mute inglorious Miltons'.

However, she offers hope for those 'souls whom boundless Fancy warms', provided they show proper homage to her 'darling's tomb' as they attempt to win (and wear) the bays:

So may that wide-spread well-won praise,
Which echoes o'er my darling's tomb;
Congenial bloom amidst your bays,
And heav'n bestow a happier doom! (185-88)

The vision dissipates, leaving Balfour to wake in dismay: 'I waked – and wish'd again to sleep, / But ah! the pleasing dream was o'er' (191-92). He concludes his elegy with an apology to the 'shade' of Burns, hoping that this product of his 'infant Muse' has not displeased him: 'My infant muse, untaught to sing, / Has marr'd the vision's solemn strain' (193-94). He fears that he has 'too harshly touch'd the pensive string, / To soothe thy shade, lamented swain' (195-96). Such lines attest to the pervasive influence Burns would have on practicing Scottish poets in the immediate years after his death, as each contender sought to mobilise the posthumous support of their departed 'brother poet'.

Unlike previous elegists who sought to apologise for Burns's conduct (whether implicitly or explicitly stated), Balfour elevates him to the stature of myth by using the poet's own poetic vehicle of the 'vision'. Within Balfour's vision, however, the Scottish Muse looks kindly on her favorite son whose work as a national bard has been cut tragically short, leaving her in perpetual grief. She may be assuaged, though, by the efforts of a poet like Balfour, whose 'infant muse' was also 'untaught to sing'. Like his subject as well, Balfour's provincial origins may qualify him to write in Burns's stead. This attractive possibility emerges in the elegy's final stanza, where Balfour expresses his 'sincere' sorrow for the lost bard and takes ownership for a long, 'artless' poem which capped a year of extensive elegising. Balfour writes,

Unskill'd to frame the venal lay,
That flows not from a heart sincere;
'Tis mine, this artless meed to pay –
The heart-felt sigh – and silent tear! (197-200)

The voice that articulates this 'heart-felt sigh – and silent tear' captures the spirit of the elegies penned in 1796, all of which sought to reshape the figure of Burns to match their own perceptions and needs. Such poems initiated a process of reconstructing Burns's image and reputation that would continue unabated throughout the nineteenth century. As already evident in these early elegies, the posthumous figure of Burns had little correspondence with the actual historical person who inhabited the persona of the 'heaven-taught ploughman'. However, as will be shown in the next chapter, this persona would also undergo significant moderation as later critics, editors, writers, and readers increasingly evaluated Burns's perceived moral failings as a 'poetic genius'.

---

[1] After 1788 and until his death in 1796, Burns overwhelmingly worked on songs instead of poems. See *The Poems and Songs of Robert Burns*, ed. by Kinsley, I, pp. xvi-xxviii, for evidence of this change in direction. Quotations from Burns's poetry refer to this edition and will be cited by volume, poem, and line numbers in the text.

[2] See Ferguson and Roy, Vol II (1985: 149).

[3] Currie (1845: li).

[4] Ferguson and Roy, Vol I (1985:74).

[5] For discussion of Burns's stays in Edinburgh, see Crawford (2009) pp. 237-90. See also Franklin B. Snyder, *The Life of Robert Burns* (New York: Macmillan, 1932), pp. 186-234: 256-77.

[6] For instance, he is quite open about this in the dedication of the Edinburgh Edition to the Caledonian Hunt, where he states: 'A Scottish Bard, proud of the name, and whose highest ambition is to sing in his Country's service, where shall he so properly look for patronage as to the illustrious Names of his native Land'. See Andrew Noble and Patrick Scott Hogg, eds, *The Canongate Burns: The Complete Poems and Songs of Robert Burns* (Edinburgh: Canongate, 2003), pp. 169-70 (p. 169).

[7] For discussion of such poets, see Carruthers, 'Robert Burns's Scots Poetry Contemporaries', in Sergeant and Stafford (2012), pp. 39-52.

[8] Ferguson and Roy, Vol I (1985: 382).

[9] See *DNB* for further information on Graham.

[10] James Graham, *Poems, in English, Scotch, and Latin* (Paisley: Neilson, 1794), p. 43, ll. 1-4. Further references to this edition will be noted in-text by line numbers.

[11] 'The lowly train in life's sequestered scene' refers to line 6 of 'The Cottar's Saturday Night' (I, 72), while 'for leave to toil' refers to line 60 of 'Man was Made to Mourn' (I, 64).

[12] See Starr and Hendrickson (1966: 39, l. 59). For more on Gray's influence on Burns, see Gorji, 'Burns's Sentiments: Gray, Milton and "To A Mountain Daisy"'.

[13] For discussion of Thomson's continuing influence throughout the century, see Mary Jane Scot, *James Thomson, Anglo-Scot* (Athens: University of Georgia Press, 1988).

[14] Burns used this term to describe David Sillar in 'Epistle to Davie, a Brother Poet'. See chapter two of the present work for further discussion of this term's relation to Burns's fellow poets.

[15] Johnson, ed. (1984: 66).

[16] For evidence of this drop in critical interest in the periodical press, see Moffatt (1941: 37-67).

[17] Burns was very keen to present himself as financially independent. See for instance the already-cited instance of Burns's refusal to accept payment from George Thomson (n. 2). See also his letter to Thomson (12 July 1796), where he writes that 'after all my boasted independance [sic], curst necessity compels me to implore you for five pounds' (*Letters of Robert Burns*, II, 389).

[18] For more on this period of Burns's life, see Snyder, pp. 294-353. For a more general discussion of Burns's 'livelihood', see DeLancey Ferguson (1939: 188-233).

[19] See Thornton, *William Maxwell to Robert Burns*, p. 157 for discussion of Burns's financial difficulties at this time. Thornton notes that 'the worse Burns's fortune as Nithside farmer had become, the greater had been his dependency upon the Excise as the only way of supporting himself and his family' (157).

[20] Ibid., p. 158. In particular, the notorious 'Ça ira' episode was dangerous to his livelihood; see Crawford (2009: 356, 358, 362, 367, 383).

[21] Johnson (1993: 7).

[22] Ibid., p. 78.

[23] For more on Blacklock, see *DNB* and Ross (1927: 29-30).

[24] Low (1974: 61-62). Further references to this edition are given after quotations in the text.

[25] Ferguson and Roy, Vol I (1985: 145).

[26] For a brief recounting of these tumultuous years, see Ferguson (1939: xiv-xvii).

[27] Blacklock died in 1791, and the poem was published posthumously in Joseph Robertson, *Lives of the Scottish Poets*, 3 vols (London: Boys, 1822), Vol II, pp. 44-45 (ll. 1-6). Hereafter cited by line numbers in-text.

[28] *The Rules of Art: Genesis and Structure of the Literary Field*, trans. by Susan Emanuel (Stanford: Stanford University Press, 1996), p. 218.

[29] For more on this aspect of Burns's contemporaries, see Carruthers in Sergeant and Stafford (2012: 39-42), and Roy in Simpson (1997'"The Mair They Talk, I'm Kend the Better": Poems about Robert Burns to 1859'.

[30] See Colin Affleck, 'Windows of Opportunity: The Scottish-English Career of Robert Kellie Douglas', *The Drouth*, 38 (2010-11), p. 40.

[31] For more on these critical/artistic tendencies, see Moffatt (1941: 232-41).

[32] *Literary Magazine and British Review* (May 1789: 297, ll. 1-2). Further citations will be noted by line numbers in-text.

[33] *Gazetteer and New Daily Advertiser* (14 August 1790: 29, ll. 1-4). Further citations will be noted by line numbers in-text. I have assumed the author of this poem is male, owing to publication conventions of the time. Women's verse addressed to Burns was often announced even in anonymous works (such as 'By A Lady').

[34] For more on the demands of readers upon writers, see William St. Clair, 'At the Boundaries of the Reading Nation', in Shafquat Towheed, Rosalind Crone, and Katie Halsey, eds, *The History of Reading: A Reader* (London: Routledge, 2011), pp. 220-30. See also his book on the subject, *The Reading Nation in the Romantic Period* (Cambridge: Cambridge University Press, 2004).

[35] Johnson (1993: 114).

[36] *Morning Chronicle* (6 September 1791: 5, ll. 1-2). Further citations will be noted by line numbers in-text.

[37] Robert Fergusson also expressed a disdain for 'foreign influences' in his poetry, particularly the taste for Italian music. For a discussion of his linguistic nationalism, see Wickman, 'Tonality and the Sense of Place in Fergusson's "Elegy, on the Death of Scots Music"'.

[38] Johnson (1993: 30).

[39] Ibid., p. 60.

[40] For a still useful discussion of Burns's song-collecting project, see Thomas Crawford, *Burns: A Study of the Poems and Songs* (Stanford: Stanford University Press), pp. 257-336. For analysis of Burns's critical remarks on Scottish song, see Andrews, in Carruthers (2009: 110-24).

[41] McGuirk (1994: xxvii).

[42] For more on the genesis of this poem, see Robert D. Thornton, *William Maxwell to Robert Burns* (Edinburgh: Donald, 1979), p. 156. The only other work that resembles the narrative framework of 'Tam O'Shanter' is 'Love

and Liberty', which was likely composed in 1785 but remained unpublished until 1799.

[43] On this period of Burns's life, see Snyder (1932: 354-441).

[44] See Kinsley (1968: xvi-xxviii), Vol I.

[45] In his letter to George Thomson (16 Sept 1792), Burns writes, 'As to any remuneration, you may think my Songs either above, or below price; for they shall absolutely be the one or the other.—In the honest enthusiasm with which I embark in your undertaking, to talk of money, wages, fee, hire, &c. would be downright Sodomy of soul!'. This high-principled decision proved to be a poor one on Burns's part. See Ferguson and Roy (1985: 149), Vol II.

[46] See chapter two of the present work.

[47] Qtd. In Henry Roscoe, *Life of William Roscoe*, 2 vols (London: Cadell, 1833),Vol I, p. 234. I have been unable to determine the first name of the letter's recipient, the Rev. Mr. Edwards of Birmingham, but he does appear on many subscribers' lists from the period.

[48] Stuart Curran, ed., *The Poems of Charlotte Smith* (Oxford: Oxford University Press, 1993), p. 71, ll. 4-7. All citations refer to this edition and are noted by line numbers in-text.

[49] Johnson (1993: 24).

[50] *Gentleman's Magazine* (August 1796: 684, ll. 1-4). Further citations will be noted by line numbers in-text.

[51] See Thornton (1979: 157-58) for details on Burns's living conditions in Dumfries.

[52] p. 13, ll. 3-4. Further citations will be noted by line numbers in-text.

[53] For more on this unusual facet of Burns's afterlife, see Carol McGuirk, 'Burns and Nostalgia', in Kenneth Simpson, ed., *Burns Now* (Edinburgh: Canongate, 1994), pp. 31-69. For the phrenologists' take on Burns, see Luke R. J. Maynard, 'Hoddin' Grey an' A' That: Robert Burns's Head, Class Hybridity, and the Value of the Ploughman's Mantle', in Aruna Krishnamurthy, ed., *The Working-Class Intellectual in Eighteenth- and Nineteenth-Century Britain* (Farnham: Ashgate, 2009), pp. 67-84.

[54] See line 73 of Burns's first 'Epistle to Lapraik' (I, 57): 'gie me ae spark o' Nature's fire'.

[55] p. 12, ll. 1-3. Further citations will be noted by line numbers in-text. The identity of E. Hyslop is a mystery; he does not appear in the bibliographies of Egerer and Gibson, nor are there other works by this author concerning Burns. The only Hyslop I have been able to find in connection with Burns is Mrs. William Hyslop, who was the landlady of the Glove tavern in Dumfries and a friend to Burns and his family (see Ross, *Who's Who in Burns*, pp. 163-64).

[56] See chapter one of the present work for discussion of these definitions of *genius*.

[57] See chapter four of the present work for analysis of this trend.

[58] p. 247, ll. 1-4. Further citations will be noted by line numbers in-text.

[59] See Starr and Hendrickson (1966: 40, l. 73) for this allusion.

[60] The phrase 'fair Edina's lofty towers' can be found in *The Giant's Causeway* by William Drummond of Hawthornden. It should be noted that in its original context, the 'towers' of Edinburgh are highly praised and seen as 'blest towers! Whose genius eagle-winged pursues / The boldest flights of science, and the Muse'. See William Hamilton Drummond, *The Giant's Causeway: A Poem* (Belfast: Longman, Hurst, Rees, Orme, & Brown, 1811), p. 90. There may also be an allusion to Burns's 'Address to Edinburgh' in these lines.

[61] For Burns's own subversive use of a 'court of equity', see Corey Andrews, *Literary Nationalism in Eighteenth-Century Scottish Club Poetry* (Lewiston: Mellen, 2004), pp. 258-62, 265-68.

[62] See Starr and Hendrickson (1966: 43, l. 118) for this allusion.

[63] Line 47 alludes to Burns's 'Despondency: An Ode' (I, 94).

[64] For more on Balfour, see *DNB*.

[65] 'Elegy', p. 465, ll. 1-4. Further citations will be noted by line numbers in-text. This poem also appeared in Balfour's collection of poems entitled *Contemplation* (Edinburgh: Watson, 1820), pp. 104-15.

[66] For analysis of Burns's 'The Vision' and its significance for his poetic self-construction, see chapter one of the present work.

[67] Balfour alludes to Burns's early song 'Behind yon hills where Lugar flows' (I, 4), which had initially used the name Stinchar for the stream of the song's title. Burns allegedly changed it to Lugar because it was a more poetical name than Stinchar. Balfour includes both (misspelling Lugar as well), presumably to avoid confusion for his readers.

[68] Starr and Hendrickson (1966: 40, l. 76).

Chapter Four

'The Powers and Failings of Genius': Constructing Burns's Posthumous Reputation, 1796-1816

1. 'Impaired by Excess': Burns's First Obituary

Of all people to comment publicly in print on the death of Robert Burns in 1796, perhaps the least-qualified (George Thomson, Burns's collaborator in the *Select Songs* project) made the most lasting impression.[1] J. DeLancey Ferguson has claimed that Thomson's obituary of the poet in *The London Chronicle* (28-30 July 1796) 'set the tone, long before the appearance of even Robert Heron's biography, for all the public comment on Burns's life and character'.[2] Although Thomson corresponded frequently with the poet, the two never met and frequently did not see eye to eye. This fact shows in the overall tone and character of Thomson's obituary, which blends approbation of the poet's talents with thinly-veiled disapproval of his lifestyle.

On the surface, Thomson's obituary is largely admiring, with clear approval of Burns's distinctive national character. For example, Thomson remarks that although the poet 'was literally a ploughman', he was 'neither in that state of servile dependence or degrading ignorance which the situation might bespeak in this country'.[3] Instead, Burns 'had the common education of a Scottish peasant […] and that spirit of independence, which, though banished in that country from the scenes of aristocratic influence, is sometimes to be found to a high degree in the humblest classes of society' (99). Along with such marks of distinction, the poet's singular difference from other Scottish peasants is emphasised by Thomson: Burns was 'a man who was the pupil of nature, the poet of inspiration, and who possessed in an extraordinary degree the powers and failings of genius' (100).

As Ferguson rightly observes, the groundwork for Burns's posthumous reputation can be found in such statements; in particular, his *genius* is frequently seen thereafter as a source of both power and weakness. As in the elegies published in 1796 (see chapter three), Burns is perceived as a figure of national importance whose loss is immeasurable for Scottish literature. However, in the prose commentary on Burns's death starting in 1796 (and continuing throughout the early nineteenth century), the poet's character becomes increasingly assailed by critics and editors who find his 'immoral' and 'irreligious' lifestyle a regrettable by-product of his *genius*. This begins as early as Thomson's obituary, in which he remarks that Burns's genius was the undeniable source of his appeal: 'proofs of such uncommon genius in a situation so humble, made the acquaintance of the author eagerly sought after' (100).

However, such genius conveys a fatal weakness: 'His nights were devoted to books and the muse, except when they were wasted in those haunts of village festivity, to which the Poet was but too immoderately attached in every period of his life' (99). In addition to the influence of such behaviour, Burns's reputation gains further notoriety by references to his eventual profession as an excise collector and his unseemly conduct among the gentry. Although the poet was 'everywhere invited and caressed', Thomson bluntly states that 'probably [Burns] was not qualified to fill a superior station to that which was assigned him. We know that his manners refused to partake the polish of genteel society' (100). This echoes other criticism of the poet's lack of 'polish' among 'genteel society', about which Dugald Stewart had claimed that 'his dread of anything approaching to meanness or servility, rendered his manner somewhat decided and hard'.[4]

In Thomson's eyes Burns appears as a driven, untoward prodigy whose demise was largely self-inflicted: 'His talents were often obscured and finally impaired by excess' (100). Despite the bitter ending of such talent, Thomson asks readers to pay 'a tribute of respect to the genius of a Poet' (101). Although Thomson did Burns many favours in the last years of the poet's life, his 'tribute of respect' here was decidedly double-edged.[5] The initial cast of Burns's posthumous reputation in prose commentary can be found within this obituary; that it had little correspondence with Burns's actual life and character is worth noting. As Ferguson indignantly records, Thomson's view of Burns as a 'dissipated' character 'was first given publicity by a man who had never met Burns, who had never been in Dumfries, and whose statements were hotly resented by some Dumfriesians who knew Burns best'.[6]

After Burns's death, the process of reputation-building begun in the early reviews and elegies began to crystallise, with certain key features becoming prominent in each account. Assessments of Burns's body of work continued to herald his 'original poetic genius' as an overriding character trait, seeing it as a source of both power and weakness. This representation derived in large part from changing perceptions of 'poetic genius' in the literary marketplace, in which *genius* became increasingly characterised as a character trait possessed by alienated outsiders from the labouring classes. It was often most evidenced in the (generally tragic) biographies of those imbued with 'poetic genius' as much as it was embedded in their works. In this respect, Burns's posthumous reputation was greatly influenced by his representation as a dissolute *genius* whose own excessive appetites led to his early demise.[7]

Rather than viewing Burns as a 'legitimate' producer in the literary field, his posthumous critics primarily found his social difference to be the key marker of his value; the concept of 'poetic genius' was paramount in validating the works of presumed outsiders like Burns. An important aspect that must be recognised about this process is the means by which a poet like Burns was granted only *conditional* legitimacy by those with power and influence in the literary field; this was especially the case after his productions necessarily ceased. In granting Burns limited legitimacy, critics asserted their authority by applying standards of literary judgment that relied upon existing exclusionary categories. In some respects, this can be seen a continuation of the 'heaven-taught ploughman' reception that Burns experienced during his lifetime, but it gained greater currency after his death as aspects of his life story became as much (if not more) central to his poetic legacy. As Nick Crossley notes, acquiring such legitimacy (commensurate with 'cultural capital') is based upon the existing social stratifications of the field itself: 'the value of any form of capital depends [...] upon social recognition'.[8] For Burns's posthumous reception, 'social recognition' became (and remained) an integral component of his reputation as a 'poetic genius'. As Romantic theories of poetry and creativity assumed greater currency in the literary marketplace, Burns served a pivotal role as a 'tragic' labouring-class precursor possessed of 'poetic genius'.[9]

This process of reputation-building reinforces the competitive nature of the field itself, revealing the methods by which an author's 'distinction' can be conferred or withdrawn. Bourdieu states that

The more the field is capable of functioning as a field of competition for cultural legitimacy, the more individual production must be oriented towards the search for culturally pertinent features endowed with value in the field's own economy. This confers properly cultural value on the producers by endowing them with marks of distinction.[10]

In Burns's case, his posthumous reputation was constructed by various 'producers' who sought to select and highlight 'marks of distinction' that derived from his 'poetic genius'. Several of these resulting representations often display deliberate misconstructions of Burns's life and works, which are then distorted to conform to the notion of a poet who possessed the 'powers and failings of genius'.

The role of critics and editors in culturally producing Burns's posthumous reputation was considerable, especially those who contributed to its development soon after his death. As Randal Johnson states, an author's work depends greatly upon the 'recognition of the functions of artistic mediators (publishers, critics, agents [...] and so forth) as producers of the meaning and value of the work'.[11] The role of 'artistic mediators' extends beyond the interpretation of an author's works, having extensive and long-lasting influence upon how an author is situated in the literary marketplace; in the case of posthumous authors, the influence of critics, biographers and editors is substantial. Such producers were also consumers, constructing a representation of Burns that accorded with their own interests and needs; Michael Grenfell observes that 'cultural consumption never exists in some pure realm of aesthetic appreciation, but is always an expression of a certain way of being in the world – of taste – and the ontological status this behaviour claims'.[12]

For Burns, his reputation changed dramatically after his death due to this ongoing process of cultural production and consumption, gaining negative associations that would trouble his admirers into the nineteenth century. The perception of Burns's numerous 'failings' derived largely from the initial wave of biographies and editions, where the representation of the poet as a 'heaven-taught ploughman' began to undergo revision in light of Burns's numerous 'indiscretions', both personal and political. Even sympathetic critics and editors felt the need to address Burns's reputation as a *genius* whose excessive appetites overwhelmed him and led to his premature death. Such views had little correspondence with the actual events of Burns's life, particularly his last years which were spent busily working as an

excise officer and living with his large family in Dumfries. His crea-
tive energies were spent on the song-collecting projects he had begun
in 1787 with James Johnson and in 1792 with Thomson, for which he
sought neither payment nor personal recognition.[13]

In contrast to the early years of Burns's fame in Scotland and
abroad (1786-1788), his last decade was decidedly anticlimactic as far
as his reputation as a 'poetic genius' was concerned. Having re-
trenched from the society of Edinburgh elites, Burns spent his time
pursuing farming at Ellisland before moving on to work solely for the
excise in Dumfries.[14] Despite the continuing popularity of his *Poems,
Chiefly in the Scottish Dialect* (which appeared in a second edition in
1793), Burns never published another volume of similar verse. It can
be argued that these years represented a deliberate retreat from fame, a
conscious attempt on Burns's part to shed his persona as a 'heaven-
taught ploughman'. Its novelty had waned considerably over the
1790s, although critics and admirers continued to express approbation
of Burns in this guise. Burns's decision to pursue song-collecting in
lieu of writing verse may be interpreted as his attempt to repudiate the
'heaven-taught ploughman' persona and craft a different one more
conducive to his interests and ambitions: that of the 'Scotch Bard'.[15]

Despite his efforts to the contrary, Burns discovered that he
could not control the personæ used to understand and interpret him as
a literary producer. In fact, his efforts to be recognised as a 'Scotch
Bard' – a poet of his nation like Blind Harry, a Scots Makar like
Dunbar or Henryson – were actively resisted by those who wished
him to remain only an exceptional prodigy from the labouring class.
After his death, this process became entirely a matter of critical debate
over the nature of Burns's *genius*, particularly its 'powers and fail-
ings'. This chapter explores the varied critical, editorial, and poetic
responses to his death and their extensive contribution to Burns's
emerging posthumous reputation as the brilliant but deeply flawed
genius of Scotland.

2. 'Poetry Was Actually Not His Forte': Maria Ridell's Sketch of Burns

In response to representations of Burns's life and character like
George Thomson's obituary, the poet's friend Maria Riddell (writing

under the pseudonym 'Candidior') produced a character sketch of Burns in the *Dumfries Journal* of August 1796. In the estimation of Burns's late nineteenth-century editors W. E. Henley and T. F. Henderson, Riddell's sketch was 'so admirable in tone, withal so discerning and impartial in understanding, that it remains the best thing written of him by a contemporary critic'.[16] Robert Thornton argues, however, that Riddell's memoir of Burns added more to the work of character assassination that was growing stronger in the immediate aftermath of the poet's death rather than offering a defense of his character. Thornton writes,

> To make matters still worse, Maria Riddell published her Memoir. She had written it within a fortnight of Burns's death as a defense [...] Within a few hundred words, Maria's tribute admits that Burns was 'candid and manly in the avowal of his errors', that his had been 'the frolic of the flowing bowl', that he had 'irregularites' and 'frailties', 'frequent errors' and 'misfortunes', 'imprudencies that sullied' and such 'inconsistencies' as alternately exalt and debase one's nature.[17]

As Thornton rightly observes, such a 'character sketch' was especially damaging to the efforts of the poet's friends William Maxwell and John Syme in finding subscribers for an edition of Burns's works to aid his family: 'the heart of the public does not vibrate with sympathy for a man eulogised as a débauchee who dies of his excess'.[18]

In her work, Riddell represents the poet's life and achievements from a privileged vantage point, that of a 'candid' friend who is out to rebut the 'injustice done to Burns's character' present in other responses to the poet's life, death, and body of works. That she composed the sketch less than a month after his death speaks to the gaining momentum of negative commentary on his life. As Thornton noted, Riddell's sketch perpetuates key elements of Burns's character as an aberrant poet of *genius*. She announces her purpose to clarify and defend the poet early in her sketch, acknowledging the inevitable hue and cry that follows the death of 'every rare & celebrated personage':

> The attention of the public is much occupied at present with the irreparable loss it has recently sustained in the death of the Caledonian poet, Robert Burns. It is not probable that this mournful event, which is likely to be felt severely in the literary world, as well as in the circle of private friendship which surrounded him, shall fail to be attended with the usual profusion of posthumous anecdotes and memoirs that commonly spring up at the death of every rare & celebrated personage.[19]

She seeks to differentiate her account from the 'usual profusion of posthumous anecdotes and memoirs' by establishing her own credentials as an author. There is a certain irony to this claim to authority, one which she reveals as based entirely on the privilege of friendship with the 'rare & celebrated personage' – it is expressed by an 'anonymous' author.

Her character as an anonymous author is delineated early in the sketch, before she can turn her attention to Burns. Although she claims that 'I shall not attempt to enlist with the numerous corps of biographers who may, without possessing a kindred genius, arrogate to themselves the privilege of criticising the character and writings of Burns' (7), she does insist that she is capable of 'judging' him. She asserts her capacity for judgment by means of rhetorical negation, displaying a craftiness of style exhibited throughout her sketch:

If it be true that men of genius have a claim, in their literary capacities, to the legal right of a British citizen in a court of justice – that of 'being tried only by his peers' (I borrow here an expression I have frequently heard Burns himself make use of), God forbid I should assume the flattering and peculiar privilege of sitting upon his jury! (7)

Her assertion that she cannot claim the 'flattering and peculiar privilege' of sitting on Burns's 'jury' rings false, especially when expressed in close proximity to a clear attestation of personal authority in the matter. Her offhanded remark that she heard Burns 'frequently' say he wanted to be tried 'only by his peers' reveals Riddell's shrewd self-presentation throughout the sketch, which should make all of her appeals to authority particularly worth scrutiny.

For instance, once she turns her attention directly to Burns, Riddell issues a counter-intuitive claim about the famed poet by declaring that he should not be remembered because of his verse alone. She writes:

It will be an injustice done to Burns's reputation in the records of literature, not only as respects future generations & foreign countries, but even with his native Scotland & some of his contemporaries, that he is generally talked of & considered with reference to his poetical talents only. (8)

Thus begins Riddell's objective to evaluate Burns's significance not only for Scottish but world literature. She repeatedly strives to clarify and establish the standards by which he should be assessed; interestingly, they are not so much 'literary' as performative criteria, able to have been judged and appreciated fully only by those who (like the anonymous author) knew the poet personally. This judgment yields diminishing returns, as will be further discussed.

As a purported friend of the deceased poet, Riddell delivers a severe judgment of Burns's literary talents and further reinforces the 'heaven-taught ploughman' persona as an explanatory tool. She claims that

Much certainly is due to the merit of a self-taught bard, deprived of the advantages of classical tuition and the intercourse of congenial minds till that period of life when his native fire had already blazed forth in all its wild graces of genuine simplicity and energetic eloquence of sentiment. (8)

Representing Burns as 'self-taught' and 'deprived' of education may seem at first glance to be merely an example of rhetorical oversimplification that Riddell employs for effect, in order to distinguish his exceptionality.[20] However, we learn that Burns was not actually an exceptional poet: 'The fact is, that even when all his honours are yielded to him, Burns will perhaps be found to move in a poetical sphere less splendid, less dignified, and less attractive [...] than some other writers have done' (8).

This leads Riddell to her first major judgment: 'I hesitate not to affirm – and in vindication of my opinion I appeal to all who had the advantage of personal acquaintance with him – that Poetry was actually not his forte' (8). This estimation of Burns's talents, so contrary to other contemporary accounts of his reputation, reveals Riddell's motivation to use personal acquaintance as the ultimate source of her critical authority. Her asides to those 'who have had the advantage of being personally acquainted with [Burns]' form the basis of a retort to those who sought to impugn Burns's character and posthumous reputation. However, such an approach diminishes the poet's accomplishments beyond the temporal realm, where personal remembrance of his character is necessarily limited.

The following comment is characteristic of her approach, where her recourse to authority based solely on personal knowledge of her subject is strikingly displayed:

If others have climbed more successfully the heights of Parnassus, none certainly outshone Burns in the charms – the sorcery I would almost call it – of fascinating conversation; the spontaneous eloquence of social argument, or the unstudied poignancy of brilliant repartee. His personal endowments were perfectly correspondent with the qualifications of his mind. (8)

This representation suggests that Burns's 'greatness' was evident only to those who had the opportunity to experience it in person; however, not all who conversed with the poet (as has been noted with Dugald Stewart) found him as impressive and congenial as Riddell. Regardless, she primarily concentrates on representing Burns as an aberrant figure, emerging from the labouring class due solely to the force of his exceptional personality. In fact, the further one reads Riddell's sketch, the more it diminishes Burns's literary productions as the basis for his posthumous reputation. Instead, Riddell implies that the poet must be ultimately judged only by those who had extensive personal knowledge of his character, not only of his exceptionality but also his failings. These 'failings' come increasingly to bear on Riddell's ultimate judgment of her subject's character.

Personal knowledge allows Riddell to focus on how Burns's character was revealed by and through his person, particularly how the singularity (or strangeness) of his appearance made his differentiating traits apparent to his acquaintances. She states that

His features were stamped with the hard character of independence, and the firmness of conscious, though not arrogant, pre-eminence. I believe no man was ever gifted with a larger portion of vivid avis animi [sic]: the animated expressions of his countenance were almost peculiar to himself. (8-9)[21]

Riddell is very insistent upon highlighting Burns's 'peculiarity'; she writes that 'though his appearance and manners were always *peculiar*, he never failed to delight, and to excel' (8). Notwithstanding such abilities, Burns 'seemed rather moulded by nature for the rough exercises of agriculture, than the gentler cultivation of the Belles Lettres' due to the 'authentic impress of his birth and original station in life' (8).

Similar to Thomson's observations about Burns's eventual profession as an excise collector, Riddell finds that Burns's class status (one she defines as 'moulded by nature') ultimately defined his core identity. Despite his assiduous yet 'peculiar' excellence in 'appearance and manners', Burns fundamentally remained a labourer best suited for the 'rough exercises of agriculture'. However, to Riddell, his exceptionality only emerged when he was engaged in animated conversation. She writes that 'the rapid lightnings of his eye were always the harbingers of some flash of genius, whether they darted the fiery glances of insulted & indignant superiority, or beamed with the impassioned sentiments of fervent and impetuous affections' (9). In such detailed descriptions, Burns's personality appears to be embedded in the very fabric of his body itself, making him easily read and interpreted by those privileged enough to witness his performances. However, despite her use of personal knowledge as the source of her authority, Riddell chooses generic qualities to depict Burns's 'unique' nature. For instance, the notion of his 'conscious, though not arrogant, pre-eminence' speaks to his persona as 'heaven-taught ploughman' and its simplistic character traits. Her reference to Burns's 'insulted & indignant superiority', however, leads her to the next major judgment of her sketch, which details the friction he initiated during social intercourse with his 'betters'.

In Riddell's account, Burns's social awkwardness (and occasionally brazen misconduct) resulted from his status as a 'poetic genius' with purportedly unpredictable behaviour.[22] Burns may not have intended for his actions and conversations to be so regarded, but for Riddell, his company was eagerly sought by those in higher social stations expressly for his *genius*, warts and all. The most signal instance of this behaviour involved the poet's taste for satire, a propensity which (according to Riddell) did not serve him well. She states that

I am almost at a loss to say whether the keenness of satire was the forte or foible of Burns; for though Nature had endowed him with a portion of the most pointed excellence in that 'perilous gift', he suffered it too often to be the vehicle of personal, and sometimes unfounded animosities. (9)

According to Riddell, his 'keenness of satire' led Burns to commit many social indiscretions, where he directly offended those with whom he disagreed. She writes, 'The darts of ridicule were frequently directed as the caprice of the instant suggested, or the altercations of parties or of persons happened to kindle the restlessness of his spirit into interest or aversion' (9).[23] After having satisfied the 'interest or aversion' of the moment, in Riddell's account Burns would experience stinging regret and abject self-hatred, to which the poet's well-known letter 'from the regions of Hell' attests.[24]

Because his 'enthusiasm' directed his conversation, Burns's volatility ensured the discomfort of his listeners, who were liable to serve as the target of his satire at any moment.[25] For Riddell, such actions confirmed Burns's outsider status, based as much upon his self-aware class difference as that of his interlocutors. Riddell judges this aspect of Burns's character with some compassion, forced though it seems: 'He paid the forfeit of his talents as dearly as any one could do' (9). Such aberrant behavior testified to the 'failings' of his *genius*, allowing audiences like the Riddells to reconcile his exceptionality with actions associated with his low social status. This stereotyping becomes more evident as the sketch continues, as she increasingly relies more upon Burns's identity as a labouring-class 'poetic genius' than her personal knowledge to represent the poet to her readers. In particular, her understanding of his career is gravely distorted by her recourse to his initial celebrity as a means of explanation; for instance, her depiction of the state of his finances throughout his life is inaccurate, as is her description of his relationships with others in his own class.

Such distortion is prominent in her discussion of Burns's 'penury', which she imagines in a highly sentimentalised fashion:

His soul was never languid or inactive, and his genius extinguished only with the last sparks of retreating life; but the vivacity of his wishes and temper was checked by constant disappointments which sat heavy on a heart that acknowledged the ruling passion of independence, without having ever been placed beyond the grasp of penury. (10)

As has been noted in chapter three, Burns led a rather more complicated life than this passage suggests, and his experience of 'penury' was not as dire as Riddell would have us believe. In addition, she describes his mental capacity as if he were motivated by 'two classes of objects' alone. She writes that 'he acknowledged in the universe but two classes of objects – those of adoration most fervent, or of aversion the most uncontrollable' (10). This 'bipolar' view of Burns leads her to speculate that 'much indeed has been said of his inconsistency and caprice; but I am inclined to believe they originated less in a levity of sentiment, than from an extreme impetuosity of feeling which rendered him prompt to take umbrage' (10). She insists, however, that 'he was candid and manly in the avowal of his errors, and his avowal was a reparation' (11).

She continues to use key elements of the 'heaven-taught ploughman' persona in her character sketch, even self-consciously avowing its accuracy as an explanatory tool. Her discussion of the persona seeks to account for its allure and applicability to Burns, and she contends that the 'Ayrshire ploughboy' was not 'an ingenious fiction':

> It has sometimes been represented, by those who, it would seem had a view to depreciate, though they could not hope wholly to obscure, that native brilliancy which this extraordinary man had invariably bestowed on every thing that came from his lips or pen, that the history of the Ayrshire ploughboy was an ingenious fiction, fabricated for the purposes of obtaining the interests of the great, and enhancing the merits of what in reality required no foil. (11)

Although she claims that this 'extraordinary man' needed 'no foil', Riddell does not discount the utility and verity of the 'heaven-taught ploughman' persona, finding it to be a convenient explanatory tool that certainly helped to promote his writing. She is more equivocal about the estimation of Burns's works if he had been 'more dignified in the ranks of society': she writes, 'Had his compositions fallen from a hand more dignified in the ranks of society than a peasant, they had perhaps bestowed as unusual a grace there, as even in the humbler shade of rustic inspiration from when they really sprung' (11). Of paramount importance throughout her sketch, however, is the fact that Burns was a 'peasant' writing in 'the humbler shade of rustic inspiration'.

Thus, although Riddell grants Burns a degree of sophistication in positioning himself in the literary field, she does not grant him cultural legitimacy as an 'authentic' producer. As she had regarded him previously as 'moulded by nature' for farming rather than 'Belles Lettres', Riddell also finds Burns wanting the necessary cultural capital to achieve lasting recognition in the field. Referring to the 'obscure scene of Burns' education', Riddell exposes the poet's inability to compete in the literary field on its own terms:

> That Burns had received no classical education, and was acquainted with the Greek and Roman authors only through the medium of translations, is a fact that can be indisputably proven. I have seldom seen him at a loss for conversation, unless where the dead languages and their writers were the subjects of discussion. (11-12)

Such a statement affirms Riddell's view of Burns's disqualifying weaknesses as a legitimate producer of 'literature' and the oddity (and perhaps even marginality) of his ultimate appeal. Bourdieu notes how the acquisition of cultural capital (here symbolised by 'classical education') distinguishes producers and consumers of literary texts: 'The whole history of the field is immanent in each of its states and to be equal to its objective requirements, as a producer but also as a consumer, one must possess a practical or theoretical mastery of this history'.[26] Riddell's pointed remark that Burns was 'at a loss in conversation' when 'dead languages and their writers' were discussed serves to reinforce the class boundaries that she erects throughout her character sketch.

She concludes by examining the concept of genius in detail, expounding upon the 'irregularities' that must be accorded, acknowledged, and allowed to men of *genius* like Burns. She offers a disclaimer in which she claims that she will not be an 'apologist' of genius, which she promptly ignores in her valorisation of men of *genius* over those of 'plain sense':

I will not [...] undertake to be the apologist of the irregularities even of a man of genius, though I believe it is as certainly understood that genius was never free of irregularities, as that their absolution may in great measure be justly claimed, since it is evident that the world must have continued very stationary in its intellectual acquirements, had it never given birth to any but men of plain sense. (12)

In this rather circular argument, Riddell endorses the view of creativity and intellectual advancement which holds that progress depends largely upon the accomplishments of extremely gifted thinkers and/or writers. This notion of genius would prove to be influential in Riddell's era, which was captivated by the ideology surrounding 'great' individuals and their impact on history.[27]

Though she allows for the necessary presence of Burns's 'irregularities' due to his overriding *genius*, Riddell intends to expose them nonetheless, linking his character and biography to her interpretive framework. She alludes to the attacks of the poet's 'censors', which she does not disavow:

The penchant uniformly acknowledged by Burns for the festive pleasures of the table, and towards the fairer and softer objects of Nature's creation, has been the rallying point where the attacks of his censors, both religious and moral, have been directed; and to these, it must be confessed, he showed himself no stoic. (12)

As Thomson had hinted of the poet's 'dissipation', so too does Riddell allude to an 'immoral' side to this poet of *genius*, one displayed in his works as well as his life. Concerning his verse, she rather glibly wonders, 'Who would wish to reprove the failings he has consecrated with such lively touches of nature?' (12). Her defense of his aberrant genius anticipates the fervor with which Romantic poets would be drawn to Burns's posthumous character; she writes that 'the eccentric intuitions of genius too often yield the soul to the wild effervescence of desires, always unbounded, and sometimes equally dangerous to the repose of others as fatal to its own' (13).

Claiming somewhat disingenuously that 'a critique, literary or moral, I do not aim at', Riddell describes her guiding intentions at the sketch's conclusion, where she hopes that 'I have been able to delineate any of those strong traits which distinguished him of those talents which raised him from the plough' (13). She embroiders his upbringing with sentimental fringes, depicting his native Ayrshire as the place 'where he passed the bleak morning of his life, weaving his rude wreaths of poesy with the wild field-flowers that sprung around his cottage' (13). Riddell also declares her wish for Burns's continuing national recognition, which she sees as a duty owed to the poet by his nation. She affirms that Scotland will proudly 'remember that beneath her cold sky, a genius was ripened without care or culture, that would have done honour to climes more favourable to the development of those luxuriances of fancy & colouring in which he so eminently excelled' (13-14). Evoking her *nom de plume* of Candidior, Riddell states that 'I still trust [...] that honest fame will be permanently affixed to Burns's character – a fame which the candid and impartial of his own countrymen, and his readers everywhere, will find he has merited' (14).

Such recognition would finally grant Burns the 'enviable eminence of literary fame, where Scotland will long cherish his memory with delight and gratitude' (14). Whether 'literary fame' is 'honest fame' is open to question, but Riddell is confident in her judgment that Burns merits the approbation of 'his own countrymen' (if not 'readers everywhere'). Her appraisal of Burns's character was influential in establishing certain key features of Burns's nineteenth-century reputation.[28] As has been noted, her affirmation of key elements of the 'heaven-taught ploughman' persona served to diminish the extent of his creative activity, as well as to distort aspects of his character and biography. Riddell's focus on personal knowledge as the principal source of her critical authority was also problematic. It did not contribute to a character sketch that accounted for the poet's fecund productivity, nor did it offer an evaluation of Burns that general readers could appreciate. There is a certain insider quality to the character sketch as well, particularly in its allusions to 'irregularities' witnessed by the author but undisclosed to the audience. With this rhetorical strategy, Riddell constructs an interpretive template that other critics and editors would frequently employ to accuse Burns of unspecified 'moral failings' and other 'irregularities'.

The sketch ends by affirming one last time the irregularities of Burns as a poet of *genius*, glossed here as 'imprudences'. Riddell asks 'kindred bosoms' to acknowledge 'the imperfection of all human excellence' before judging her subject too harshly:

Whenever a kindred bosom is found that has been taught to glow with the fires that animated Burns, should a recollection of the imprudences that sullied his brighter qualifications interpose, let such an one remember the imperfection of all human excellence, – let him leave those inconsistencies which alternately exalted his nature into the seraph and sunk it again into the man, to the Tribunal which alone can investigate the labyrinths of the human heart. (14)

To this she appends the last stanza of Thomas Gray's 'Elegy Written in a Country Churchyard', of which two lines – on the poet's 'merits' and 'frailties' – are exceptionally apropos: 'No farther seek his merits to disclose / Or draw his frailties from their dread abode'.[29] However, regardless of Riddell's wishes for her subject's evolving reputation, the commentators who followed her were often quite keen to draw the poet's 'frailties from their dread abode' as their primary objective. The next of these, Robert Heron, produced a widely-read and influential biography of the poet that openly promoted a view of Burns as a 'dissipated' alcoholic whose excessive tastes led to the squandering of his talents and an early grave.

3. 'The Expiring Genius of an Ancient and Once Independent Nation': The Early Biographies of Robert Heron and James Currie

In his *Memoir of Burns* (1797), Robert Heron explores the effects of Burns's genius upon his life, particularly the role it played in leading to his untimely death. Although Heron's memoir has been criticised by almost all subsequent biographers for its many errors and misrepresentations, his analysis of Burns's poetic legacy is actually more nuanced than has been credited.[30] Like Thomson and Riddell, Heron isolates Burns's *genius* as the *modus vivendi* of his life; although it imbues him with exceptional poetic ability, his genius also makes him prey to moral failings. William Duff had argued in *On the Writings of the Most Celebrated Geniuses in Poetry* (1770) that genius could shield its bearer from such an outcome, remarking that 'the man of true Genius possessing talents happily turned to contemplation or composition, will find in the exercise of these an effectual resource against that deplorable satiety and lassitude of mind which are the consequences of a life of sensual indulgence'.[31] Heron saw genius rather differently, describing his endeavour in the *Memoir* as 'an honest though humble tribute to the merits of illustrious genius', which seeks 'to recommend that steady VIRTUE, without which even genius in all its omnipotence is soon reduc'd to paralytic imbecility, or to maniac mischievousness'.[32]

Along with examining the attributes of Burns's *genius*, Heron also repeatedly stresses his growth as a poet, resisting the impulse to represent him as a fully-formed, 'untaught' poet from the very beginning. Looking at the material conditions of Burns's upbringing in rural Scotland, Heron discusses the influence of the local parish schools upon the young poet. Without their aid, Heron suggests that 'the infant energies of this young genius might never have received that first impulse by which alone they were to be excited into action' (4). Heron further claims that learning was a constant feature of the poet's upbringing:

[Burns] returned from labour to learning, and from learning went again to labour; till his mind began to open to the charms of taste and knowledge; till he began to feel a passion for books and for the subjects of books, which was to give a colour to the whole thread of his future life. On nature, he soon began to gaze with new discernment and with new enthusiasm. (5)

These statements are an accurate account of Burns's early exposure and 'passion' for books, evidenced in the letters and biography.[33] The relevance of this element of his upbringing is most obviously evident in the later course of his poetic career, when he began to explore areas of interest initiated by his early education.

Heron also offers a pragmatic assessment of the results of such learning (particularly attained by reading literature) upon any young person, genius or not:

> It is impossible, that there should not be occasionally some souls among them, awakened to the divine emotions of genius, by that rich assemblage which these books present, of almost all that is interesting in incidents, or picturesque in imagery, or affectingly sublime or tender in sentiments and character. (6)

As Bourdieu claims, such reading is a necessary precondition for participation in the literary field that enables one to gain recognition among fellow writers: 'A practical mastery of the specific attainments of the whole history of the genre which are objectified in past works [...] becomes part of the conditions of entry'.[34] Indeed, the importance of reading is repeatedly stressed by Heron; he remarks that Burns's works are 'the true effusions of genius, *inform*ed by reading and observation, and promoted by its own native ardour, as well as by friendly applause' (15, emphasis mine).

Further, Heron isolates the influence of specific authors and texts upon Burns's development as a poet, stating that Thomson's *Seasons*, Blair's *The Grave*, Gray's 'Elegy', *Paradise Lost*, Ossian, and Beattie's *Minstrel* were 'commonly read, even among those with whom Burns would naturally associate' (9). For Heron, Burns's maturation as a writer was a deliberate, time-intensive process of inculcation: 'With such means to give his imagination a poetical bias, and to favour the culture of his taste and genius, Burns *gradually* became a poet' (9, emphasis mine). Even though it may not have always been a 'conscious' process, it was profoundly important for Burns's growth as a writer: 'He slowly and unconsciously acquired a poetical temper of soul, and a poetic cast of thought' (10). Besides the acquisition of necessary cultural capital, Heron isolates *genius* as the poet's key differentiating trait. Alluding to Burns's 'native strength, ARDOUR, and delicacy of FEELINGS, passions, and affections' (47), Heron lists and describes the key attributes of the poet's *genius*. He writes, 'It is originality of genius, it is soundness of perception, it is delicacy of passion, it is general vigour and impetuosity of the whole mind' (50).

Without such a poetic sensibility, Burns would not have been able to gain the sudden, widespread adulation of his readers:

Never could Burns, without this delicacy, this strength, this vivacity of the powers of bodily sensation, and of mental feeling, which I would here claim as the indispensible native endowments of true genius; without these, never could he have poured forth those sentiments, or pourtrayed those images, which have so powerfully impressed every imagination, and penetrated every heart. (49)

Burns's difference as a poet of *genius* resides not only in his extraordinary sensibility but also his skills in execution: Heron states that 'what with Burns awes or fascinates; in the hands of others, only disgusts by its deformity, or excites contempt by its meanness and uninteresting simplicity' (50). In addition, Burns was also furnished with 'extraordinary intelligence, good sense, and penetration', which made him a 'master of powers of language, superior to those of almost any former writer in the Scottish dialect' (10).

This leads him to suggest that 'what appear to me to have been Burns's real merits, as a poet and as a man' were to be found in his 'enlarged, vigorous, keenly discerning, COMPREHENSION OF MIND' (45). This assertion is similar to Riddell's claim about Burns's powers of conversation, although to Heron, the poet's perspicacity extends beyond the realm of public performance and permeates the entirety of his works. Along with such impressive powers and 'the studious bent of his genius' (10), Heron adds yet another demonstrative character trait of his subject: 'a lofty-minded CONSCIOUSNESS of his own TALENTS and MERITS' (52). This 'consciousness' engineers (or underwrites) the powerful impact of Burns's poems upon readers, which allows them to witness and experience the operations of *genius*: 'He exalts, for a time, the genius of his reader to the elevation of his own; and, for the moment, confers upon him all the powers of a poet' (50). Hans Jauss claims that such a necessary interaction between author and reader, writing that a literary work 'predisposes its audience to a very specific kind of reception by announcements, overt and covert signals, familiar characteristics, or implicit allusions'; Jauss describes this interaction as 'a corresponding process of the continuous establishing and altering of horizons'.[35] Burns's texts work on such principles of reception, constructing a 'predisposition' for readers' interpretations and their corresponding 'elevation' to the level of the poet.

Such complexity leads Heron to insist that Burns should not be classified as a novel anomaly but should rather be regarded as a legitimate/legitimised producer in the literary field. In a striking passage, Heron 'consecrates' Burns by granting him recognition as a 'legitimate' poet with 'distinction', gained by active participation in the literary field and despite labouring-class origins that had tended to diminish Burns's reputation for other critics:

Shoemakers, footmen, milk-maids, peers, stay-makers, have all written verses, such as deservedly attracted the notice of the world. But in the poetry of these people, while there was commonly some genuine effusions of the sentiments of agitated nature, some exhibition of such imagery as at once impressed itself upon the heart; there was also ever much to be excused in consideration of their ignorance, their want of taste, their extravagance of fancy, their want or abuse of the advantages of a liberal education. Burns has no pardon to demand for defects of this sort. He might scorn every concession which we are ready to grant to his peculiar circumstances, without being, on this account, reduced to relinquish any part of his claims to the praise of poetical excellence. (46-47)

Thus, Burns is an exceptional poet among exceptional poets: 'He touches his lyre, at all times, with the hand of a master. He demands to be ranked, not with the Woodhouses, the Ducks, the Ramsays, but with the Miltons, the Popes, the Grays' (47).

Heron also desires to rebut the 'heaven-taught ploughman' persona, starting that Burns is 'not a merry-andrew in a motley coat, sporting before you for your diversion: but a hero [...] little caring, at the moment, whether you do, or do not, cordially sympathize with his feelings' (53-54).[36] Up to this point, Heron appears to accord Burns the type of legitimacy in the literary field that he had never been so openly granted during his lifetime. However, when Heron turns to the perils of Burns's acclaim, he offers testimony to the 'failings' of the poet's *genius* for which his biography is largely remembered. At the same time that he accords Burns 'distinction' in the literary field, Heron describes the practical problems facing the poet: 'It seemed to be forgotten, that a ploughman thus exalted into a man of letters, was unfitted for his former toils, without being regularly qualified to enter the career of any new profession' (33). For Heron, the poet's 'consciousness of his own talents and merits' made it impossible for him to live within the confines of his class. His interaction with those

above his social class led him down the path of dissipation, starting
with his Masonic brothers who initiated Burns into the world of
convivial debauchery. They were 'men of convivial dispositions, and
of religious notions rather licentious than narrow; who encouraged his
talents, by occasionally inviting him to be the companion of their
looser hours' (12). His descent to the state of 'paralytic imbecility'
and 'maniac mischievousness' was complete upon his entry into
Edinburgh, where 'for the dissipated, the licentious, the malignant
wits, and the freethinkers, he was so unfortunate as to have satire, and
obscenity, and ridicule of things sacred, sufficient to captivate their
fancies' (20).

These overpowering influences led to the poet's ultimate decline,
which Heron imagines as the inevitable result of such utter depravity
and 'immoral' behaviour: 'Too many of his hours were now spent at
the tables of persons who delighted to urge conviviality to
drunkenness, in the tavern, in the brothel, in the lap of the woman of
pleasure' (27). He concludes that Burns 'suffered himself to be
surrounded by a race of miserable beings who were proud to tell; that
they had been in company with BURNS; and had seen BURNS as
loose and foolish as themselves' (27). Asking 'what more remains
there for me to relate', Heron describes the ending of Burns's life in
Dumfries as the sad finale of wasted *genius*: 'At last, crippled,
emaciated, having the very power of animation wasted by disease,
quite broken-hearted by the sense of his errors, and of the hopeless
miseries in which he saw him and his family depressed [...] he died'
(43). Thus, despite its high praise for Burns's poetry, Heron's
biography (the first on record) is now remembered largely for its
inaccurate representation of the 'dissipation' that led to the poet's
death. As Franklin Snyder notes, Heron 'seems to have taken great
delight in blackening the poet's character, and by so doing furnished
the starting point for the tradition of alcoholism and debauchery'.[37]

Though not as notorious as Heron, Dr. James Currie occupies a
similar position in Burns criticism as a promulgator of negative
stereotypes.[38] However, as in Heron's memoir of the poet, Currie's
'Criticism of the Works of Burns' from his edition of the poet's *Works*
(1800) offers a complex description and analysis of Burns's *genius*.
Although not nearly as admiring as Heron, Currie also accords Burns
legitimacy as a poet who is conscious of the models and methods
intrinsic to his craft. He is willing to accord Burns 'poetic genius', but

he qualifies it by recourse to the poet's class status and its attendant 'coarseness'. He states that Burns had 'a genius which comprehends the human mind', while admitting that 'in approaching him, the first impression is perhaps repulsive: there is an air of coarseness about him, which is difficultly reconciled with our established notions of poetical excellence'.[39] To his credit, Currie admits his reservations about Burns's character from the start, envisioning readers who may have shared his class prejudices. Nevertheless, there is a strong element of thinly-veiled disgust throughout Currie's account of Burns, for the poet seems to represent a type of exceptionality which is greatly disturbing to the doctor's sensibility.[40]

Such ambivalence tempers Currie's representation of Burns's *genius* without forsaking the concept altogether. Like Riddell, he is determined to keep Burns within his class boundaries; the poet may be more than a novelty, but in Currie's view that still does not fully legitimise him as a literary producer. He writes of Burns that 'his poems, as well as his letters, may be considered as the effusions of his sensibility, and the transcript of his own musings on the real incidents of his humble life' (lxxix). He expands upon this point by noting that 'the incidents which form the subjects of his poems, though some of them highly interesting and susceptible of poetical imagery, are incidents in the life of a peasant who takes no pains to disguise the lowliness of his condition' (lxxix). That the milieu of the 'lowly peasant' should be productive of verse seems to astonish Currie, who frankly admits that the 'real incidents of his humble life' do not appear fit subject matter for poetry. After a discussion of 'To a Mouse' and 'To a Mountain Daisy', he states (with no small measure of disbelief) that 'to extract out of incidents so common, and seemingly so trivial as these, so fine a strain of sentiment and imagery, is the surest proof, as well as the most brilliant triumph, of original genius' (lxxxviii).

When Burns occasionally transcends the paltriness of his subject matter, Currie finds that he is 'carried on to exert the higher powers of imagination' (lxxxvi). The wording here is instructive; Burns is passively 'carried on' (as if by accident or without volition) to higher reserves of imagination. 'In such instances', Currie writes, '[Burns] leaves the society of Ramsay and of Fergusson, and associates himself with the masters of English poetry, whose language he frequently assumes' (lxxxvi). Such descriptions of Burns's *genius* are intermittently conditional, seen as 'marks of uncommon genius' that 'impress' upon various rural subjects 'the stamp of his understanding' (lxxii).[41] Elsewhere he is more absolute in his depiction of Burns as a 'man of genius', whose 'temperament of devotion, and the powers of memory co-operated [...] with the sensibility of his heart, and the fervor of his imagination' (lxxxix). Despite such high praise, Currie is resolute in containing Burns's *genius* within the strict boundaries of his class, locale, and language. For instance, he remarks on the difficulty of Burns's Scots usage, claiming that 'the greater part of his earlier poems are written in the dialect of his country, which is obscure, if not unintelligible to Englishmen' (lxxix). This invites criticism of Burns's class status, for Currie remarks that although the Scots dialect 'still adheres more or less to the speech of almost every Scotchman, all the polite and ambitious are now endeavouring to banish [it] from their tongues as well as their writings' (lxxix). It is important to recognise the staying power of the 'Scotticism', which was a linguistic concern dating from the mid-eighteenth century that continued to bedevil 'polite and ambitious' Scots.[42]

If Currie cannot pardon Burns's lack of 'grace', he can acquit the poet for other temperamental excellencies: 'If he is deficient in grace, he is distinguished for ease, as well as energy; and these are indications of a higher order of genius' (xcv). This 'higher order of genius' is on display in such poems as 'The Cotter's Saturday Night', for which Currie's lavish praise set the critical standard for much later nineteenth-century adulation of the poem.[43] Currie claims that this poem is 'an original and truely interesting pastoral. It possesses every thing that is required in this species of composition' (lxxxix). Remarking upon the lack of other works similar to 'The Cotter's Saturday Night' in Burns's oeuvre, Currie claims that 'it is to be regretted that Burns did not employ his genius on other subjects of the same nature, which the manners and customs of the Scottish peasantry would have amply supplied' (lxxxix). Stating that 'out of such materials have been reared the fairest and the most durable of the monuments of genius' (xcv), Currie promotes a severely circumscribed depiction of Burns's *genius* that is expressed only in subjects and styles appropriate to the poet's class and place. This meant reinforcing the poet's representation as a 'heaven-taught ploughman', whereby his exceptionality was clearly delimited with reference to his status as a 'peasant'. As noted earlier, approaching such a 'peasant' occasioned a degree of 'disgust' on the doctor's part due to the poet's 'coarseness'.

Currie was profoundly ambivalent about the effects of Burns's class on his character and his writing; in his edition of the poet's *Works* – the first to be commissioned on behalf of the remaining family – he offered detailed 'prefatory remarks on the character and condition of the Scottish peasantry' which appeared before his 'life' of the poet. These remarks tend to amplify and restate pre-existing representations of Burns as a 'heaven-taught ploughman' by situating the poet squarely in the milieu of the Scottish labouring class. To this end, Currie aims to define and evaluate the 'lowliness' of Burns's condition by examining the character of the Scottish 'peasant'. He affirms that 'Burns was in reality what he was assumed to be, a Scottish peasant' (xvii). In order to 'render the incidents of his humble story generally intelligible', Currie decided to offer 'some observations on the character and situation of the order to which he belonged' – a class that the editor suggests is 'distinguished by many peculiarities' (xvii).

Affirming that the subject is 'in a great measure new' (xvii), Currie begins to anatomise the 'Scottish peasantry' as a distinctly national type of labouring class. His use of Scottish history is interesting, to say the least; he argues that the 'present character' of the Scottish peasantry has only been formed during the period of 'comparative tranquility' that followed the Jacobite uprising in 1745 (xvii). Imagining 'tranquility' in the aftermath of the 'Forty-Five is a dubious proposition for registering the temperament of all Scots, to say the least. Currie continues by arguing that the 'present character' of 'tranquility' distinguishes Scottish peasants from those of other countries, claiming that they 'possess a degree of intelligence generally not found among the same class of men in the other countries of Europe' (xvii). This distinction is evident despite 'their uncouth appearance, and [...] their peculiar manners and dialect' (xvii). In fact, Currie asserts that they owe their 'present character' to the establishment of the parish schools in 1646 by act of Parliament, a law that the editor claims 'may challenge comparison with any act of legislation to be found in the records of history' (xvii).

Such esteem does not continue throughout Currie's examination of the Scottish peasantry, however, as he ultimately finds little (if any) connection with this class of Scots. As with Riddell, Currie's own class status (considerably above that of his subject) tends to influence his perception of the Scottish labouring class in sometimes jaw-dropping fashion. For instance, his tendency to generalise without evidence is apparent when he suggests that the 'peace and security' brought by the Union of 1707 had produced the 'extraordinary change in favour of industry and good morals, which the character of the common people of Scotland has since undergone' (xviii). His rather overblown estimation of the Scottish peasantry also includes an encomium of the 'respectable character of a school-master' in the parish, to whom students owed 'the means of a classical education' (xix). Currie is careful to qualify this, adding that that 'many of the farmers, and some even of the cottagers, submit to much privation, that they may obtain for one of their sons at least, the precarious advantage of a learned education' (xix). Such passages indicate the doctor's uncertainty about the 'precarious' advantages of an educated peasantry.

Throughout his 'remarks on the character and condition of the Scottish peasantry', Currie often displays a willful misunderstanding of both their 'character' and their 'condition'. His remarks should be closely scrutinised, for they plainly reveal the doctor's political and cultural biases. In addition, his view of Scotland derives from a lack of personal knowledge and/or experience, despite the considerable exchange between Currie's native Liverpool and the southwest of Scotland.[44] For instance, he argues against the institution of 'Poor Laws' in Scotland, claiming that it would corrupt Scottish peasants by enticing them not to labour for their own sustenance. In addition, he attempts to account for the Scottish 'passion for dancing' by declaring it a 'contradiction' of the national character of a people 'deeply tinctured with the spirit and doctrines of Calvin' (xxi). Other doubtful ventures in the preface include Currie's attempt to explain the 'amatory character in the rustic muse of Scotland' (xxii), 'the state of the intercourse between the sexes' (xxii), and 'the manners and appearance of the Scottish peasantry' (xxiii), among many others. Currie attempts to link Burns to his labouring-class compeers by establishing standards of conduct to which the poet conformed (or should have conformed). To wit, Currie claims that labouring-class families exhibit a 'striking particular' in the 'strength of their domestic attachments' (xxiv). He asserts that 'our poet partook largely of this amiable characteristic' (xxiv). In addition, he finds that Burns shares 'a partiality for his native country' with fellow labouring-class Scots, which can be judged as either 'a selfish prejudice' or a 'generous affection' (xxiv).

Burns's difference resided in his *genius*, which is depicted as the primary source of the poet's 'faults and failings' (xxv). Currie suggests that 'his virtues and his failings had their origin in the extraordinary sensibility of his mind' (lxxii). In his edition, Currie includes one of Burns's letters (to Mrs. Graham of Fintry) that addresses the poet's 'failings'. Burns describes them in the following light-hearted manner: 'Whatever may be my failings, for failings are a part of human nature, may they ever be those of a generous heart, and an independent mind' (62). To Dr. Currie, though, Burns's 'failings' are of a much more sinister nature. He writes, 'In relating the incidents of his life, candour will prevent us from dwelling invidiously on those faults and failings which justice forbids us to conceal' (xxv). However, he assures the reader that 'we will tread lightly over his yet warm ashes, and respect the laurels that shelter his untimely grave' (xxv). As with Heron, Currie is most concerned to represent the dangers of the poet's 'excesses', particularly drunkenness. As a medical doctor, Currie was especially attuned to the consumption of alcohol and had been a heavy drinker in his youth.[45] In spite of (or perhaps because of) his personal history, Currie did not grant Burns even a degree of empathy regarding this sore topic. His thoughts on Burns's drinking are invested with 'clinical' overtones: it is 'necessary for men of genius to be on their guard against the habitual use of wine, because it is apt to steal on them insensibly' (lxxv). He warns men of *genius* that 'the temptation to excess usually presents itself to them in their social hours, when they are alive only to warm and generous emotions, and when prudence and moderation are contemned as selfishness and timidity' (lxxv).

Currie's final verdict on Burns's 'failings' due to excessive drinking asks readers to judge the poet 'fairly' by accepting that his aberrant behaviour resulted from his exceptional nature. Burns's death should serve as a *memento mori* to all who read his work; Currie writes that

It is, indeed, a duty we owe to the living, not to allow our admiration of great genius, or even our pity for its unhappy destiny, to conceal or disguise its errors. But there are sentiments of respect, and even of tenderness, with which this duty should be performed; there is an awful sanctity which invests the mansions of the dead; and let those who moralise over the graves of their contemporaries, reflect with humility on their own errors, nor forget how soon they may themselves require the candour and the sympathy they are called upon to bestow. (lxxv-vi)

Beyond the usefulness of Burns's manner of death in pointing a moral, Currie admonishes 'men of reflection' not to 'think it a superfluous labour to trace the rise and progress of a character like his' (xxv). Instead, only after accounting for Burns's origins in the Scottish peasantry can 'men of reflection' truly understand his 'distinction and influence' as a poet and a man: 'Born in the condition of a peasant, he rose by the force of his mind into distinction and influence, and in his works has exhibited what are so rarely found, the charms of original genius' (xxv). When he considers Burns's poetry as a whole, Currie claims that 'it displays, and as it were embalms, the peculiar manners of his country' (xxv).

Currie's use of 'embalming' imagery extends into his discussion of the ultimate value of Burns's poetry, where he argues that 'it may be considered as a monument not to his name only, but to the expiring genius of an ancient and once independent nation' (xxv). To Currie – the first editor of the poet's works, consequently a figure whose views commanded much influence throughout the nineteenth century – Burns is the epitome and terminus of the 'genius of Scotland', embodying all the 'expiring' traits that constitute its peculiar, 'independent' character.[46] Seen in this light, Burns is a relic of a bygone age, with little use for the future of his nation; his manners and means of death speak only of a past that must be acknowledged but ignored in the more 'virtuous' present of Scotland. Currie goes so far to encourage readers to remember Burns solely as a 'monument' to his nation's past, an evanishing of distinctive Scottish culture best expressed and embodied by the peasants among whom the poet lived and died. In this conception of Burns, his death on the verge of a new century was not premature but predictive of a better future.

4. 'The Disepensing Power of Genius': The Critical Reviews of Francis Jeffrey, Walter Scott, and Josiah Walker

Other nineteenth-century editors and critics employed similar terminology to calculate Burns's posthumous place in the literary field. Francis Jeffrey's influential review of R. H. Cromek's *Reliques of*

Robert Burns (1808) in the *Edinburgh Review* (January 1809) blends appreciation with acerbic wit to measure the worth of Burns's poetic achievement, with much attention paid to Burns's place among labouring-class as well as mainstream poets.[47] Noting that 'Burns is certainly by far the greatest of our poetical prodigies – from Stephen Duck down to Thomas Dermody', Jeffrey insists that such judgments diminish him as a poet:

So much indeed are we impressed with a sense of his merits; that we cannot help thinking it a derogation from them to consider him a prodigy at all; and are convinced he will never be rightly estimated as a poet, till that vulgar wonder be entirely repressed which was raised on his having been a ploughman.[48]

In fact, Jeffrey finds Burns to have been neither 'uneducated or illiterate' and compares his learning to that of Shakespeare: 'He had as much scholarship, we imagine, as Shakespeare, and far better models to form his ear to harmony, and train his fancy to graceful invention' (179). Despite such high approbation, Jeffrey claims that there are 'peculiarities' in Burns's works, 'which remind us of the lowness of his origin, and faults for which the defects of his education afford an obvious cause, if not a legitimate apology' (181).

This strain of thought leads to Jeffrey's articulation of a key critical conundrum facing many other critics such as Heron and Currie: how to gauge Burns's poetic worth despite the glaring presence of his supposed moral 'failings'. Jeffrey recognises these 'failings' and offers a strident moral judgment that is characteristic of the early years of the nineteenth century:

The leading vice in Burns's character, and the cardinal deformity indeed of all his productions, was his contempt, or affectation of contempt, for prudence, decency, and regularity; and his admiration of thoughtlessness, oddity, and vehement sensibility; -- his belief, in short, in *the dispensing power* of genius and social feeling, in all matters of morality and common sense. (182)

The notion here of the 'dispensing power' of genius offers an intriguing variation on the concept's eighteenth-century connotations; where genius had formerly been seen as the source of both power and weakness, to Jeffrey it also offers license to offend. He writes, 'Men of the highest genius have frequently been hurried by their passions into a violation of prudence and duty' (182). For this reason genius must be simultaneously praised and condemned, forcing critics to fully separate the life from the work. Thus, for Jeffrey there is no contradiction in stating that Burns the poet is 'entitled to the rank of a great and original genius', while the man must be condemned for his 'contempt' of 'prudence, decency, and regularity' (184-85).

Such an overriding critical judgment might lead one to infer that Jeffrey will validate Burns as a leading British poet. Nothing could be further from the truth; in Jeffrey's review, Burns is venerated exclusively as a Scottish poet writing in Scots. Jeffrey writes of the difficulties facing non-Scottish readers of Burns's poetry: 'All his best pieces are written in Scotch; and [...] it is impossible [...] to form any adequate judgment of their merits, without a pretty long residence among those who still use that language' (186). In this paradigm, Burns is an acquired taste, to be fully savored only by native Scots. Jeffrey insists that this is nothing for Scottish readers to be ashamed of, but nevertheless it is an 'infantile' taste:

This Scotch is not to be considered as a provincial dialect, the vehicle only of rustic vulgarity and rude local humour. It is the language of a whole country, – long an independent kingdom, and still separate in its laws, character and manners. It is by no means peculiar to the vulgar; but is the common speech of the whole nation in early life. (186)

Although a 'great and original genius', Burns appeals primarily (or perhaps, only) to those Scots who have not progressed beyond the 'early life' of the nation. He is regarded in the same light as 'all the great poets of every country', whom Jeffrey contends 'have appeared in an early stage of their history, and in a period comparatively rude and unlettered' (181).

Although he may lay claim to an ancient pedigree of national poets, Burns was still fundamentally flawed as a man in Jeffrey's estimation, his 'vices' leading to a corruption of key elements of his verse. In particular, Jeffrey isolates the poet's seeming 'generosity' and 'sentimentality'. He states that while Burns 'expressed admirably the feelings of an enamoured peasant', his 'passion' and 'character of immorality, at once contemptible and hateful' led him to a 'violation of prudence and duty' (182). His tendency to 'represent himself as a hairbrained sentimental soul' was purposeful, the result of a 'deliberate system' that justified the poet's 'immoral' behaviour (183). Jeffrey delivers an absolutely scathing critique of the poet's character during the last years of his life:

It is a vile prostitution of language, to talk of that man's generosity or goodness of heart, who sits raving about friendship and philanthropy in a tavern, while his wife's heart is breaking at her cheerless fireside, and his children pining in solitary poverty. (183)

To this 'pitiful cant of careless feeling and eccentric genius', Jeffrey remarks that it is 'humiliating to think how deeply Burns has fallen into this debasing error' (183). Despite his disreputable character, Burns's achievements as a poet are worth the appreciation of judicious readers. Jeffrey states this quite unmistakably: 'It is impossible to read the productions of Burns, along with his history, without forming a higher idea of the intelligence, taste, and accomplishments of the peasantry, than most of those in the higher ranks are disposed to entertain' (194).[49] Thus, readers may choose to 'submit to be admonished by a self-taught and illiterate poet, who drew from Nature far more directly than they can do' (195).

In his unsigned review of Cromek's *Reliques* in the first number of *Quarterly Review* (February 1809), Walter Scott offers another influential interpretation of Burns and his body of work at this time.[50] Unlike Jeffrey, Scott begins with the worst of Burns and describes the effects of the poet's moral 'failings' upon those in his purview:

The extravagance of genius with which this wonderful man was gifted, being in his later and more evil days directed to no fixed or general purpose, was, in the morbid state of his health and feelings, apt to display itself in hasty sallies of virulent and unmerited severity.[51]

In Scott's view, Burns also suffered from the excessive 'dispensing power' of his genius, which led him to injure those around him. Due to such displays of errant temper, Burns needed 'the pious care with which the late excellent Dr. Currie had performed the task of editing the works of Burns' (196). In Scott's estimation, Currie's editorial emendations and acts of censorship were necessary post-mortem operations required in order to create and preserve a suitable literary reputation for the poet. Scott writes that Currie 'excluded every thing approaching to license, whether in morals or in religion, and thus rendered his collection such, as doubtless Burns himself, in his moments of sober reflection, would have most highly approved' (196).

Owing to the fact that Burns had 'the character of one of the most singular men by whose appearance our age has been distinguished' (198), he was not an ordinary (or even extraordinary) labouring-class 'prodigy', as Jeffrey had noted. Rather, Scott considers Burns to be exceptional in a much different way: 'His character was not simply that of a peasant exalted into notice by uncommon literary attainments, but bore a stamp which must have distinguished him in the highest as in the lowest situation of life' (199). Unlike those theories which sought only to explain the origins of Burns's *genius* in his contemporary class status, Scott postulates a transhistorical theory that seeks to account for the emergence of such a poet of *genius* from the labouring classes from other places and periods of time. He writes that

The dignity, the spirit, the indignation of Burns was that of a plebeian, of a high-souled plebeian indeed, of a citizen of Rome or Athens, but still of a plebeian untinged with the slightest shade of that spirit of chivalry which since the feudal times has pervaded the higher ranks of European society […]. The lowness of his birth, and habits of society, prevented rules of punctilious delicacy from making any part of his education. (201)

Burns's 'plebeian' status thus accounts for his unruly behaviour as well as his thoroughly emotional responses to the world around him. Where Heron had praised Burns's 'delicacy' of feeling, Scott finds only embarrassing plebeian excess.

Of the poet's politics, Scott dismisses them out of hand by observing that 'the political predilections, for they could hardly be termed principles, of Burns, were entirely determined by his feelings' (203). As in Jeffrey's review, Scott prefers Burns's Scots productions, although his view of Burns's verse in English is more nuanced. Where Jeffrey had stated that Burns had taken 'much greater pains with the beauty and purity of his expressions in Scotch than in English' (187), Scott suggests that there may be a paucity in English itself that prevented Burns's *genius* from being expressed in that language:

There are a few attempts at English verse, in which, as usual, Burns falls beneath himself […]. His use of English was *voluntary*, and for a short time; but when assumed as a primary and indispensable rule of composition, the comparative penury of rhimes, and the want of a thousand emphatic words which his habitual acquaintance with the Scottish supplied, rendered his expression confined and embarrassed. (208)

It is partly his lack of facility that causes Burns's English verse to fall below expected standards, but the verse also fails due to the linguistic inflexibility of the English language.[52] Although he himself wrote much poetry in English, Scott valorises Burns's facility in Scots in a subtle nationalist gesture. Scott does not expand upon this point, concluding his review by simply praising 'the character of this wonderful and self-taught genius' (209). Suggesting that Burns is an autodidact allows Scott to firmly situate Burns within Scottish literary history alone, apart from 'foreign' influences that would allow the poet to be appreciated and understood by those beyond Scotland's borders.[53]

In 1811, Josiah Walker published his 'Miscellaneous Remarks on the Writings of Burns', which was printed in his edition of Burns's *Poems*; this 'long and important critique' examined the poet's legacy by assessing the influence of his class background upon his literary production.[54] Walker proposes to evaluate Burns's 'pretensions to genius' in his critique by focusing on the poet's representation of 'character' and 'affections' in his verse. Walker writes, 'From the power of Burns, in delineating character, if we ascend to a higher region of poetry, and try his pretensions to genius by his exhibition of the stronger affections of the mind, we shall still find our scrutiny successful'.[55] The critic's 'success' in this endeavour is verified by evidence of Burns's style – 'In his delineations of softer and brighter scenery, we shall easily discover the pencil of genius' (219) – as well as diction, which he employs 'to express the meaning which [words] had conveyed to himself, and they come by his authority and adoption to be legitimated' (220). Walker claims that Burns's style alone proves his *genius*, writing that 'it has a penetrating and original poignancy, which genius alone can bestow' (224). It is so 'original' that it acts as 'a kind of 'sorcery', seeking to 'disengage us from the power of the senses, and to transport us to imaginary scenes, where the vision for the time has all the power of actual existence' (225).

As with Jeffrey and Scott, Walker is eager to interpret the influence of class upon his subject's writing. He believes that Burns's authenticity as a poet derived from his 'accurate' observation of 'practices and modes' in the 'subdivision' of society in which he lived: 'Another province of the genuine poet is to seize with interesting accuracy, the practices and modes which prevail in certain subdivisions of society' (221). Such observation is the root of Burns's distinction as a poet, for Walker contends that 'the mind of Burns was a magazine of ideas, collected by the activity of his observation, aided by a memory which treasured only what possessed some species of interest' (226). It is important to note at this point that Walker is a clear proponent of the 'heaven-taught ploughman' persona as an explanatory tool, for he believes that the poet's talents are even more exceptional due to his lack of education. Burns's occasional usage of common conceits or ideas derives entirely from his class identity; Walker observes that while Burns's poems 'abound with original thoughts, and with images of his own creation [...] it must be remembered that an author, whose reading was so limited, might frequently produce, by a second invention, what, unknown to him, had been invented before' (224). This unhappy event of unintended imitation does not occur in the poet's Scots productions, which were rather sprung fully-formed from the poet's mind without need of further development: 'From the first fruits of the genius of Burns, we see that it very suddenly shot up to maturity; and that in the use of the Scottish dialect little subsequent improvement was to be expected' (228). Walker accords with many other critics from this period in finding little praiseworthy in Burns's English verse, which he seemed to write 'under constraint'.[56]

As a decidedly 'Scots' poet, then, Burns's role appears to be largely communal in its observational capacity. It is not enough, however, that he merely record the cultural life of his community, but he must also be able to express the powerful feelings within him that are spurred on by his *genius*. For example, Walker claims that 'in his own breast he might always find some passion domineering with a force, and indulged with a freedom, which rendered its operations singularly distinct' (222). Such 'domineering' passions needed an outlet and/or excuse, which Walker readily finds in the poet's life: 'The events of his life, and the manner in which they had affected him, furnished abundant exercise for his power in displaying the passions' (223). Owing to the poet's class background, Walker imagines that his life must have been grim indeed, suggesting that 'the views of human life which Burns habitually indulged, were dark and cheerless' (223). This depressing existence inevitably led to 'immoral' behaviour, which is recorded in the poems as the result of 'domineering' passions. Walker claims that even such examples of Burns's verse of which we 'disapprove' still have the power to 'attract' readers, in spite of their wishes to turn away: 'Even where he deviates into a strain which we disapprove, we may condemn, but cannot quit him; and generally find the attraction of his talent stronger than the repulsion of his immorality' (226).

This leads to Walker's final accounting of Burns's 'literary defects'. As noted in the previous reviews, such apparently 'literary' judgments were often strongly influenced by the critic's perspective of the poet's character and life story. Walker insists that the 'most striking' instances of Burns's 'literary defects' were 'incorrectness of taste, and carelessness in exercising the judgment which he possessed' (234). Already the lines are blurred that distinguish the poetry from its producer, for 'carelessness in judgment' refers more to Burns's character than his creative choices. This leads to Walker's direct confrontation with the 'immorality' that Burns practiced due to his 'careless' judgments. As Scott had praised Currie's censorship of the poet's works, Walker examines the issue of whether all of Burns's writing was intended (or fit) for publication:

Apologists may urge, that his poems were originally written without any prospect of their publication; and that, to the circle of his acquaintance, from the rusticity of the lower class, and the libertinism of the higher, he knew, by their taste in conversation, the indelicacy of his wit would be half its charm. (234)

Vowing not to be one such 'apologist', Walker points to the entirety of Burns's corpus and avers that one cannot deny 'that, after he had reached a distinction, which might have convinced him that whatever he wrote was written for the public, he shows little amendment, some of his latest productions being as offensive as the earliest' (234).

Seen in this light, the deliberate desire to offend in Burns's 'latest productions' is offered as proof of his continually poor judgment. While Walker does not specify the poet's 'immoral behaviour', by this time enough had been written of Burns's purported alcoholism and libertinism that the critic could be assured that his readers would get the idea. Intriguingly, Walker ends his critique by deconstructing some of the key facets of the 'heaven-taught ploughman' persona, which had otherwise been endorsed in his judgment of the poet's talents. Although he had previously stated that Burns's lack of learning may have led to unintended repetition of common literary tropes, Walker now states that 'Burns, like Milton, Butler, and many others, was sometimes led to display his knowledge, at the hazard of

impairing the progressive admiration of his reader' (236). In fact, due
to the extensive allusiveness of his verse, Walker finds that Burns
'wished to gain credit for more erudition than he possessed' (236). He
offers a theory of genius that accounts for Burns's limitations as a
self-taught poet who displayed the little 'knowledge' he possessed in
order to deceive readers.

Walker's conceptualisation of this process is somewhat unique in
criticism of the poet from this period: he writes, 'In works of genius,
as in the works of nature, the limit of power should never appear, the
imagination being thus led to conceive it much greater than its effects
display' (235). By sustaining the appearance of limitless 'power', a
poet can deceive his readers into regarding his productions with awe,
in the same manner they might regard a simple shower of rain in the
distant ocean as the approach of a maelstrom. This trickery is essential
for maintaining the illusion of the poet's 'power', and Walker advises
that a poet should 'abandon every idea, which he has not expressed
both with clearness and energy; because the boundaries of his ability
are thus discovered, and the deception of its indefinite extent re-
moved' (235). If poets are unable to perform this necessary operation
to fool readers' imaginations, they often resort to attacks on rivals who
can produce such effects with greater success. Walker claims that such
'pretenders to genius are frequently detected by their false judgments
of the productions of rival artists, and by envious struggles to lower to
their own level, that merit to which they perceive themselves unable to
rise' (237).

'Pretenders to genius' thus engage in the competitive battle tak-
ing place in the literary field, as they seek to gain recognition through
successful imitation and/or vanquishing of rivals. This is a necessarily
zero-sum game, though; Bourdieu describes the end result of this
process as a search for 'the illusion of the absolute', in which perfect
art forms are conceptualised by creators striving to achieve (or recre-
ate) such forms' 'absolute essence'. He writes,

What they have in common is to take as object – whether tacitly or explicitly [...] –
the subjective experience of the work of art which is that of the analyst, meaning of a
cultivated person of a certain society [...] without paying attention to the historicity of
this experience or of the object to which it is applied.[57]

Those who have 'true genius' do not need to participate in this un-
seemly and impossible struggle for dominance, for their poetic imita-

tions express sincerest flattery; Walker writes, 'It is commonly in imitation that genius, if preceded by any near approaches to its own conception of excellence, begins its exertions' (237). Indeed, he claims that 'the characteristic of true genius, is to feel with vehemence, to admire with enthusiasm, and to emulate with vigour and with hope, the excellence of those who have preceded them' (237).

For Walker, Burns fits into this pattern of imitation and emulation, this searching for the 'illusion of the absolute' art form. However, Burns's development was necessarily much slower than that of others who belonged to classes with greater access to education (to wit, 'cultivated persons of a certain society'). Because of his status as a rural labourer, Burns 'set out without a guide: his understanding had to discriminate and form rules for itself: and the spark of his genius, with no gentle breath to cherish it into a flame, waited to be kindled by the passing breeze' (238). Because of this limitation, Burns was unable to wholly develop his talents as 'poetic genius', for 'he seems always to have been conscious of a strength of talents beyond what he observed around him, but he was ignorant of its extent, and afraid to listen to the persuasions of his consciousness' (238).

This led him to deprive himself of cultivating his *genius* to the fullest extent possible, leaving him in a class of poets whose claim to 'true genius' was compelling but incomplete. Walker ends his critique with a direct comparison of Burns to William Cowper, his English contemporary. Stating that 'their genius possessed many features in common' (245), Walker argues that 'Burns excels Cowper in genius, less than he is excelled in taste' (248). However, he is careful to qualify Burns's *genius* one last time, asserting that the poet 'betrays, in the effusions of his genius, a stern and haughty discontent with a portion so unworthy of his claims and capacity of enjoyment' (248). This representation of Burns – a figure whose *genius* was inhibited by his class, whose character was that of a proud malcontent – influenced generations of readers in the coming decades and helped shape their understanding of his life and works.[58]

5. Burns's 'Monumental Consecration' as the Genius of Scotland

Following his death, some of Burns's critics openly defended the poet's character as an integral element of his legacy. One of his most vocal supporters was Alexander Peterkin, who sought to challenge the poet's detractors in his *Review of the Life of Robert Burns, and of Various Criticisms on his Character and Writings* (1815). In particular, Peterkin singles out Currie, Jeffrey, Scott and Walker for their assaults on the poet's character:

Various individuals, who talk and write with authority, have affected to represent the joint tendency of Burns's personal character and writings as morally pernicious. Much unwarrantable assumption, calumny, and drivelling fanaticism have been wasted, to stain unworthily the memory of Burns; while the sweetest flowers in his writings have yielded to the enemies of his fame, the venom which issues from their stings.[59]

In Peterkin's account, these critics have willfully misread Burns; what should be the fragrance of the poet's 'sweetest flowers' is used instead to 'poison' his 'personal character and writings'. Peterkin will have no truck with those who seek to despoil the poet's reputation with their 'stings'. He writes, 'By their public and voluntary assertions and reflections of an injurious tendency, they have, successively, thrown down the gauntlet to every Scotchman who takes an interest in the honour of his country, of its literature, and of human nature' (268).

Defending Burns in this manner – as a fellow 'Scotchman' who 'honours' country, literature, and 'human nature' – allows Peterkin to calumniate the poet's critics with a very broad brush indeed. Peterkin's use of hyperbolic accusation appears throughout his review, as he claims that any opponent of Burns must necessarily be an opponent of Scotland. Scots themselves are the worst offenders, for theirs is a national betrayal. Peterkin argues that 'no man shall be permitted to assert, without evidence in support of his allegation, that Burns was a worthless wretch, if there be one untrammelled press in Scotland' (270). As it is the duty of Scots to defend their national poet, so too is it the business of 'untrammelled' Scottish presses to print only the truth about Burns: namely, that he was not a 'worthless wretch'. Peterkin ends his *cri de guerre* with a call for all Scots to support the movement to erect a monument in the poet's honour:

Some of the rigidly righteous tremble at the mere sound of praise to his genius, and seem to think that because he had the failings of humanity, there should be no monument to his memory. It is not to his failings that a monument can be consecrated by any rational being; but to his transcendent genius as Poet of Nature. (270)

It is hard to say whether this bit of propaganda worked in Burns's favour. As will be shown, a monument for the poet was built in Dumfries in 1816 and was the first of many to be erected throughout the century. However, Peterkin's allusion to Burns's 'failings' is not a refutation of the charge, but rather an admission that must be counterbalanced by the 'transcendent genius' of the poet. Peterkin acts as Burns's defense attorney to the very end, where his final flourish is delivered in the hopes that the jury – fellow Scots all – will move to 'acquit' the defendant due to insufficient evidence: 'We retire from public notice, with a perfect conviction, that as Burns has been tried he will be acquitted by his country' (270).

Once he was duly acquitted, Burns was free to be monumentally consecrated by his fellow Scots. Poet Thomas Campbell offered an effusive tribute, written for a Burns dinner held in London on 25 May 1816; the aim of the dinner was to persuade patrons to contribute to the building of a monument for the poet in Dumfries.[60] In Campbell's ode, Burns enjoys happiness in death that was denied to him in life:

Soul of the Poet! wheresoe'er
Reclaim'd from earth, thy genius plume
Her wings of immortality!
Suspend thy harp in happier sphere,
And with thy influence illume
The gladness of our jubilee.[61]

In this tribute, Campbell invokes Burns as a spiritual presence, able to consecrate jubilees held in his honour; the dead poet is depicted as wholly benign, whose *genius* is proof of his 'immortality'. We learn that 'discord and strife' (8) at the mention of Burns's name 'fly like fiends from secret spell' (7), for they are 'excorcis'd by his memory' (9). This unusual notion – Burns as holy relic, capable of casting out 'demons' – is further delineated, as the poet's life is cleansed of wrongdoing altogether: 'He was chief of bards that swell / The heart with songs of social flame' (10-11). To this Campbell adds, 'And high delicious revelry' (12). Within this vision of Burns's posthumous reputation, social pleasure and conviviality are not condemned but seen as a key method for unifying all Scots.[62]

For Campbell, Burns's influence allows Scots to recognise and celebrate their own national character: 'What patriot pride he taught! –

how much / To weigh the inborn worth of man!' (27-28). Burns is also
capable of transforming the misery of 'rustic life' into a thing of
beauty: 'rustic life and poverty / Grow beautiful beneath his touch'
(29-30). Campbell represents the poet as a kind of martial hero who
defies all opposing forces, even death itself:

It is the Muse that consecrates
The native banner of the brave,
Unfurling, at the trumpet's breath,
Rose, thistle, harp; 'tis she elates
To sweep the field or ride the wave, –
A sunburst in the storm of death. (61-66)

Campbell's evocative imagery illustrates the influence of Romantic
theories of poetic identities as well as a veiled nationalist agenda that
proffers Burns as protector of 'the native banner of the brave'.[63] He
concludes his tribute by disavowing the attempts of 'Envy' to despoil
the poet's grave – 'Farewell! and ne'er may Envy dare / To wring one
baleful poison drop!' (85-86) – before welcoming future 'pilgrims' to
the site of Burns's monument in Dumfries: 'Still may the grateful pil-
grim stop / To bless the spot that holds thy dust' (89-90).[64]

    Less than two months later, the ceremony of the opening of the
Dumfries monument was recorded in detail by *The European Maga-
zine and London Review* in July 1816. Like Campbell's ode, the anon-
ymous author of this article discussed the need for a monument in
Burns's honour. Writing that 'no one has been more deservedly pop-
ular than Robert Burns', the author describes the attributes that make
the poet worthy of public commemoration:

His wildly original, though uncultivated genius, arising superior to all restraints of
adversity, and the shackles of situation, blazed like a meteor on the poetic world, and
was hailed with the same enthusiasm which greets a newly discovered planet of the
astronomer.[65]

Such a prodigious figure demands national attention, yet the author
opines that 'the slave of his passions – neglectful of himself – Burns
was neglected by others' (5). Such 'neglect' has extended into the
present, for the author observes that 'though TWENTY YEARS have
this day elapsed since his decease until now, no public monument has
marked his resting place, no national cenotaph has pointed out the
sepulchre of native genius' (5). The author's emphatic 'twenty years'

of neglect underscores the perceived need for Scots to construct a physical monument in honour of the poet. He writes, 'Large […] was the debt of gratitude due to his undying fame, and nobly now has Scotland redeemed the pledge' (5).

The author describes the peculiarly national character of Burns – 'Scotsmen, indeed, may well be vain of his talents and his name, for his genius was truly national' (5) – before laying the blame for the poet's neglect. As with Peterkin, it falls heaviest on the Scots, for the author claims that 'the hard fate of BURNS, while living, and the comparative obscurity in which he closed his days' are proof of his nation's irresponsible treatment of its national poet: 'While among them he was not sufficiently valued, and [this] in some degree turns their very pride into a reproach' (5). Therefore, the author calls for all of Britain to venerate this Scottish poet, claiming that 'Britain owes to his memory a long arrear of admiration' (5). In order to clear this debt, all Britons should join in the commemoration of Burns: 'The only way we can discharge this debt is by uniting to do honour to his tomb' (5).

The linking of 'monument' and 'tomb' in this passage suggests that the process of consecrating the poet involved interring his literary remains within public structures that would attest to his continuing fame. This process – best termed as 'monumental consecration' – works to affirm the continuing value of Burns as public figure as well as national icon, who is apotheosised as monument *and* tomb. Bourdieu observes that the power of consecration exists 'outside the network of relations of exchange through which it is produced and circulates', further stating that there is an 'endless struggle for a power of consecration'.[66] In Burns's case, the 'endless struggle' for consecration can be overcome by his monumental consecration, embodied in public structures that clearly exist 'outside the network of relations' in the literary field. The author of the *European Magazine* article affirms the ongoing need for the poet's monumental consecration, claiming that poets, even more than 'heroes' and 'kings', deserve this form of cultural acclamation. He writes that it is the bard 'who may be said to make kings and heroes what they ultimately become in the eyes of the world, by inciting them to deeds of virtue, and by animating them to pursue the paths of fame and glory' (5).

Finding that poetry 'leads us to the noblest efforts of which the human mind is capable', the author attests to the expressly Scottish interest evoked by Burns's verse. He also addresses the burgeoning

Scottish tourist industry focused on Burns's life and works, describing the sensation of reading the poet's works and then feeling 'a new and superior interest to every spot which his muse has loved to celebrate' (5). He wonders if any 'who has ever visited the rivers, the valleys, the mountains which he sang, and felt not the glow of enthusiasm which animated the poet they admired' (5). He continues by reminding would-be tourists that 'these were the objects which he once delighted to contemplate' (5). Describing the Burns Cottage and various Scottish battlefields as 'sanctified by his verse', the author ends his case for Burns's consecration by discussing the poet's unique contribution to Scotland and Britain together: 'Some mark of public gratitude – some lasting record of admiration [...] must be due to the memory of that great original – untutored – and inimitable because untutored poet, whose name we have attempted to commemorate' (5). The author's stress on Burns as 'untutored' suggests the staying power of the 'heaven-taught ploughman' persona, that abiding perception of the poet's *genius* as necessarily 'natural' and 'untaught'.

The remainder of the article provides an account of the principal Scots involved in the business of funding and erecting the Burns Monument, among whom numbered several notable Scots such as William Grierson, the Marquis of Queensbury, and the Earl of Selkirk. Its architect was Thomas F. Hunt, who was chosen among sixty other entrants for the monument's design; his 'most classic design' is praised by the author, who finds it to be 'truly elegant' (6). The efforts of local masons in constructing the monument are praised, as is the choice of a fitting passage from Burns's work to be inscribed on the exterior: 'The poetic genius of my country found me – as the prophetic bard Elijah did Elisha – at the plough, and threw her inspiring mantle over me!'(6).[67] For the author of the *European Magazine* article, such monumental efforts as that in Dumfries testify to the lasting fame of Burns, whose consecration will be complete once a traveler can 'pay the arrear of monumental fame, / [and] muse and linger o'er the TOMB of BURNS' (7).

The 'monumental consecration' of Burns begun in Dumfries spread throughout Scotland, where similar sentiments led to the erection of statues, greater and lesser monuments, as well as other types of testimonials to the poet's memory. The view of Burns as a 'heaven-taught ploughman' continued to exert much influence on how he was depicted and remembered in these instances, where his status as a 'poetic genius' relied on being 'untaught' and attuned to 'nature'. The judgment of Burns's 'moral failings' by his critics from this period is not evident in the monuments themselves, which assess the poet solely as a 'bard' of great national importance whose memory must be commemorated. His 'failings' are silently elided in lieu of patriotic, self-congratulatory sentiments that consecrate the 'heaven-taught plough-man' as national 'bard'.

This 'monumental' version of Burns and his legacy would be his most conspicuous representation for many Scots from this period, often serving as the *de facto* attraction for tourists seeking to encounter Burns in his 'native' environment. Such a representation relied on a gross oversimplification of the poet's life and works, one that essentially arrested his development after 1786. His *genius* became an object for the veneration of Scots and Britons alike, for the narrative of his life and death was both compelling and instructive for his admirers. His 'failings' could be attributed to the Scottish nation itself, blinded to the needs of its 'bard'. In this scenario, his death alone provoked the nation to atone for its neglect by commemorating the poet (though 'twenty years' late). The 'poetic genius' of Scotland throws a shroud over Burns, rather than a mantle, thus completing the work of consecration. As the 'genius of Scotland', Burns can be redeemed only through public commemoration which finally pays Scotland's 'debt' to his 'talents and his name'.

---

[1] For a discussion of Thomson's relationship to Burns, see Carol McGuirk, 'George Thomson and Robert Burns: With Friends Like These', *Eighteenth-Century Scotland*, 9 (1995), pp. 16-20.

[2] J. Delancey Ferguson, 'The Earliest Obituary of Burns: Its Authorship and Influence', *Modern Philology*, 32.2 (1934), pp. 179-84: 184.

[3] Low (1974: 99). Citations of this obituary refer to this edition and are given after quotations in the text.

[4] James Currie, ed., *The Complete Works of Robert Burns* (Halifax: Milner, 1845), p. li.

[5] Thomson settled some of Burns's debts at this time and later helped to raise money for the erection of the Burns Monument at Calton Hill in Edinburgh. For more on Thomson, see Maurice Lindsay, *The Burns Encyclopedia*, 3rd edn (New York: St. Martins, 1980), pp. 356-62.

[6] Ferguson (1934: 184). Ferguson's article persuasively debunks the 'dissipated' character imputed to Burns in Thomson's obituary. See also Thornton (1979: 195-96) for an account of the immediate, nearly irreparable

damage that Thomson's obituary caused for the poet's supporters in Dumfries.

[7] For more on this emerging paradigm, see chapter two of the present work. See also Burke, in Rodger and Carruthers (2009: 13-24).

[8] Crossley, in Grenfell (2011: 88).

[9] For more on Burns's significance for Romantic poets, see chapter five of the present work.

[10] Johnson (1993: 117).

[11] Ibid., p. 11.

[12] Michael Grenfell, in Grenfell (2011: 161).

[13] For more on Burns's contributions and practice collecting Scottish songs, see chapter three of the present work.

[14] For more on these years, see Thornton (1979: 105-40).

[15] For more on Burns's attempts to be recognised as a 'Scotch Bard', see chapter two of the present work.

[16] Henley and Henderson (1896: 422), Vol II.

[17] Thornton (1979: 196-97).

[18] Ibid., p. 196.

[19] Thomas Rae, ed., *Robert Burns: A Memoir* (Greenock: Signet Press, 1966), p. 7. Hereafter cited in-text by page numbers.

[20] It may also be the strained relationship between Riddell and Burns emerging through her characterisation of the poet here, especially as it relates to education. Riddell was very well-educated and had published an account of her travels at the age of twenty with the help of Burns. She was also an aspiring poet, which may have also complicated her feelings about her subject.

[21] Riddell intends to cite Lucretius – *vivida vis animi* (strong force of mind) – but transliterates her source quote.

[22] There has been much critical discussion of Riddell's part (if any) in the infamous Rape of the Sabine Women episode that occurred at the home of Robert Riddell. Whether she or her sister-in-law Elizabeth was the subject of Burns's bad behavior is debatable, although most commentators suggest it was Elizabeth. Nevertheless, Maria may have carried a grudge with Burns beyond the grave. See Lindsay (1980: 300-03).

[23] Riddell is probably thinking here of the topical satire Burns wrote about her family after the Sabine Women incident. See Thornton (1979: 196).

[24] For more on this letter, as well as the relationship between Riddell and Burns, see J. DeLancey Ferguson, 'Robert Burns and Maria Riddell', *Modern Philology*, 28.2 (1930), 169-84.

[25] Walter Scott in a later review of Burns also refers to the poet's disarming, often offensive satirical wit in mixed company. See Low (1974: 261-62).

[26] Emanuel (1996: 243).

[27] See most prominently Thomas Carlyle's *Of Heroes and Hero-Worship* (1841).

[28] Riddell's sketch was reprinted in a number of important nineteenth-century editions of Burns's works; among others, it was published in full in Robert Chambers's edition from 1852, Currie's edition from 1835 which included Lockhart's *Life*, and William Scott Douglas's edition from 1895. For more on Riddell's sketch, see J. DeLancey Ferguson, 'Maria Riddell's Sketch of Burns'.

[29] See *The Complete Poems of Thomas Gray*, ed. by Starr and Hendrickson, p. 43, ll. 125-26.

[30] Edward Cowan made this point in a keynote lecture entitled 'The Philosopher, The Physician, The Fanatic, The Fraudster, and the First Secretary: The 'Doonhame' Creation of Robert Burns' at the Robert Burns at 250: An International Conference at the University of South Carolina on 2 April 2009.

[31] p. 362.

[32] p. 3. Hereafter cited in-text by page numbers.

[33] For analysis of Burns's reading habits, see John Robotham, 'The Reading of Robert Burns', in Carol McGuirk, ed., *Critical Essays on Robert Burns* (London: Prentice Hall; New York: G.K. Hall, 1998), pp. 281-97.

[34] Bourdieu, in Emanuel (1996: 242).

[35] Hans Jauss, *Toward an Aesthetic of Reception*, trans. by Timothy Bahti (Minneapolis: University of Minnesota Press, 1982), p. 23.

[36] This is the earliest mention I have found of Burns as a 'hero' in contemporary criticism of the poet.

[37] Snyder (1932: 479).

[38] For an extended analysis of Currie's relationship to Burns, see Thornton, *James Currie, the Entire Stranger, and Robert Burns* (Edinburgh: Oliver & Boyd, 1963). See also Jeffrey Skoblow, 'Dr. Currie, C'est Moi', *Studies in Scottish Literature*, 30 (1998), 109-15; Davis, 'James Currie's *Works of Robert Burns*: The Politics of Hypochondriasis', *Studies in Romanticism*, 36.1 (1997), 48-66; and Carol McGuirk, 'James Currie and the Making of the Burns Myth', in Steven R. McKenna, ed., *Selected Essays on Scottish Language and Literature* (Lewiston: E. Mellen Press, 1992), pp. 149-62.

[39] Currie (1835: lxxix). All citations hereafter refer to this edition and will be noted in-text by page numbers.

[40] For a different view of this relationship between editor and subject, see Thornton (1963: 314-23).

[41] The imagery of the 'stamp' or 'impression' of *genius* is frequently found in the early critical responses to Burns.

[42] For more on Scotticisms, see the introduction of the present work.

[43] See Andrew Nash, 'The Cotter's Kailyard', in Robert Crawford, ed., *Robert Burns and Cultural Authority* (Edinburgh: Edinburgh University Press, 1997), pp. 180-97 for a detailed examination of the legacy of 'The Cotter's Saturday Night'. See also his book on the subject, *Kailyard and Scottish Literature*, (Amsterdam: Rodopi, 2007).

[44] For more on Currie's relationship to Scotland, see Thornton (1963: 229-58).

[45] See Thornton (1963: 60).

[46] For more on Currie's influence as an editor, see Thornton (1963: 479-82).

[47] Jeffrey's role in constructing and disseminating 'standards of taste' by means of the *Edinburgh Review* has been well-documented; see for instance Philip Flynn, *Francis Jeffrey* (Newark: University of Delaware Press, 1978) and *Jeffrey's Literary Criticism*, ed. by D. Nichol Smith (London: Oxford University Press, 1910). For a more general account of the influence of the Edinburgh periodicals, see Charles A. Knight, 'The Created World of the Edinburgh Periodicals', *Scottish Literary Journal*, 6.2 (1979), 20-36. For more on Cromek's role in stimulating critical debate of Burns at the time, see Dennis M. Read, *R. H. Cromek, Engraver, Editor, and Entrepreneur* (Farnham: Ashgate, 2011).

[48] Low (1974: 178). All citations of this review refer to this edition and are given after quotations in the text.

[49] As in Currie's preface, Burns is praised here as an exemplar of 'hardy' Scottish peasants who excel all others. This tendency may owe to the desire to 'naturalise' labouring-class populations as sentimentalised and non-threatening.

[50] Along with Jeffrey's, Scott's review influenced many nineteenth-century perceptions and representations of Burns. It did not take long for Scott to be identified as the author of this review. For an account of Scott's importance as a critic of Burns, see Margaret Ball, *Sir Walter Scott as a Critic of Literature* (New York: Columbia University Press, 1907), pp. 81-107 (especially pp. 87-88).

[51] Low (1974: 196). All citations of this review refer to this edition and are given after quotations in the text.

[52] Scott's complaint about the English language is a somewhat unique statement in nineteenth-century criticism of Burns. For more on Scottish views of English during this time, see J. Derrick McLure, *Language, Poetry and Nationhood* (East Linton: Tuckwell, 2000), pp. 14-24.

[53] For more on Burns as a 'self-taught' poet, see Prandi (2008: 152-60).

[54] Moffatt (1941: 128).

[55] Low (1974: 222). All citations refer to this edition and are given after quotations in the text.

[56] Moffatt (1941: 133).

[57] Emanuel (1996: 286).

[58] Walker's assessment of Burns has not received much critical attention, although his edition was reprinted throughout the century and his criticism discussed in depth in John Wilson's *The Genius and Character of Burns* (New York: Wiley and Putnam, 1845). Moffatt describes Walker's critique as 'one of the best estimates of Burns that had at yet appeared' (1941: 135).

[59] Low: 1974: 267. All references will be to this edition and are given after quotations in the text.

[60] See Gibson (1969: 157). Campbell's ode was reprinted frequently in his own collections, as well as within later nineteenth-century editions of Burns's works (most notably, that of Allan Cunningham).

[61] 'Ode to the Memory of Burns', p. 7, ll. 1-6. Further citations will be noted in-text by line numbers.

[62] For the use of conviviality as a nationalist unifying strategy, see Andrews (2004: 115-214).

[63] For more on Burns's influence on practicing Romantic poets, see chapter five of the present work.

[64] The extent to which the ode directly contributed to the fund-raising for the Dumfries monument is uncertain, but Campbell's name recognition certainly must have helped the effort. In *Specimens of the British Poets* (London: Murray, 1819), Campbell defends Burns from the charges of 'libertinism' leveled against him by Francis Jeffrey, further underscoring his view of Burns as an appropriate figure for national veneration.

[65] 'Frontispiece. The Monument of Burns', p. 5. Further references will be cited in-text by page numbers.

[66] Emanuel (1996: 230).

[67] There is some irony in these lines from Burns's preface to the Edinburgh edition, which is dedicated to the members of the Caledonian Hunt. He adopted his 'heaven-taught ploughman' persona in this dedication in order to maximise his appeal to his club of Edinburgh notables for future patronage. He would later repudiate this club for the boorish behavior of its members, as well as for their lack of financial support after his appeal.

Chapter Five

'Great Shadow! Hide Thy Face': Scottish Poetry after Burns, 1797-1819

1. Writing in the 'Great Shadow' of Burns

As a part of his famous 'Walks in the North' with Charles Armitage Brown, John Keats visited several Scottish sites that were associated with Robert Burns. In July 1818, Keats wrote the first of three poems dealing with Burns's legacy for living poets, entitled 'On Visiting the Tomb of Burns'. This sonnet explores Keats's feelings about the departed poet's presence in the churchyard in Dumfries, which he described in a letter to his brother Tom: 'You will see by this sonnet I am in Dumfries [...]. Burns's tomb is in the church-yard corner, not very much to my taste, though on a scale large enough to show they wanted to honour him'.[1] In his efforts to 'honour' Burns as well, Keats considers his own presence in this 'sacred' place, emphasising the 'strangeness' he feels there: the landscape of town, churchyard, trees, and hills seems to him 'though beautiful, cold – strange – as in a dream, / I dreamed long ago now new begun' (285, 3-4). The alterity of this landscape imbues Dumfries with Keatsian ambiguity, leading to the speaker's uncertainty about the reality of the experience itself.

Thinking perhaps of his recently-composed sonnet 'The Human Seasons', Keats depicts the harsh Scottish landscape through recourse to imagery of seasonal weather, writing that 'the short-lived, paly Summer is but won / From Winter's ague, for one hour's gleam' (5-6).[2] In such a place where winter's 'ague' reigns supreme, the poet declares that 'All is cold Beauty; pain is never done' (8). This unforgiving vision of winter's severity mirrors its central role in 'The Human Seasons', where the season provides humans with bleak recognition of their mortality: 'He hath his Winter too of pale Misfeature, / Or else he would forget his mortal nature' (248, 13-14).[3] Although Burns has yet to be mentioned in 'On Visiting the Tomb of Burns', his presence becomes discernible as the sonnet nears its conclusion. Keats ponders the concept of 'cold Beauty' as he stands before the tomb, recollecting the 'pain' he imagines Burns to have felt throughout his life. As a fellow poet, Keats reflects on the mind of his Scottish forebear, wondering if Burns had 'mind to relish, Minoswise, / The Real of Beauty' (285, 9-10). As in other poems in which he addresses abstractions, Keats represents the concept of 'Beauty' here by defining it through negation: he writes that the 'Real of Beauty' must be 'free from that dead hue / Sickly imagination and sick pride' have cast upon it (10-11).

At this point, Burns finally appears in the sonnet, summoned to be duly 'honoured' by the poet: 'Burns! with honour due / I oft have honoured thee' (12-13). Keats was certainly not the first (nor the last) poet to stand before the grave of Burns in order to pay homage to a 'brother poet'.[4] In fact, fifteen years earlier, William Wordsworth had written his tribute 'At the Grave of Burns'. However, for Keats, Burns casts a dark shadow upon his poetic descendants, reminiscent of the pall of a cloudy Scottish winter. Keats's state of mind at the sonnet's close suggests his unease in the presence (or absence) of the great poet in his tomb: he writes, 'Great shadow! hide / Thy face; I sin against thy native skies' (13-14). In his letter to his brother, Keats reflects upon the sonnet he has enclosed, writing that 'this sonnet I have written in a strange mood, half-asleep. I know not how it is' (285).

For Scottish poets in particular, writing in the 'great shadow' of Burns was both exigent and unavoidable in the years immediately after his death. Following the wave of tributes and elegies prompted by Burns's death in 1796, his 'brother' and 'sister' poets confronted his legacy just as Keats had done at the poet's grave. As Burns's body of work began to be disseminated widely in the early nineteenth century, competing versions of the poet's character and *genius* emerged and exerted varying levels of influence. James Currie's edition was highly significant in establishing key elements of the poet's popular conception; in this work, his multiple personæ began to give way to an abiding preconception of Burns as the 'heaven-taught ploughman' (albeit one with numerous moral failings, as befits an 'untaught' genius).[5] The critical reception of Burns in the early nineteenth century, as noted in the previous chapter, complicated the 'heaven-taught ploughman' persona without entirely dismissing the fundamental tenets which assessed the poet's skills as 'natural' and uneducated. For fellow Scottish poets, this perception of Burns made him an inspirational yet forbidding figure. Inasmuch as he was 'mortal', Burns could be approached by admirers who visited his tomb. To imitate his success, however, was another undertaking altogether, one that many poets from this period despaired to achieve.

Writing in Burns's shadow invited inevitable comparisons, particularly when one wrote in Scots and/or came from a labouring-class background. The need to justify one's works was felt personally by such poets, who (like Keats) frequently addressed the matter in poems to or about Burns. Much of this body of verse has been critically dismissed as inferior imitations of Burns's preferred modes (epistle, song, dialogue, et al.), and some critics have gone so far as to claim that Scottish verse virtually disappeared after Burns's death.[6] In this light, Burns might be envisioned as one of Harold Bloom's mighty agons, forcing his successors to continually appraise their relationship to him and inevitably find their own efforts wanting.[7] On the surface, this seems to be the case, especially since Burns obviously could not control or influence the critical and popular perception of his legacy as the most famous Scottish poet of recent times. Like Walter Scott's, Burns's 'shadow' kept many of his fellow Scottish poets in the dark, at least as far as public recognition and literary accolades were concerned.[8]

Despite this reality facing his successors, Scottish poets produced a high volume of verse that explored Burns's influence and legacy in the early nineteenth century. The first wave of elegies was followed by further reflections on the implications of the poet's death for Scottish poets (and Scotland as well), lasting well into the first decade of the nineteenth century.[9] Thereafter, the focus on Burns began to shift from elegiac expressions of loss and mourning to celebratory invocations of his presence in various Scottish locales. As has been noted about the debates surrounding the need for the poet's 'monumental consecration', there was substantial public interest in Burns as a national figure who deserved recognition by fellow Scots.[10] This desire to publicly commemorate Burns was addressed quickly by the proliferation of Burns Clubs less than a decade after his death, with Paisley/Greenock's Club being founded in 1805.[11] The notion of Burns's 'Immortal Memory' – still the byword for his consecration in Burns Clubs and beyond – was born in such surroundings, as was the veneration of certain 'Burnsian' places and things. There was a movement to preserve the 'auld clay biggin' where the poet was born, and the location of various monuments to his fame depended greatly for funding on the poet's presence within (or poetic depiction of) the place.[12]

All over Scotland Burns Clubs provided occasions for poetic tributes to the departed *genius*, at least once a year for the celebrations of his birthday. Most practicing Scottish poets from the period tried their hand at such tributes, as did well-known poets abroad such as James Greenleaf Whittier, Oliver Wendell Holmes, and Henry Wadsworth Longfellow.[13] However, for Scottish poets, the need to confront Burns – either formally through such tributes or informally through occasional verse – often served as a rite of passage and initiation, whereby their verse could be publicly sanctioned by their explicit recognition of Burns's *genius*. This process of literary inculcation continued throughout the century, and it is worth bearing in mind the overall effects of such recognition and consecration on Scottish poets writing during these years. Did Burns's influence negate the work of all who immediately followed him, forcing poets to try to reproduce his distinctive and idiomatic Scots verse in a failed bid for recognition and fame? Few poets from the period emerged as 'legitimate' challengers to Burns. With the exception of James Hogg, no one tried to claim the mantle of Burns in the same manner that Burns had sought to demonstrate his superiority over Fergusson (and less dramatically, Ramsay). Such major Scottish poets as Walter Scott and Thomas Campbell avoided the comparison altogether by writing verse almost exclusively in English, as if Scots poetry was not a métier in which they desired to compete with their great predecessor.

Many critics viewing this evidence have concluded that Burns may have hastened the death of Scots verse by the very means he used to gain fame and recognition: in other words, his work was *too* exceptional, too much the product of his individual *genius* to be capable of instilling confidence in his followers.[14] Beyond the misleading endgame of such conclusions, there has been little critical assessment of the large body of work that Scottish poets produced during this period, particularly the verse that was written by lesser-known figures who took on the challenge of writing after Burns. Many of these poets examined the nature of Burns's influence and legacy upon their own works, finding that the departed *genius* could be used as the occasion for further reflection on the nation and the future of Scottish verse.

It is the aim of this chapter to demonstrate that Burns's influence, while powerful and abiding, did not overwhelm Scottish verse in the years following his death and into the nineteenth century. Indeed, the figure of Burns – variously imagined for often widely opposing reasons – provided Scottish poets with a common ground, upon which they could envision the future of their nation and their verse. Perceptions of Burns's *genius* began to refer once again to his role as the *genius* of Scotland, a doomed figure whose death could nevertheless serve to unite Scots in their common national interests. Along with other phenomena of popular Scottish nationalism of the time (viz., tartans and the regalia), Burns became the image of Scotland for his fellow Scots, cutting across class and gender boundaries to provide an occasion for celebration of a distinctive national character. Along with Burns Clubs, the work of Scottish poets in this process deserves more detailed consideration, for theirs was a genuinely popular poetry that was read and recited throughout the nation.

2. 'Thy Country's Glory and Her Shame': Tributes to Burns by English and Irish Poets

English and Irish poets treated the matter rather differently, and it is their efforts which often attained the most public recognition as Burns elegies. Before turning to the Scots, it is useful to survey the range of elegiac responses to Burns's death that issued from English and Irish pens. Wordsworth expressed his indebtedness to Burns in a number of works, ranging from his lengthy *Letter to a Friend of Burns* (1816) to a number of tributes and elegies.[15] Within this body of work, Wordsworth's 'At the Grave of Burns' (written in 1803) provided a model of funereal meditation for later poets like Keats; it was written a mere seven years after Burns's death during the poet's visit to the 'land of Burns'.[16] In this elegiac tribute, Wordsworth addresses a 'Spirit fierce and bold' who attends the grave 'where Burns is laid'; the speaker seeks to summon Burns's own spirit, yet is frustrated by the ineluctable truth of mortality: 'And have I then thy bones so near, / And thou forbidden to appear'.[17] This leads Wordsworth to the same 'dark thoughts' (14) that Keats later expresses in his graveside sonnet, but such thoughts do not deter him from performing the duty he has bidden for himself:

With chastened feelings would I pay
The tribute due
To him, and aught that hides his clay
From mortal view. (15-18)

The remainder of the poem recounts Burns's distinction as a fellow poet, whose 'genius "glinted" forth' (20) to express the mind beneath 'the thoughtful brow' (25) and the feelings of 'the struggling heart' (26).[18]

Wordsworth's elegy relies on prior models to frame his tribute to the departed poet, most notably Thomas Gray's 'Elegy Written in a Country Churchyard'. As in Gray's poem, the dead poet – described here as 'Aspirant of the Plough' (27) – finds a place amid 'the obscurest, in the low / And silent grave' (29-30). Burns's difference from Gray's 'youth to fortune and fame unknown'[19] is quickly made apparent, though; Wordsworth writes that 'I mourned with thousands' (31). In typical Wordsworthian fashion, the speaker indicates that he is 'more deeply grieved' (32) than these thousands of fellow mourners, for Burns had shown him in his youth 'How Verse may build a princely throne / On humble truth' (35-36). He imagines the future friendship they might have enjoyed had Burns lived, claiming that they might have been 'two friends, though diversely inclined; / But heart with heart, and mind with mind' (43-44).

The elegy concludes with several stanzas recounting the speaker's disappointment, as well as his thoughts on the grave of one of Burns's sons – 'not three weeks past the stripling died' (62) – beside his father's. This additional death occasions the speaker's 'sad delight' (60), as he considers that death is the only place where one can be 'safe' (61). After such morbid reflections, Wordsworth turns one last time to Burns's grave, summoning the poet's spirit for affirmation and hoping for his ascent to heaven:

And oh for Thee, by pitying grace
Checked oft-times in a devious race,
May He who halloweth the place
Where Man is laid
Receive thy Spirit in the embrace
For which it prayed! (67-72)

As in Keats's graveside sonnet, the speaker's concentrated focus on the mourner's state of mind obscures the poetic representation of Burns, for he acts more as a prompt for evoking Wordsworth's 'spontaneous overflow of powerful feelings' rather as than the subject of the elegy.[20] This performative element of Wordsworth's elegy recurs in the final stanza, where the speaker describes a 'ritual hymn' (76) that he 'heard, or seemed to hear' (74) as he walked away from the grave. Hymning in such fashion – respectfully, but profoundly self-involved – became a ritual that many Romantic poets felt that they too must perform when visiting Burns's grave.[21]

In addition to his graveside elegy, Wordsworth also wrote an accompanying poem entitled 'Address to the Sons of Burns, After Visiting the Grave of their Father', dated 14 August 1803.[22] In this work, Wordsworth represents the poet in a much different light, not as a 'brother' poet but as a dangerous example of 'intemperance'. After standing before the 'untimely grave of Burns' (220, 2), Wordsworth offers advice to Burns's sons by admonishing them to avoid their father's cardinal sin:

Hath Nature strung your nerves to bear
Intemperance with less harm, beware!
But if the Poet's wit ye share,
Like him can speed
The social hour – of tenfold care
There will be need. (13-18)

Balancing the father's wit against his 'Intemperance' will demand the fullest efforts of his sons. If they share their father's *genius*, they must exhibit 'tenfold care' that they do not fall prey to 'intemperance'. By employing this concept, Wordsworth alludes more to Burns's purportedly excessive drinking than to his penchant for powerful feelings.[23] Where the latter is clearly significant for Wordsworth's poetics, the former invites only the repetition of their father's 'failings': he writes, 'For honest men delight will take / To spare your failings for his sake' (19-20). He next states the matter as plainly as could be: 'Your Father's name will make / A snare for you' (23-24).

How Wordsworth expected Burns's sons to respond to this rather insulting depiction of their father is open to question, but notwithstanding, he follows his moral logic to the end. He exhorts the sons to 'seek the genius of your Sire' (29) in the cottage or the field rather than 'noisy haunts' (25). He declares that while they should follow their father's 'fancy cheer' (37), they should also 'ne'er to a seductive lay / Let faith be given' (38-39). Referring to Burns's 'The Vision', Wordsworth rebuts his predecessor's assertions, insisting to his sons that they refuse to 'deem that "light which leads astray / Is light from heaven"' (41-42). The elegy ends with yet more exclamatory advice, this time delivered with another intertextual reference (to the last stanza of 'To a Mouse'):

Let no mean hope your souls enslave;
Be independent, generous, brave;
Your Father such example gave,
And such revere;
But be admonish'd by his Grave,
And think, and fear! (43-48)

Despite embodying the kind of ideal poet sketched in the 'Preface' to *Lyrical Ballads* (1800), Burns seems to exist solely for Wordsworth as a flawed inspirational figure, one whose excessive appetites led to a purposefully self-inflicted early demise.[24] Wordsworth's lack of empathy in thus hectoring Burns's sons is worth notice, particularly coming from a poet with self-professed 'powerful feelings' and a 'greater knowledge of human nature' than ordinary people.[25]

Keats's sonnet 'Written in the Cottage where Burns was Born' evinces a similar ambiguity about the imagined relationship linking living poets to their dead predecessors. Written in July 1818, the sonnet records Keats's experiences as one of many Burns tourists visiting the poet's birthplace. Like his previous effort, 'Written in the Cottage' focuses primarily on the thoughts and sensations of the speaker within this 'shrine'. There is barely-repressed awe at literally being in the cottage, coupled with typical Keatsian anxieties about death: 'This mortal body of a thousand days / Now fills, O Burns, a space in thine own room' (297, 1-2). Unlike his prior sonnet, in this poem Keats invokes Burns almost immediately, addressing him directly. He feels that the dead poet must have lived a much happier life than his own, writing that within the cottage 'thou didst dream along on budded bays, / Happy and thoughtless of thy day of doom!' (3-4). As part of this 'happy' thoughtlessness, Keats reenacts what he believes to have been Burns's experiences of pleasure in the cottage:

My pulse is warm with thine own barley-bree,
My head is light with pledging a great soul,
My eyes are wandering, and I cannot see,
Fancy is dead and drunken at its goal. (5-8)

Though not as overt as Wordsworth's imaginings of Burns's 'pleas-
ures', Keats's representation employs convivial imagery throughout,
whereby his mimicry of the dead poet terminates with his own 'dead,
drunken' Fancy spiraling across the floor.

In a letter accompanying the poem written to his brother Tom,
Keats describes his visit to the Burns cottage, writing that 'we drank
some toddy to Burns's memory with an old man who knew him.
There was something good in his description of Burns's melancholy
the last time he saw him' (297). While certainly Keats was likely not
as inebriated as the sonnet suggests, it does highlight the perception of
Burns as dependent on drink for pleasure. As seen in Wordsworth's
poem to the sons of Burns, there is an admonitory aspect to this ele-
ment of Burns's character.[26] As the sonnet nears its end, Keats contin-
ues to emphasise his sensory experiences within the cottage; he de-
scribes his continuing awed response to simply being in a place where
Burns had been. He writes:

Yet can I stamp my foot upon thy floor,
Yet can I ope thy window-sash to find
The meadow thou hast tramped o'er and o'er –
Yet can I think of thee till thought is blind. (297, 9-12)

Whether this experience is 'pleasurable' is questionable, but Keats's
narrow focus on his sensations tends to adumbrate the sonnet's tribu-
tary function. The couplet presents further evidence of the mixed po-
etic strategies at work: 'Yet can I gulp a bumper to thy name, – / O
smile among the shades, for this is fame!' (13-14). An imagined
friendship like that Wordsworth felt would have indissolubly united
him with Burns – 'heart with heart, and mind with mind' – appears to
be evident in these lines, yet the dead poet can only 'smile among the
shades' who surround him in death. The living poet seems incapaci-
tated – his thoughts 'blind' as he 'gulps' a drink – and his view of
Burns's 'fame' is uncertain at best. Is this fame merely the drunken
reenactment of Burns's own drinking? Are such foolish actions really
a testament to the Scottish poet's fame and legacy? As with many
other of Keats's poems, there may be considerable 'negative

capability' informing both the composition and reception of this ele-
giac tribute.[27]

Two of the best-known Burns elegies by English poets were
authored by less familiar figures. The first, entitled 'To the Memory of
Burns', appeared in Edward Rushton's *Poems* (1806); however, as
James Gibson notes, the poem was printed in Currie's edition of
Burns's *Works* (1800) and thus found a wide readership throughout
the century.[28] Rushton was a fellow Liverpudlian of Currie and had
already written an early elegy for Burns that was published in the New
York paper *The Time-Piece* in 1797. The version that found its way
into Currie's edition had been revised in some depth from the earlier
elegy, running to 102 lines while still retaining the 'standard Habbie'
stanza from the original. As with the above poems, Rushton's elegy
begins with a speaker at the graveside of 'dear nature's child', this
time accompanied with 'youths and maidens mild' who 'sigh' over the
poet's tomb.[29] The speaker avers that 'Scotia's sons shall hear no
more / Thy rapturous flow' (11-12), while remarking upon the poet's
labouring-class origins that 'From the rough plough thou didst aspire,
/ To make a sordid world admire' (14-15).

He expresses wonder over such an anomaly among the 'rude',
uncultivated Scottish folk among whom Burns lived and died:

So, when to life's chill glens confin'd,
Thy rich, tho' rough, uncultur'd mind,
Pour'd on the sense of each rude hind,
Such dulcet lays,
That to thy brow was soon assign'd
The wreath of praise. (25-30)

Rushton describes Burns's aspirations for recognition as the workings
of a 'fervid mind / Toward fame's proud turrets boldly press'd' (34-
35). The inevitable outcome for such an aberrant class anomaly ap-
pears in the form of penury, leading to a familiar pattern of recrimina-
tion against Scottish gentry that attended Burns's reputation from the
very beginning.

The only new variation is the inability for the poet's suffering to
be redressed (except through patronage of his extant family). With
bitter sarcasm Rushton expresses his contempt for the narrow-minded
Scots who 'applauded' Burns but refused to support him: 'Applause,
poor child of minstrelsy, / Was all the world e'er gave thee' (43-44).

There is evidence here of national prejudice on the Englishman Rushton's part, particularly his invocation of 'penny-pinching' Scot stereotype – 'Unmoved, by pinching penury / They saw thee torn' (45-46). Burns's formerly disinterested Scottish audience now acts the part of the sanctimonious mourner: 'Now, (kind souls) with sympathy / Thy loss they mourn' (47-48). Rushton makes his contempt for such hypocrites quite explicit – 'Oh how I loathe the bloated train' (49) – and adds that 'true genius scorns to flatter knaves, / Or crouch amid a race of slaves' (61-62). Nevertheless, Rushton claims that Scots will cherish the legacy of Burns wherever they are in the world, which is far flung indeed:

Where Ganges rolls his yellow tide,
Where blest Columbia's waters glide
Old Scotia's sons, spread far and wide,
Shall oft rehearse,
With sorrow some, but all with pride,
Thy witching verse. (85-90)

Thus, despite their complicity in his early death, Scots will regard him as an iconic figure whose 'witching verse' unites them in an expression of national 'pride'. This conclusion encapsulates Rushton's rather toothless critique of the Scottish gentry, which is particularly odd when considering his ties to radical politics and abolitionism throughout his career.[30]

Rushton's rather maudlin tribute is matched by William Roscoe's contributions to the growing Burns elegy tradition, the first of which appeared as 'Lines to the Memory of R. Burns' in *The Scots Magazine* 59 (January 1797). Like Rushton and Currie a fellow Liverpudlian, Roscoe was not known for his verse at this time, having achieved more renown for such historical works as his celebrated *Life of Lorenzo de Medici* (1796).[31] Nonetheless, Roscoe's Burns elegies were widely circulated throughout the nineteenth century and helped to establish dominant features and elements that were copied by other elegists. His first elegy represents Burns as the 'sweetest minstrel' and 'Nature's child', one whose favoured status could not help him escape the clutches of 'the ghastly tyrant' Death: the speaker wonders why 'Could not thy native wood-notes wild / […] The ghastly tyrant have beguil'd'.[32] Adding to the Miltonic allusion, Roscoe employs imagery

borrowed from Gray's 'Elegy' to further distinguish Burns's differ-
ence from the common lot of the dead, oblivion:

But not for thee, O Bard, the lot
In cold oblivion's shade to rot,
Like those unhonour'd and forgot,
Th' unfeeling great
Who knew thy worth, but hastened not
To sooth thy fate. (25-30)

The anger of Rushton's elegy against 'th' unfeeling great' is felt but
muted here, giving place instead to consideration of Burns's *genius*.

Throughout the remainder of the elegy, Roscoe pits the concept
of 'Nature' against that of *genius*, which is aided by 'Pity' (33) to
ensure the continuing fame of the 'immortal Bard': 'Whilst Genius
shall with Nature vie' (32), the speaker claims that 'Thy honour'd
name shall never die, / Immortal Bard' (35-36). 'Nature' in this in-
stance seems commensurate with mortality, epitomised by the decay-
ing body in the grave. This body is still attended by its angered spirit,
one which must be 'soothed' by the work of mourning:

But thou, O! bard, in Silence laid,
Ah! what shall soothe thy pensive shade,
For worth of genius ill repaid,
With bounty scant;
And hours of sorrow unallay'd,
And pain, and want! (85-90)

The only suitable recompense is enduring fame, accorded to the bard
by all Scots (especially those who neglected the nurture of such
'worth of genius'). Roscoe writes, 'Go, builder of a deathless name, /
Thy country's glory and her shame' (133-34). He tasks Burns's spirit
with the charge to 'th' immortal guerdon claim / To genius due!' (135-
36). As in Rushton's elegy, there is a national prejudice animating
these lines, which declare that Scotland must share both 'glory' and
'shame' in the mistreatment of Burns. Only in so doing can the poet
claim 'th' immortal guerdon' owed to his genius and truly be regarded
as a 'deathless name'. Once this 'guerdon' is claimed, Roscoe assures
Burns's spirit that 'rolling centuries thy fame / Shall still renew' (137-
38).[33]

Roscoe's second effort, entitled 'Elegy on the Death of the Scottish Poet Burns' and published in *The Morning Chronicle* (28 July 1800), is the better-known of the two. Frequently anthologised, this elegy employs similar diction and imagery to achieve similar ends; as in the first, there is a clear desire on Roscoe's part to shame Scotland for its poor treatment of Burns.[34] The second elegy is more indirect, opening with description of an expressly-imagined Scottish landscape (for Roscoe rarely left his native Liverpool): 'Rear high thy bleak, majestic Hills, / And shelter'd Vallies proudly spread'.[35] Such generic imagery is quickly clarified by reference to the nation in which it is found: 'SCOTIA, pour thy thousand rills / And wave thy Heaths with Blossoms red!' (3-4). Despite its sublime majesty, the landscape lacks a vital figure, the 'sweetest Bard' who inhabited it:

But, ah, what Poet now shall tread
Thy airy heights, thy woodland reign,
Since he, the sweetest Bard, is dead
That ever breath'd the soothing strain? (5-8)

The speaker observes the evidence of loss which has silenced the landscape: 'his wild Harp lies all unstrung – / And cold the hand that wak'd its sound!' (15-16).

In much the same manner as Wordsworth's speaker exults in the landscape in 'Tintern Abbey', Roscoe envisions the youthful Burns gamboling in the wild Scottish terrain: 'Thy lonely wastes and frowning skies / To him were all with rapture fraught' (33-34). As content as a pastoral shepherd, Burns exhibits all the health and glory of youth until he is approached by Spenserian 'dark conceits', embodied yet abstract:

Now, Spells of mightier pow'r, prepare –
Bid brighter Phantoms round him dance: –
Let FLATT'RY spread her viewless snare,
And FAME attract his vagrant glance. (65-68)

Allegory guides the remainder of the elegy, where Burns increasingly becomes the object of critique as well as pity. In this respect, Roscoe's elegy more closely resembles Currie's narrative of Burns's life rather than Rushton's. Of particular concern for Roscoe is the poet's susceptibility to 'Pleasure': 'Let sprightly PLEASURE too advance, / Unveil'd her eyes, unclasp'd her zone' (69-70). Against the advance of such forthright sexuality, the young Burns does not stand a chance: 'Lost in Love's delirious Trance, / His scorns the joys his Youth has known!' (71-72).

Like Redcross Knight's captivation by Duessa in the *Faerie Queene*, Burns is entranced (and ensnared) by sensual delight, here none too subtly glossed as the symbol of pleasure 'unclasping' her 'zone'.[36] Roscoe codes such pleasures with the register of class, made explicit in the following sarcastic lines, in which sensual enjoyment – which is 'beyond the Peasants humbler joys, / And freed from each laborious strife' (85-86) – ensnares the youthful poet: 'Let him learn the Bliss to prize / That waits the Sons of polish'd Life!' (87-88). Along with sexual pleasure, conviviality wreaks havoc on the young shepherd exposed to the 'bliss' enjoyed by the 'Sons of polish'd Life':

Then, whilst his throbbing veins beat high
With ev'ry impulse of Delight,
Doth from his lips the Cup of Joy –
And shroud the scene in shades of Night! (89-92)

The inevitable result, depicted with the same forthright simplicity of Hogarth's 'progress' series, is the grave: 'Tis done – the pow'rful Charm succeeds; / His high reluctant Spirit bends' (105-06). Once his spirit 'bends', he is corrupted and dies: 'In bitterness of Soul he bleeds, / Nor longer with his Fate contends!' (107-08).

Thus, the poet is ruined by his own appetites, the 'pow'rful Charm' which has rendered him corrupt and mortally injured him. Roscoe represents Burns's descent into death with obscure diction, magnifying the extent of the 'degradation' suffered by his *genius*:

An Ideot-laugh the welkin rends
As Genius thus degraded lies,
'Till pitying Heav'n the veil extends
That shrouds the Poet's ardent eyes! (109-12)

With the doom-laden sky rending its 'welkin' and echoing an 'ideot-laugh', the depiction of the poet's death verges on hysteria.[37] Indeed, Roscoe's elegy has little bearing to the actual world in which Burns lived and died, offering instead only allegory that indicted the poet's character and manner of death. In this respect, his representation of Burns in the elegy may have contributed more greatly to views of the poet's 'dissipation' and 'moral failings' than even the biographies of

Heron and Currie. Roscoe repeats elements of Burns's supposed 'moral' decline without referring to actual events, which allows for readers to imagine the worst. In addition, Roscoe's elegy was more likely to have been read in its entirety than the prose accounts of Heron and Currie, thus reaching a larger reading audience of Burns's works.

Other poets would rush to Burns's defense, imploring readers to revere him despite his manifold 'failings'. One such defender was Irish poet William Hamilton Drummond, who wrote an extensive tribute to Burns entitled 'The Sighs of Genius: An Elegiac Ode, Occasioned by the Death of Robert Burns, The Ayrshire Poet' (1798). Drummond felt deep kinship with Burns, having studied briefly at the University of Glasgow in 1794, before returning to his native Belfast where he worked as a tutor and studied for the Presbyterian ministry. His poetry of the period, particularly *The Man of Age* (1798), reveals an abiding interest in nationalist politics and revolutionary principles, for which Drummond was almost shot by a loyalist officer in 1798.[38] 'The Sighs of Genius' explores the relationship between a country's *genius* – its distinct, national character – and the poets who express that *genius* in their verse.[39] As in Burns's 'The Vision', Drummond's *genius* is embodied and articulate: 'Deep in a laurel-cinctur'd glade, / His votive lay bold Genius sung'.[40] Gendered as female, she asserts a proprietary interest in the fate of her 'sons' like Burns, championing him in death as Coila had in life in Burns's own 'The Vision'. Because the tribute is an elegy, however, such enunciation – even if 'boldly' sung – can only provoke a 'votive lay' in Burns's honour. Beyond this tributary function, Drummond's *genius* can only testify to feelings of irreparable loss occasioned by the poet's death.

After fulfilling the work of mourning, the 'song' of *genius* transforms into a monologue that extends throughout the poem. It eventually devolves into an elaborate series of questions that cannot be answered. The first inquiry of *genius*, however, begs a reply:

Still is my offspring doom'd to bleed?
Still doom'd the voice of song to raise,
Contented with th'extorted meed,
Of fruitless and penurious praise? (9-12)

The notion of 'penurious praise' is intriguingly expressed in these lines, without Rushton's moral outrage at 'penny-pinching' Scots. To

Drummond's *genius*, praise itself seems to be 'penurious', 'extorted' by poets who seek fame. The *genius* declares, 'For who among that tribe of death / Is churlish of uncostly fame?' (17-18). All such praise is rather dismissively described as 'heaping honors to a name' (20). The deliberate oxymoron of 'uncostly fame' finds its clearest expression once the *genius* finally names the subject of the ode, a poet whose entry into the 'tribe of death' epitomises the ultimate cost of literary renown.

At this point, the *genius* sighs as strongly as ever in offering up the name of her son Burns, a figure whose fame invited the envy of 'insect mortals' :

So glow'd, my honor'd BURNS, thy praise,
So shone among my sons thy name,
While envy sicken'd at the blaze,
And insect mortals buzz'd thy fame. (33-36)

The peculiar diction heightens the ode's insistent unreality in a manner akin to Roscoe's second elegy; however, it is Rushton's sentiments that are conveyed most ardently by Drummond's *genius*. She addresses Burns at the grave: 'Could all the wonders of thy art / Avert the poignant shafts of pain?' (57-58). Her questions gain greater urgency once they take on the dimension of class, once more summoning the spectre of Burns's neglectful patrons. She asks if his art could 'warm the cold unfeeling heart / Of pride, and opulent disdain?' (59-60). Such class-based criticisms are fairly generic statements in Burns elegies, but Drummond inflects them with the overlying nationalist rhetoric of Rushton's elegy. He attempts to indict the whole of Scotland for its 'cold, unfeeling' treatment of its 'untutored' bard.

Borrowing imagery from Burns's 'To a Mountain Daisy', Drummond reinforces key elements of the 'heaven-taught ploughman' persona before turning his attention to the poet's nation. Genius declares,

Let wealth, and pow'r, and grandeur blush,
They saw my glory's fainting stem;
They saw – and suffer'd want to crush
Untutor'd nature's loveliest gem. (61-64)

With the death of 'untutor'd nature's loveliest gem', Scotland has suffered an apparently irretrievable loss: 'But ah! no more shall greatness scorn / Thy like, lamented, honor'd name!' (65-66). From Drummond's nationally-minded Irish perspective, the complicity of Scots in contributing to the poet's early death should be a source of national shame, worthy of the censure of permanent loss. The following lines sound almost like a threat to the Scottish nation, who will find its voice silenced after the loss of such an inimitable poet like Burns: 'Nor shall thy equal e'er be born, / For Scotland's glory or her shame' (67-68). Losing its voice in this way leads the *genius* of Scotland to 'sigh' indeed.

Drummond expresses a modicum of hope for Scottish poets, though. He writes, 'Yet may some young advent'rous bard, / Aspire to emulate thy lays' (69-70). Such aspiration may yield unhappy results, for the *genius* counsels the 'young advent'rous' Scottish bard who seeks to emulate Burns that 'like thine, may be his poor reward, / But not like thine shall be his praise' (71-72). A young Scottish bard may have found Drummond's grim prognosis for his own 'poor reward' to be depressingly accurate. As will be shown, the 'Scottish' brand of Burns elegy reveals the many frustrations and obstacles facing those who wrote in the shadow of a great dead poet.

3. 'Parnassus' Bastards': Scottish Poets Writing after Burns

During the first decade following Burns's death in 1796, Scottish poets focused almost exclusively on producing elegies in his memory. In similar manner as birthday odes in honour of Burns became *de rigeur* for Scottish poets, trying one's hand at the elegy often served as a necessary step to publication. Scottish journals and newspapers continued to print such elegies throughout the nineteenth century, but the first decade proved the most abundant.[41] While death provided the occasion, exploring the nature of Burns's continuing renown was as much the object of the elegy as offering public testimony of one's mourning for the loss of a great national poet. Such strategies are, of course, not uncommon in other elegies for similar personages, while the elegy as an ancient poetic mode bespeaks its own familiar terrain.[42] That said, the elegies to Burns from this period offer intriguing variations on common themes and techniques, finding commonality in the recourse to shared national identity as a source for commemorating loss while also affirming continuity. The very act of writing the elegy testifies to the poets' need to affirm their own presence as mourners and their own vitality as fellow writers.

Such recognition is often implicit in the elegies which issued from the press and became anthologised in volumes of verse. They were presented to the public as necessary acts of homage to a departed *genius* whose blessing they sought through the elegy itself. The fact that such blessing cannot be literally granted is diminished by the elegy's publication, an act of recognition by the literary marketplace which grants the elegists cultural legitimation. As Pierre Bourdieu states, however, such legitimation is judged by the 'criterion of temporal success measured by the indices of commercial success [...] or social notoriety'. In this schema, 'pre-eminence' is only granted to those 'who are known and recognised by the "general public"'. Scottish poets may seek to gain this type of recognition, but it comes with a price. Bourdieu argues that commercial success tends to prevent writers from being granted 'consecration' within (or by) the community of artists 'who owe their prestige, at least negatively, to the fact that they make no concessions to the demand of the "general public"'.[43] This circular logic informs this cycle of literary production for Scottish poets during this period, whose very insistence upon commemorating Burns was an attempt to gain their own recognition and validation from fellow producers as well as the general public. Although they were seldom successful in both endeavours, writing a Burns elegy allowed living Scottish poets to affirm their own practice while simultaneously bereaving the loss of their dead mentor.

In 1797, Scottish printer and occasional poet William Reid anonymously published his 'Monody on the Death of Robert Burns' in *The Scots Magazine* 59 (May 1797). He would later reprint the poem in a short collection entitled *Poetry: Selected and Original*, in the series of Brash and Reid chapbooks. While Reid's tribute expresses many sentiments common to the increasing horde of elegies written to commemorate Burns, it also provides insight about his self-aware difference as poet and publisher. Reid asks plainly, 'For sterling genius, blyth and free, / Fam'd Robin's match when shall we see?'[44] Following the typical model of elegiac commentary on Burns's exceptionality, Reid notes that 'the pith and saul o' mirth and glee / Wi' Burns are fled' (11-12). He later returns to the concept of 'pith' (slightly reconfigured from the above) as he attempts to locate the precise difference(s) that made Burns such a 'sterling genius'. He first tackles the important issue of Burns's supposed religious heterodoxy, assessing the poet's satirical targets and techniques:

He lash'd the canting, whining race
Wha wear an artificial face,
Tho' blest wi' kirks, or out of place,
Rab did na care,
Hypocrisy weel could he trace,
And ne'er did spare. (31-36)

Like other supporters of the poet, Reid is careful to distinguish the exact nature of Burns's satire of the religious community. While he affirms the poet's whole-hearted support – 'Na, na, Religion, heav'nly Fair! / Thy dictates Rab did ay revere' (49-50) – he acknowledges that 'tho' he did na practice mair' (51). In fact, in tune with Burns's 'Address to the Unco Guid', Reid declares, 'Whare dwells the man didna err / As well as he?' (53-54).

Alluding to Burns's numerous yet unspecified 'errors', Reid recognises the ready complaints lodged by the poet's critics about his 'immoral' and/or 'irreligious' behavior in life.[45] Later in the elegy, Reid expands upon this facet of Burns's biography, conjuring the apparent simplicity of the rural life of the 'heaven-taught ploughman' that was despoiled by his sudden fame. He exclaims that 'O dool! that e'er he left the plough' (97), for this 'took him to a trade was new, / And bade sweet Temperance adieu!' (98-99). Reid's invocation of 'temperance' works in concert with the unspecified 'errors' of Burns's conduct to summon the burgeoning posthumous representation of the poet as an 'immoral' drunkard. Reid concludes his disquisition on this regrettable aspect of his subject:

Let us not, as chatt'ring fools,
Proclaim his faults, like envy's tools,
Wha seek out darkness just like owls,
Dark, dark indeed;
But a' his failings co'er wi' mools,
Now since he's dead. (103-08)

Despite having just 'proclaimed' the poet's 'faults' and 'failings', Reid advises readers to forget them entirely by burying the poet anew (covering him with 'mools', or lumps of earth). Indeed, the finality of Burns's death is reinforced with one last remembrance of his distinc-

tion as a national *genius*: 'As bright a genius death has torn / As thee
fram'd Scotia did adorn' (109-10).

Reid's 'monody' conforms to many of the standard features of
the Burns elegy, particularly with its references to the poet's 'ques-
tionable' character as well as his clear difference as a superior artist.
What distinguishes the 'monody' is a lengthy examination of the state
of Scottish poetry after Burns, extending for several stanzas and obvi-
ously written from Reid's professional point of view as a printer
(especially of Scottish poetry).[46] Reid sees only a limitless horizon of
pallid imitators, poets whose productions invariably fail in comparison
to the great original. He writes, 'Let poor dull rhymers rack their
brains' (61) to imitate Burns, whose 'native, wild, enchanting strains /
Shall charm all Caledonia's swains' (62-63). Reid has no sympathy
for such 'dull rhymers', further disparaging their attempts at verse by
describing them as 'ambitious fools [who] ha'e mony a time / Striven
to outrival Robin's rhyme' (73-74). In order to clarify exactly what
distinguishes the verse of 'ambitious fools' when set against 'Robin's
rhyme', Reid returns to the concept of 'pith':

Pith was wanting – poor dull chyme
Was a' they gied;
Rab was the boy hit a' things prime,
But ah! he's dead. (75-78)[47]

In this formulation, 'pith' connotes poetic substance as well as mas-
tery of material and form.[48] In its stead, Burns's imitators offer only
'poor dull chyme' which fails to qualify as verse of formal or material
substance.

The crucial difference in this respect is addressed by Reid the
printer, for whom the subject is more a matter of professional than
personal concern:

Parnassus' bastards, mony a gelping,
Ha'e deev'd us wi' their dinsome yelping;
But his sweet sangs ne'er needed helping,
To send to prent. (79-82)

These intriguing lines derive from an editor's point of view, one that
is motivated by professional considerations (i.e., lack of copyediting
required) and annoyances (being besieged by 'Parnassus' bastards'
and their 'dinsome yelping'). To Reid, the state of Scottish poetry

after Burns is obvious; the literary marketplace is being overrun by a surplus of versifiers whose works show no unique or original distinguishing traits. As with any surplus in an operating market, the product becomes invariably devalued, especially when compared with the 'sterling genius' of Burns.

In fact, Burns's works gain in value due to their necessarily finite nature. Just as the value of any artist's output increases posthumously, Burns's extant works become 'inimitable': no matter how strenuously they are imitated by his successors, they retain their intrinsic worth. In a different context, Walter Benjamin described this as the 'aura' of an original artwork, which becomes lost as it is mechanically produced *ad infinitum*.[49] For Reid, this means that Scottish poetry – at least to its contemporary publishers – must evolve or simply end after Burns's death. The last stanza of the 'monody' records Reid's skeptical point of view, with an eye to a poetic past that will remain valuable to his business, perhaps in perpetuity: he writes, 'The winter nights I've cheer'd by turns, / Wi' Ramsay, Fergusson, and Burns' (107-08). Noting that 'the first twa cauld are in their urns' (109), he declares that 'now weeping Caledonia mourns, / Him last and best' (111-12). Given this scenario, Reid was able to capitalise on printing Burns's works in his chapbooks, which he had started publishing in 1796 with 'Alloway Kirk' and continued throughout the early nineteenth century.[50]

Other poets expressed similarly grim sentiments, though in less self-interested fashion than Reid. Often these elegists were poised (sometimes literally) over the grave of Burns. In his 'Dirge, to a Person who lamented that no Monument had been erected on the Grave of Robert Burns', Scottish labouring-class poet John Struthers assessed the state of affairs for those writing verse after Burns, as well as the ongoing perceived need for the poet's monumental consecration. The son of a shoemaker in Lanarkshire, Struthers found an early patron in Joanna Baillie who encouraged his efforts in verse; as an adult, he settled in Glasgow and worked in his father's trade. Through Baillie's agency, Struthers enlisted Walter Scott's help in negotiating with the printer Archibald Constable. His first works, including *The Poor Man's Sabbath* (in which his 'Dirge' was reprinted), sold well and led him to keep writing throughout his life. However, he continued working as a shoemaker until the early 1820s and even anonymously published a treatise entitled 'Essay on the State of the Labouring Poor, with some Hints for its Improvement' in 1816.

Despite his financial difficulties, Struthers enjoyed success as a poet and anthologist in later life. He published the anthology *The Harp of Caledonia* (1819) as well as a two-volume *History of Scotland from the Union* (1827). He held the post of librarian at Stirling's Public Library from 1833 to 1848, during which time he contributed many biographies for Robert Chambers's *Biographical Dictionary of Eminent Scotsmen* (1835).[51] Indeed, had Burns lived, he might have enjoyed receiving the kind of public and artistic recognition afforded to Struthers. However, despite his literary contributions throughout his life, Struthers has been all but forgotten in the history of Scottish poetry.

In his 'Dirge', Struthers confronts the situation facing Scottish poets who have had the misfortune to outlive Burns. He perceives his auditor's question about the lack of a monument over Burns's grave as both impertinent and immaterial:

Why sigh'st thou, my friend! for a monument great,
To point where the poet fills, cold, the clay urn,
Whom Nature profuse, in a peasant's estate,
Gave with all the bold ardour of genius to burn?[52]

As Keats deemed his urn a 'cold pastoral', so Struthers considers it foolish to construct a 'monument great' over a simple 'clay urn' filled with poet's remains. In an incidental pun, the 'bold ardour of genius' is seen to have 'burned' the poet to ashes. As many critics and editors believed, the 'failings' of *genius* had wrought just such a deleterious effect on Burns the man.[53] The refrain at the end of all four stanzas underscores such perceived 'failings', glossed here as 'folly': of the visitor to the grave, Struthers writes, 'Sad, he laments, by folly undone, / In the cold tomb he lies, all untimely laid low!' (7-8). The speaker isolates the key elements of Burns's verse that made it the work of 'burning genius', stating that 'his powers of description each bosom shall own, / Consenting emotions their wonder shall show' (13-14). The emphasis on description and emotion in these lines suggests that it is exclusively the verse itself that is 'wonderful', not the poet who wrote it. Struthers follows this praise with the refrain, adding that 'the sigh shall be heard, for by folly undone, / In the cold tomb he lies, all untimely laid low' (15-16).

In addition to his talents in evoking his readers' 'consenting emotions', Burns is praised for his ability to mobilise martial sentiment for Scotland. Struthers sketches a scenario replete with Burnsian conceits: 'When roused by the coward insults of the vile, / His anger is up, and his arms dreadful gleam!' (21-22). Into the fray the 'bard' appears – 'the strength of the strains of our bard shall be known' (23) – and deploys his arsenal of verse: 'In a torrent of fire it shall burst on the foe!' (24). Such enthusiastic rhapsodies are counterbalanced with the dirge's persistent refrain, here modified for the occasion: 'The hero shall weep, for by folly undone, / In the cold tomb he lies, all untimely laid low' (25-26). The repetitive stress on the 'cold tomb' serves as a *memento mori* for future poets, who are implicitly advised to defer to Burns's *genius* while regretting the nature of his life and death.

Addressing the poor in the poem's final stanza, Struthers makes a critical judgment on the verse of his fallen 'hero', dissecting it for fellow labouring-class poets who might wish to follow Burns's example:

While the trust of the poor man is placed upon heaven,
While devotion the breasts of the wise can inspire,
While to virtue and calm contemplation is given,
In his works the Creator to see and admire;
His cottar shall live. (27-31)

At this point a caesura follows, stretched to a full stop before the line resumes, 'But the good shall bemoan' (31). And what shall they bemoan exactly? The character of the poet himself, deceived and deceiving, undone by unspecified 'error' and 'folly': Struthers writes, 'The warm tear of pity unceasing shall flow; / For by error bewilder'd, by folly undone' (32-33). Struthers's dirge consolidates a number of key features common to Burns elegies, particularly the hortatory mode of moral admonition. In addition, he negates the possibility (indeed, desirability) of another poet emerging with the same great gifts. In the shadow of Burns, Scottish poetry is advised to take another path altogether, leaving no visible monument over the poet's 'cold tomb'.

In *Poems on Various Subjects* (1803), Anne Grant of Laggan offers her own gloomy perspective on Scottish poetry after Burns in an elegy entitled 'On the Death of Burns'. Although born in Glasgow, Grant spent her early years in America, where she taught herself to read and write verse. At the time of the elegy's composition, Grant (recently widowed in 1801) was living in Inverness-shire. She turned to writing to support her eight children, and due to the agency of influential friends, her *Poems* had three thousand subscribers. She moved to Edinburgh in 1810 and became even more successful for her works on Highland life. Eventually, through the aid of Walter Scott, she was granted pension from the Literary Fund in 1825.[54] As her biography makes clear, Grant considered herself as a professional writer, attuned to the demands of the literary marketplace. Her perception of Burns's legacy for Scottish poetry reflects the continuing interrogation of the nature of his *genius*, especially its relationship to formal education.

In a section preceding the elegy entitled 'Remarks on the Character of Burns', Grant speculates openly about the meaning of her great predecessor's legacy, puzzling over the range of emotions that his example provokes. She writes, 'I do not know whether to pity or admire Burns most'.[55] She describes her confused state of mind by noting that although 'it would look like gross affectation to describe' her feelings on the subject, she will nevertheless 'lay my little offering on the shrine of departed genius' (256-57). Her feelings are decidedly mixed, as she claims that 'I have invariably tried to divest myself of an idolatrous veneration for genius' because 'the instances in which intellectual superiority has been debased by vice, or degraded by absurd conduct, are so frequent' (257). Regardless of its 'degradation' and 'debasement', it still pains Grant to witness fallen *genius* being triumphed over by the 'tasteless', the 'selfish', and the 'stupid': 'How do the tasteless, the selfish, and the stupid, triumph over the splendid ruins of ill-fated Genius!' (257).

Like many previous commentators, Grant depicts the 'snares' that face 'the children of Genius' with recourse to the familiar narrative of dissipation leading to death. In her vision, such children are presented with the 'full cup of public admiration', which when imbibed results in the embrace of those with 'treachery' and 'temptation' in their hearts (257-58). Once the 'children of Genius' embark on this path, their fate is sealed; she writes that 'the snares that vanity and pleasure spread in the way of those who join exquisite sensibility and a glowing imagination, with artless simplicity and a high relish for all that flatters the senses, are [...] numerous and fatal' (258). Linking Burns's 'decline and fall' to the genre of allegory, Grant offers a moral tale that is exceedingly reductive of the poet's life story and body of works; even his status as an adult is questioned, for in Grant's vision he acts with the rash thoughtlessness of a child.

Along with expressly infantilising those in possession of *genius*, Grant believes that the only way for such exceptional, vulnerable children to be spared is to enforce their 'obscurity of retirement' as 'their only chance of safety' (258). Accordingly, she declares that 'perhaps the blooms of Genius are too delicate to bear the unhallowed breath of the world' (258). Before she turns her attention more closely to her subject at hand – Burns's character – she concludes her initial thoughts by claiming that poets are not 'necessarily less virtuous than others', but that 'they are less prudent, less firm, more susceptible, more simple' (259). Asking 'why were such people made', Grant rehearses the by-now rote catalogue of Burns's dissipation by 'false friends', usually unnamed gentry who preferred to 'debase' the poet rather than patronise him.[56] It is useful to recognise once more that Grant's essay appeared in 1803, a mere seven years after Burns's death; as in the works of previous elegists, Grant's extremely vague accusations of the poet's misconduct seem largely designed to provoke outrage at those who abused him, as well as ruefulness over Burns's unnamed moral indiscretions.

She follows these thoughts with a lengthy rumination on the nature of Burns's *genius*, which she finds inimical to a 'thorough education':

Ask me of his genius! I have not power to do justice to its vigour, extent, and versatility [...]. It is nauseous to hear people say what he would have been if he had got a more thorough education. If he had, he would not have been Burns; he would not have been that daring, original, and unfettered genius, whose 'wood-notes wild' silence the whole chorus of modern tame correctness, as one of our mountain blackbirds would a number of canaries. (259)

Given Grant's own self-taught background, it is perhaps predictable that she felt that Burns's *genius* had little or nothing to do with his 'learning'. In praise of this 'untaught' facet of his character, Grant claims that 'he did know his own strength, as such a superior intelligence necessarily must' (259). Despite the self-knowledge accorded by such a 'superior intelligence', Burns is believed to have known 'his own weakness', which 'did not answer the purpose of self-defence' (259-60). 'Self-defence' is only bolstered by 'self-command'

and 'self-denial', skills which he needed to have 'learned and habitually practised' (260).

Because of his lack of control and will-power, Burns himself was the agent of his own downfall. In this theory of Burns's character and *genius*, it was not only his exposure to the larger world which ensured his 'debasement', but also (and more importantly) it owed to his 'weakness' for enjoying illicit pleasures. Stating that 'this theme is endless' (260), Grant asks readers to reconceptualise Burns by remembering only that part of him which displayed his true *genius*. She finds this in his correspondence with his patron Frances Dunlop, writing that these letters are where 'his heart truly opens, from his effusions to his gay companions, – that unaffected scorn of the world and its vain pursuits, – that sublime melancholy, – that aspiration (tho' struggling through doubts and darkness) after what the world does not afford' (260). She summarises her thoughts on Burns's character by elevating the ideal of his *genius*, which is best represented through his 'sensibility' and 'manly sincerity'; both qualities work in concert to capture his 'essence', emphatically and evocatively exclaimed as 'every thing, in short, that characterises genius, and exalts humanity!' (260).

Grant's elegy 'On the Death of Burns' opens with extensive intertextual referencing, examining a 'whole chorus' of poets who serve as the 'tuneful train' to which Burns rightly belongs. She begins with an exclamation – 'What adverse fate awaits the tuneful train!' (261, 1) – followed by a speculative assay of the 'fates' of Otway, Spenser, Collins, Savage, and Shenstone. The dismal 'fates' of this diverse group of poets are seen to have resulted from their lack of 'prudence' and the insistent demands of 'Fancy' upon 'thoughtless bards':

His warning Muse to Prudence turn'd her strain,
But Prudence sings to thoughtless bards in vain;
Still restless Fancy drives them headlong on
With dreams of wealth, and friends, and laurels won –
On Ruin's brink they sleep, and wake undone! (13-17)

This rumination leads her to her real subject, another poet whose 'fate' led him to 'Ruin'. She writes, 'See where CALEDONIA's Genius mourns, / And plants the holly round the grave of BURNS!' (18-19). His distinction derives from the guiding influence of his exclusively national *genius*, which is both the source and subject of his verse: 'With manly force and native fire / He wak'd the genuine Caledonian lyre' (22-23).

His influences are also clearly Scottish, for she finds that 'RAMSAY, once the HORACE of the North, [...] / Bequeath'd to him the shrewd peculiar art' (32, 34). Praising 'The Cottar's Saturday Night', Grant asserts that Scots can find pleasure in Burns's representation of Scotland's 'virtuous' rural denizens – 'Our "virtuous populace"' (46) – which she claims should be a source of national pride: 'a nobler boast / Than all the wealth of either India's coast' (46-47). Despite Burns's greatness as a Scottish poet coming from such a 'virtuous populace', however, Grant claims that he was just as doomed as his fellow English poets listed at the elegy's beginning. She highlights the extremity of the 'misfortune' that overwhelmed his gifts in the manner of a hero burdened with *hamartia*, his own tragic error or flaw:

Yet while our hearts with admiration burn,
Too soon we learn that 'Man was made to mourn'.
The independent wish, the taste refin'd,
Bright energies of the superior mind,
And Feeling's generous pangs, and Fancy's glow,
And all that liberal Nature could bestow,
To him profusely given, yet given in vain;
Misfortune aids and points the stings of pain. (49-56)

Despite (or perhaps because of) a 'superior mind' animated by taste, 'Feeling', and 'Fancy', Burns is destined for suffering. In this respect, it may seem that, like the reckless Richard Savage, Burns was imbued with his own tragic flaw, an inherent gift that served as a source of distinction as well as 'Misfortune'.

However, the notion of *hamartia* also implies a tragic 'error' or mistake in judgment, and it is this meaning which applies most readily to Grant's view of Burns's character.[57] Indeed, being 'made to mourn' seems more a matter of choice for Burns as the elegy proceeds. She recounts his sudden rise to fame – 'Fond admiration spread his name, / A candidate for fortune and for fame' (59-60) – as a fatal misstep that led him directly to a fallen world: 'In evil hour he left the tranquil shade / Where Youth and Love with Hope and Fancy play'd' (61-62). Grant places the blame upon the Edinburgh gentry, whom she believes deceived the poet and led him to a premature death wrought by convivial excess:

Convivial hours prolong'd awake the morn,
Even Reason's sacred pow'r is drown'd in wine,
And Genius lays her wreath on Folly's shrine.
Too sure, alas! the world's unfeeling train
Corrupt the simple manners of the swain. (68-72)

Although his death is 'untimely', it is at the same time inevitable in this scenario, regarded as the irrevocable *peripeteia* provoked by the poet's *genius*: she writes, 'Low on earth he lays his sorrowing head, / And sinks untimely midst the vulgar dead' (75-76). As in other elegies written at this time, Grant concludes with an appeal to 'ye whom honour Genius' (89) to 'let the stream of pity flow' (94) for the poet's widow and orphans. Together with her essay on his 'character', Grant's tribute heightens the sentimental, moralising strain in the Burns elegy by representing the poet as a flawed *genius*, an exceptional figure whose poor judgment and susceptibility to flattery led to his own death and the impoverishment of his family.

In 1813, Margaret Chalmers published a collection of poems in Newcastle due to 'circumstances of severe domestic affliction'. She had hoped the novelty of her situation – namely, being 'the first British Thulian quill' due to her upbringing in the Shetland Islands – would help redress her family's dire financial difficulties.[58] One year older than Burns, Chalmers felt his presence and influence strongly in her verse. For Chalmers, Burns represented a touchstone as well as an impediment owing to his ongoing posthumous celebrity. In her poem 'Verses in Humble Imitation of Burns', Chalmers examines the matter in self-deprecating style, offering a lengthy epigraph which assesses the situation she faces in 'humbly imitating' the poet:

I beg it may not be supposed, that these Verses express my ideas respecting the information and intelligence of the Ayrshire Bard with regard to this country. But the thought striking me, that had he been alive, he might, perhaps, have been amused with the novelty of a poetic essay from a Zetland authoress; my feeble attempt is made on the supposition of his giving the reins to his enlivening vein of raillery and burlesque. Well am I convinced, although I have attempted the Imitation, that he is inimitable. Why then embark in the vain pursuit of imitating the inimitable? I stand reproved.[59]

Chalmers captures the ambiguous nature of Burns's legacy for living Scottish poets in this passage, for she acknowledges the enduring influence of his style. At the same time she recognises the challenge that living poets face when they choose to imitate such an 'inimitable' poet.

Like other labouring-class poets, Chalmers identifies key figures in the literary marketplace (which she describes as the 'rhyming trade') in order to demonstrate her fitness for participation. She states – 'What will this warld come to believe! / The rhyming trade does briskly thrive' (44, 1-2) – before mentioning how her gender has not traditionally participated in the trade: 'The tunefu' lasses lent the pen / To able hands' (7-8). Among these 'able hands' number Shakespeare, Milton, and James Thomson. Despite the preclusion of women in a literary marketplace dominated by alpha males like Shakespeare and Milton, Chalmers announces her decision to write with some trepidation:

I wat I thought it was right fair,
Whan after muckle thought and care,
On cow'ring wing,
My ain wee muse, in hamely strain,
Ettled to sing. (11-15)

Such self-presentation evokes that of John Lapraik, who also ex-pressed serious reservations about writing due to his lack of education rather than his gender.[60] Chalmers appeals for help from her own muse 'madam Thulia' who dwells 'amang thae awfu' eerie rocks, / Whar selchies, otters, gang in flocks' (51-52). Like Burns's Coila from 'The Vision', Chalmer's muse is also a 'hizzie' who 'has the pertness 'mang the Nine / To be right bizzie' (54-55).[61] Thulia is represented as forthright and confident – 'Fegs, madam Thulia, ye're no blate, / Ye want na for your ain conceit' (56-57) – but also angry: 'Ye're angry; weel, they're aft ill heard / That tell the truth' (59-60).

Her anger stems from the unequal opportunities afforded to her 'daughters'; her 'review' of Chalmers's talents extends to the end of her 'imitation', offering a much less comforting vision of her future as a poet than Coila had assured Burns in 'The Vision'. Thulia assesses her daughter's chances in the rhyming trade by acknowledging that concessions must be made before Chalmers can be judged beside the likes of Burns, Milton, or Shakespeare: 'Besides, in a' that's done and

said, / Allowances maun ay be made' (66-67). She claims that 'whar
other authors fa' a grain, / Ye claim a pound' (69-70), before
suggesting that 'sae they will, may be, let you pass' (71). Thulia's
advice to Chalmers here is hardly reassuring in its suggestion that
those with prestige in the literary marketplace will 'maybe' admit her
entry.

   Mirroring Burns's sentiments in his epistles to Lapraik, Thulia
advises her daughter instead to 'rhyme for fun', or else her work will
be ignored for its many errors:

But tak my word, my rhymin lass,
It's for the fun;
And it would hae sae mony fauts,
The task they'll shun. (72-75)

Thulia describes the added obstacles Chalmers will encounter due to
her gender, writing 'it moves my anger, I confess' (97) when people
tell her 'Poetesses' that 'twad set you better to clean fish, / Or knit
your socks' (99-100). She ends her 'humble imitation' by recounting
the last words of Thulia, who tells her daughter to stay home despite
her ambition for 'tunefu' fame': 'Since ye maun hae tunefu' fame, /
What need ye gang sae far frae hame' (121-22). Thulia's canny if
distressing advice underscores Chalmers's self-awareness of her
novelty as 'the Thulia quill' in much the same manner that Burns had
initially endorsed the 'heaven-taught ploughman' persona. For
Chalmers, however, the stakes are much higher to attain even a
modicum of success that would resemble Burns's, owing largely to
her gender and locale.

   Chalmers's 'humble imitation of Burns' exemplifies the tenuous
status of practicing poets in Scotland the first decade after his death,
when the elegiac mode began to give way to commendatory verse.
Once Burns had been 'grieved' properly by Scottish poets, it was time
to assess his poetic legacy and national reputation, usually by means
of odes and tributes written for celebratory occasions. As editors,
biographers, and critics worked to construct a palatable image of the
genius of Scotland, so too did the poets from this time. They wrote a
great volume of accessible verse often designed to be read in public
places for a wide audience of admirers. These poems were frequently
anthologised in the growing market for 'Burnsiana', an emerging
genre that compiled assorted prose and verse into multiple scrapbook-

style volumes.[62] Although the popularity of 'Burnsiana' provided a new venue of publishing opportunities for poets like Chalmers, such occasions for verse also invited unenviable comparisons to the 'inimitable' Burns. As if in response to critics and readers who had not yet perused her poetry, she simply states, 'I stand reproved' (44). Her inhibitions were well-founded, for her volume of poems sold poorly upon publication; through the agency of Walter Scott, however, she secured a grant of £10 from the Royal Literary Fund in 1816. Despite this modest degree of recognition, she never published another collection and it is not known where or when she died. As with Struthers, Chalmers simply vanished from the rhyming trade and the history of Scottish poetry altogether.

4. Poetic Defenders of Burns's 'Fallen Genius'

Other poets would confront similar challenges when considering the influence and legacy of Burns upon their own works. Robert Tannahill was no less sanguine about the future of Scottish poetry than his contemporaries; although he emerged as a significant songwriter in the early nineteenth century, like Burns he died an 'untimely' death at the age of thirty-six. Tannahill was born into a labouring-class family in Paisley and worked as a cotton weaver from the age of twelve; as with Grant and Burns, he was also largely self-taught and found much inspiration in Scottish folk songs. He published his first (and only) volume of poetry that year by subscription, but his attempt to publish a second edition with Archibald Constable was unsuccessful. Following a serious breakdown, he committed suicide by drowning himself in a culvert near Paisley in 1810.[63] Throughout his brief career, Tannahill was acutely aware of writing in the shadow of Burns, writing several poems that reflected upon the dead poet's legacy for Scottish verse.[64] Tannahill was also deeply involved in the formation in 1805 of the Paisley Burns Club, serving as its first secretary and unofficial poet laureate. However, where Burns had written poetry for various clubs that sought to unify members through national kinship, Tannahill's odes perform a different unifying function through commendation of the club's paterfamilias.[65]

His first effort in this vein is the 'Ode, Written for, and read at the Celebration of Robert Burns' Birthday, Paisley, 29th January,

1805'. Within this ode Tannahill constructs an elaborate scenario that stages the club's veneration of Burns by employing the council of the gods, that hoary epic chestnut. 'Once on a time, almighty Jove', Tannahill writes, 'invited all the minor gods above, / To spend one day in social festive pleasure'.[66] In such a setting, a stranger appears, identifying himself as the 'the guardian of that far-fam'd land, / Nam'd Caledonia, great in art and arms' (45-46). He voices a sore complaint which he expects the gods to redress:

But what avail the virtues of the North,
No Patriot Bard to celebrate their worth,
No heav'n-taught Minstrel, with the voice of song,
To hymn their deeds, and make their names live long? (54-57)

Tannahill's Burnsian keywords, particularly 'heav'n-taught' and 'bard', denote the ode's occasion as well as accentuate the poet's key attributes.[67] The 'guardian' requests that such a 'Patriot Bard' be found for Scotland, pleading for the gods to 'grant my country one true Patriot Bard' (65). As expected, the gods appease the guardian: 'Thy bard shall rise full-fraught with all the fire, / That heav'n and free-born nature can inspire' (70-71).

At this point, the guardian is revealed to be the *genius* of Scotland – 'Speechless the Genius stood, in glad surprise / Adoring gratitude beam'd in his eyes' (78-79) – before the ode turns to the disclosure of the 'Patriot Bard':

And on that morn,
When BURNS was born,
Each muse with joy,
Did hail the boy. (84-87)

Commendation of this chosen poet follows the generic formula of such verse, expressing unqualified praise: 'His merits proven – fame her blast hath blown, / Now Scotia's Bard o'er all the world is known' (91-92). However, Tannahill ends his ode as ambiguously as Chalmers had begun her 'humble imitation', expressing much self-doubt along with validation of his subject: 'Trembling doubts here check my unpolished lays, / What can they add to a whole world's praise?' (93-94). His ode ends where it had begun, with the veneration of the 'Patriot Bard' whose birth alone acts as proof of the 'Virtues of the North' and cause for Scottish 'glory'; he writes, 'Yet, while revolving time this day returns, / Let Scotchmen glory in the name of BURNS' (95-96).[68]

Other birthday odes were less self-conscious than Tannahill's, yet they often matched his efforts in idealising Burns as a national icon. In his poem 'Verses to the Memory of Robert Burns', James Aikman offers his own variation on the anniversary ode. Like William Reid and James Macaulay,[69] Aikman was a printer, working with his partner Andrew Aikman and publishing *The Edinburgh Star* newspaper (1809-16) and James Hogg's *The Spy*, nos. 14-52 (1810-11). Some of his early poems had appeared in *The Spy* before he published them in *Poems* (1816), where his commemorative ode to Burns is found. His efforts at verse extended into the 1820s with the publication of *The Cenotaph* (1821) and *Disappointment and Other Poems* (1825), although he became better known for his work on national and religious history, in particular his translations of George Buchanan and his edition of the works of Robert Leighton, Archbishop of Glasgow.[70]

Before turning to his anniversary ode, it is worth examining another poetic tribute in Aikman's *Poems*, this one dedicated to Burns's 'elder brother in the muse' Robert Fergusson.[71] His poem 'Lines to the Memory of Robert Fergusson' reviews the national reception of Burns's 'elder brother' by describing the poet's unhappy fate, a narrative that Burns himself had recalled and recounted in his tribute to Fergusson. Aikman directly addresses his readers by asking:

Heard ye that piercing maniac shriek –
That awful, wild, responsive yell;
Dread as Despair's first notes; that shook
The dreary dark concave of hell?[72]

Fergusson's death at an Edinburgh asylum is depicted with a decidedly Gothic brush, the imagery amplified with exclamatory indignation: 'Fallen genius! Thine the frantic groan – / Thus hail'd thy steps the phrenzied crew' (7-8). The notion of Fergusson as a 'fallen genius' is further dramatised by Aikman's indictment of unfeeling fellow Scots who left the poor poet to die: 'They left thee, FERGUSSON, to want, – disease; No friendly hand e'en mark'd thy grave' (37-38).

At this point, the analogy that the whole tribute has been designed to deliver is finally made plain. Fergusson's unmarked grave is properly venerated when 'kindred genius traced the sacred place – /

What BURNS now needs to thee he gave' (39-40). 'Kindred genius' demands the necessary act of homage that Burns had performed for Fergusson, one which is literal (the marker Burns placed over the grave of his 'elder brother') and figurative – the written tribute from one 'fallen genius' to the next. Thus the hortatory reminder: 'What BURNS now needs to thee he gave'. However, to whom is this call to action directed? What 'kindred genius' among living Scottish poets can respond in due course, with talents equal to predecessors like Fergusson and Burns?

Aikman's answer can be discerned in his anniversary ode, which reveals his awareness of the value of Burns's posthumous celebrity as well as his perspective on the literary marketplace as poet and printer. His ode opens with a mock-heroic scenario, the familiar monarchal anniversary ode satirised for effect and tone:

The day that marks a Monarch's birth
Is noted by the cannon's roar,
And adulation hast'ning forth,
Sings to the fawning courtly corps. (90, 1-4)

Given such 'hast'ning adulation', the presses begin to groan under the weight of insincere anniversary odes written by the king's 'minions' (10). This noble personage – apostrophised as 'worthy the head that wears the Crown' (9) – is validated by 'minions' who declare, 'Renown / Awaits the name that ne'er can die!' (11-12). These lines perhaps best bespeak Aikman's perspective as a printer, especially coming from one who may have felt quite inundated by bad verse at that time of year.

Despite its associations with the 'fawning courtly corps', the idea of 'the name that ne'er can die' gains greater currency in the ode, once Aikman gets to the real subject of 'fallen genius'. He writes:

Not so when genius sinks to rest,
When stiff the hand that struck the lyre;
When cold for aye the inspired breast,
Once glowing with celestial fire. (17-20)

He employs classical imagery and diction to represent 'fallen genius', whose 'worthy' head wears a different kind of crown, the holly or laurel. This king, though 'deaf to praise' (33), has not sunk 'with th'unhonour'd dead' (34). Rather, his grave has become a site for his followers to ruminate on his 'fallen genius', symbolised by the over-growth of holly which shrouds his monument: 'The Holly overshades his bier, / That bloom'd and blossom'd round his head' (35-36).

In considering the national value of one of the 'honor'd dead' like Burns, Aikman rehearses the narrative of his decline. While Burns's descent to death is less overtly pathetic than Fergusson's, it is no less indignantly recounted. The ode registers righteous anger at the poor patronage of privileged Scots, those who were blind or oblivious to the worth of the great *genius* in their midst:

Oh! but it rends the Patriot heart,
(While ruffians on a nation's spoil
Fatten and feed! and the last part
Wrung from th'industrious peasant's toil
A Pimp or Pander's pockets fills),
To think no portion could be spared
To him who struggling with life's ills,
Found Poetry its own reward. (61-68)

In spite of the indifference of the nation's 'ruffians' who acted no dif-ferently than 'pimps' or 'panderers', the memory of Burns alone will suffice to immortalise the poet for his fellow Scots. Aikman ends his ode with the hope that Burns's name will 'outlive his time' (69) and thus 'claim immortality his own' (72), while 'pamper'd minions die unknown' (70). Aikman's proprietary interest in preserving the poet's fame (also seen in Reid's 'Monody') can be seen to dictate his repre-sentation of Burns's legacy as an inimitable 'fallen genius'. Such a *genius* could never be equaled (or even compared) to the verse of the soon-to-be unknown 'pamper'd minions' clogging the presses.[73]

In 1819, Hamilton Paul edited a collection of Burns's poems in which he included two odes that he had written in the poet's honour. At the time of printing, Paul was a well-known member of the 'New Licht' clergy; he had also been writing and publishing verse since 1800. Among his friends was the poet Thomas Campbell, with whom Paul had taken classes at the University of Glasgow. Paul also worked as a tutor and editor of the *Ayr Advertiser* before joining the clergy.[74] His edition gained recognition for its spirited defense of Burns's character and religion, a task for which he was criticised roundly by the writers of *Blackwood's* (among several others). In the 'Extracts from Wastle's Diary' section for *Blackwood's* (1820), 'Wastle'

remarks upon the recent publication of Paul's edition with some
bewilderment and contempt: 'What a noise has been made about this
new edition of Burns, by [...] the Reverend Hamilton Paul'. He
continues by observing that

> No clergyman that has any sense of what befits his own office, will ever write a life of
> Burns – for, if he says what he ought to say, he will throw a damp upon his theme –
> and if he does not, he will infallibly injure himself.

Remarking that 'every body understands the character of Burns now-
a-days', 'Wastle' concludes his critique by declaring that 'the
Reverend Hamilton Paul's book is a most absurd one – so are all
books written by clergymen, that do not know or feel what is the na-
ture of their clerical office'.[75]

In the 'Introductory Ode' of his edition, Paul presents his 'ab-
surd' defense by estimating the poet's character through the act of
commendation. Pastoral imagery blends with hyperbolic praise to
'inweave' the 'panegyric wreath' that will crown the subject of the
ode:

> Not with more joy the cottage fair,
> Whose bosom love refines,
> The flow'ry garland for her hair
> With rosy finger twines,
> Than I, this hawthorn shade beneath,
> Whose blossoms bend the bough,
> While fragrant zephyrs round me breathe,
> Inweave the panegyric wreath
> To deck the Poet's brow.[76]

His emotional response to Burns is no less dramatic, for he contends
that he 'clasps' the volumes of Burns's work 'at rise or fall of day'
(15), embracing them like a loved one. The volumes offer Paul insight
into 'lorn love, or effusion gay, / Breath'd from the soul of BURNS'
(17-18). Such effusive veneration of Burns's 'soul' by a member of
the clergy ('New Licht' or otherwise) clearly roused the indignation of
Blackwood's 'Wastle'.

Paul's defense of Burns's character is expressed most vividly in
the vigorous assertion of the poet's 'moral page', which Paul claims
'eild and poortith mourns' (33). He exhorts his reader to 'listen to the
counsel's sage, / Or tales to soothe the woes of age' (34-35) which

have been 'penn'd by the hand of BURNS' (36). Burns's writing serves specific moral functions in Paul's estimation, working to rein-force basic tenets of the church in the manner of a holy text. Indeed, Paul goes so far as to calumniate critics like 'Wastle', whom he deems to be living in hell because of their refusal to read (and appreciate) Burns:

Can peace within his bosom dwell
Who taste and feeling spurns?
No – 'tis the residence of Hell,
Whose gloom defies th'united spell
Of music, song, and BURNS. (50-54)

Paul ends his 'Introductory Ode' by eschewing the task of compari-son, which he deems to be particularly odious when confronted with a figure of such stature as Burns. He complains that 'I've poured a melancholy strain / O'er many timeless urns' (64-65), but this one is different – so different that 'comparisons are vain' (66). The ode's last two lines are intriguing in their all-encompassing scope: 'All the pleasure and the pain / Are swallowed up in BURNS' (71-72).

In the appendix to his edition of Burns, Paul provides a short ex-planation of the origins of another ode he wrote in honour of Burns, this one having been composed with a specific audience in mind. He states that 'the posthumous fame of Burns is without parallel in the annals of poetry', before remarking upon the occasion of his second ode: 'Among the earliest of the anniversaries that were celebrated in honour of his memory, was one which took place in the Cottage wherein he was born. The party was small but select, and formed a most interesting group' (295). Numbering among this 'select' group, Paul was invited to compose an anniversary ode for their next meeting in the cottage. His invitation derived not only from his repute as a poet but also for a specific reason: to expose and debunk critics of 'Burnomania', a term coined as a critique by the Reverend William Peebles in *Burnomania: The Celebrity of Robert Burns Considered* (1811). Peebles's target was not only Burns but also his admirers, particularly the growing customs among them to celebrate the occa-sion of the poet's birth. His anger largely stemmed from his role as a member of the clergy; Peebles was outraged that fellow clergy like Paul considered an 'irreligious' figure like Burns as suitable for na-tional veneration.

For Peebles, celebrating Burns in any fashion was to 'make a mock of Sin': he writes, 'Can we bear, and hold the faith / Sporting with Heaven, and Hell, and Death'? To tolerate such 'sporting' from the poet means condoning his 'degrading holy writ; his dreaming / Profanely; and awake blaspheming'. Not only do Burns's supporters commit such blasphemy by condoning his works, but more outrageously they celebrate his life:

Let anniversaries repeat
His glories, celebrate a fete
Imbibe his spirit, sing his songs,
Extol his name, lament his wrongs,
His death deplore, accuse his fate,
And raise him far above the great.[77]

Peebles coins a name for this 'insane' behavior with a rather feeble pun: 'What call you this? Is it Insania? / I'll coin a word, 'tis Burnomania'.[78] To Paul, all that Peebles's critique consists of is 'some weak attempts […] made by narrow-minded men to expose to ridicule this Burnomania, as they term it' (296). Paul claims that such criticism can make no impact upon the affection that Scots feel for their national poet: 'Like self-love converted by the plastic power of the Poet into social affection, it is spreading wider and wider every day' (296).

In the 'Irregular Anniversary Ode, Sacred to the Memory of Burns', Paul emphasises the setting of both the poem and its recitation, 'the Cottage in which he was Born'. As in his 'introductory ode', Paul's actions are highly charged with powerful sentiments that may seem excessive in a member of the clergy. He opens the 'irregular' ode in irregular fashion, kissing the ground of the cottage: 'Here let me kneel and kiss the precious earth, / For ever hallow'd by the Poet's Birth' (296, 1-2). The cottage, 'hallow'd' by the poet's spirit, assumes the symbolic role that it will serve for Burns tourists in the years to come. Indeed, it is worth noting Paul's explicit role in sacralising the setting and preparing a narrative in which its veneration is overtly staged. In particular, he is anxious to describe the role that future Scottish poets will play in the continuance of the anniversary celebration as a tributary rite of passage. His description of this process is decidedly secular and sensual:

While youthful Bards delight to strike the lyre,
And pay their court with rapturous desire,

To objects half infernal, half divine,
Man's bane and bliss – to women, wit, and wine;
So long thine amourous ditties shall be sung,
And breathe enchantment from the virgin's tongue. (15-20)

In graver circumstances, such 'youthful Bards' join the funeral procession to 'the Poet's grave' (48), where these 'friends of genius and of song' (53) pay homage to Burns and 'wonder and weep' (54). After paying their proper (and obligatory) respects, the young poets must compose 'th'annual tributary lay' (80) as an act of initiation into Scottish verse, still ruled by the force of Burns's departed *genius*.

The young poets testify to their need to pay tribute to Burns's 'consecrated dust' (58), stating in unison that

With willing hearts to him we'll pay,
Whose ardent soul and polish'd mind,
Restor'd the purity of song
(Degraded and debas'd so long)
And love's soft dialect refin'd. (81-85)

The nameless, faceless bards aspiring to be Burns's successors coalesce into a single voice that questions whether such a feat is possible at all in the shadow of one with such exceptional poetic powers. This voice wishes that 'the lov'd Bard, ere his spirit was flown' (109) had coronated his successor, thus ensuring a stable succession; had this act been performed, 'wide over my shoulders his mantle had thrown, / I'd have breath'd a strain worthy of him and you' (111-12).

Assuming the mantle in such a ritual act – the kind of poetic coronation openly mocked in Dryden's 'Mac Flecknoe' and Pope's *Dunciad* – is not only literally impossible but highly unlikely for the poets writing in Burns's shadow. Paul is not optimistic about the possibilities of another Burns rising to wear his predecessor's mantle:

Alas cold forever's the soul kindling fire,
Mute the tongue that could captivate, ravish, inspire,
While the hands of the feeble awaken the lyre,
And the Muses sigh out, 'Our adorers are few!' (113-16)

Scottish poetry after Burns is penned by 'the hands of the feeble', imitators who cannot compare to the inimitable *genius* looming over them. Indeed, in his appendix, Paul bluntly states that 'the success of

Burns, at that time unrivalled, awakened the ambition of a myriad of servile imitators, who conceived that a facility of versifying, and a knack at rhyming, formed the Poet, and constituted the essentials of poetry' (301). Remarking that very few had 'attained to celebrity in the path which Burns had trode', he does concede that 'panegyrical effusions have proceeded from the pens of the most celebrated Poets of the age, for genius, taste, and originality' (301). In fact, he observes that 'scarcely an author of eminence has appeared since the demise of the Poet, who has not paid a compliment to the merit of Burns' (301).

Despite these asseverations, Paul ends his 'Irregular Ode' with a paean to Burns that suggests that a poetic successor will never be found who can match or even compare with Burns. This dim outlook causes very little gloominess for Paul the poet, for it stimulates even more elevation of his subject. Burns becomes a god-like poet whose great 'heaven-sent' talents are enough to ensure his immortality:

That matchless magnitude of mind,
That feeling heart, that taste refin'd,
That self-taught art sublime,
Which bid the Cottage-tenant rise,
Th'ennobled favourite of the skies,
Whose heaven-sent laurel crown defies
The withering touch of time! (299, 122-28)

Although he numbered among those poets who would be forgotten, tapped by 'the withering touch of time', Paul feels (or seems to feel) little anxiety about his own mortality. Venerating Burns as an 'immortal', 'heaven-sent' favourite allows Paul to seek recognition for his own work through the act of commendation. Thus, although living poets cannot imitate or hope to reproduce Burns's inimitable style (or else be judged 'feeble' and 'servile'), they can still gain legitimacy by praising his *genius* in a bid for national unity.

As Keats had observed, Burns's 'great shadow' loomed large in early nineteenth-century Scotland. No matter how loudly one cried for the dead poet to 'hide thy face', his presence (through absence, the essence of the shadow) could not be ignored. While some poets and editors like Hamilton Paul were content to keep blithely writing in the dark, others, like the 'Ettrick Shepherd' James Hogg, were displeased with this vision of the future. For Hogg, if Scottish poetry were to live on, it must step out of the 'great shadow' of Burns and learn to thrive on its ground. As will be shown, it was Hogg's protean creative enterprise, consisting of multiple stylistic and generic efforts, which pointed the way to a new future – and new possibilities – for Scottish writers which had not been thought possible in the shadow of Burns.

---

[1] Qtd. in *The Poetical Works and Other Writings of John Keats*, ed. by H. Buxton Forman, ed., 4 vols (London: Reeves & Turner, 1889), II, p. 285. Quotations from Keats's poetry and letters refer to this edition/volume and will be cited in-text by page and line numbers.

[2] Keats composed 'The Human Seasons' in March 1818 and sent it in a letter to Benjamin Bailey dated 13 March.

[3] I have quoted Keats's original version of 'The Human Seasons' here, which is the version he sent in his letter to Bailey. The published version of the sonnet employs a subtle change in diction in the final couplet, where 'forget' becomes 'forego': 'He has his winter too of pale misfeature / Or else he would forego his mortal nature'.

[4] This phrase was used by Burns to describe fellow poet David Sillar in his 'Epistle to Davie, a Brother Poet'. For more on this term, as well as the tradition of elegies to Burns, see chapters two and three of the present work.

[5] For more on Currie's representation of Burns, see chapter four of the present work.

[6] For discussion of this critical paradigm, see Leask, '"Their Groves of Sweet Myrtle": Robert Burns and the Scottish Colonial Experience', in Murray Pittock, ed., *Robert Burns and Global Culture* (Lewisburg: Bucknell University Press, 2011), pp. 172-88, 83.

[7] See Bloom's *The Anxiety of Influence Bloom, Harold, The Anxiety of Influence* (New York: Oxford University Press, 1973) and *A Map of Misreading* (New York: Oxford University Press, 1975).

[8] See Ian Duncan, *Scott's Shadow: The Novel in Romantic Edinburgh* (Princeton: Princeton University Press, 2007).

[9] For more on this group of elegies, see chapter three of the present work.

[10] For more on the concept of 'monumental consecration', see chapter four of the present work.

[11] See James Thomson, 'Paisley Burns Club: A Sketch of its History', *Burns Chronicle*, 5 (1927), p. 131-34.

[12] For discussion of the preservation of the Burns Cottage, see M'Bain, James, *Burns' Cottage: The Story of the Birthplace of Robert Burns* (Glasgow: Bryce, 1904).For general discussion of Burns Clubs, see Corey Andrews, 'Venders, Purchasers, Admirers: Burnsian "Men of Action" from the Nineteenth to the Twenty-First Century', *Scottish Literary Review*, 2.1 (2010), 97-115.

[13] For examples of this body of verse, see John D. Ross, ed., *Round Burns' Grave* (Paisley: Gardner, 1891; repr. New York: AMS Press, 1973).

[14] See for instance Thomas Crawford, *Burns: A Study of the Poems and Songs* (Stanford: Stanford University Press, 1960), pp. 249-50, and Daiches, *Robert Burns* (New York: Macmillan, 1966), p. 3.

[15] For discussion of Wordsworth's poetic debts to Burns, see Thomas Gill, 'Wordsworth and Burns' in Sergeant and Stafford (2012) p. 156-67; and Leask (2010: 292-98).

[16] The phrase refers to Hew Ainslie's *A Pilgrimage to the Land of Burns* (Deptford: the author, 1822).

[17] *The Poems of William Wordsworth* (London: Moxon, 1849|) p. 218, ll. 1, 6, 7-8. Quotations from Wordsworth's poetry refer to this edition and will be cited in-text by page and line numbers.

[18] Wordsworth's highlighted word 'glinted' refers to line 15 of Burns's 'To a Mountain Daisy', Kinsley (1968, poem 92).

[19] See Starr and Hendrickson (1966: 43, l. 118).

[20] The 'spontaneous overflow of powerful feelings' refers to Wordsworth's theory of poetics advanced in his 'Preface' to *Lyrical Ballads* (1800).

[21] For a differing view of this poem, see Leith Davis, *Acts of Union: Scotland and the Literary Negotiation of the British Nation, 1707-1830* (Stanford: Stanford University Press, 1999), pp. 134-35.

[22] Wordsworth also composed a poem entitled 'Thoughts, Suggested by the Following, on the Banks of Nith, Near the Poet's Residence' at the same time as the other Burns-related poems discussed in this chapter. In this poem, Wordsworth addresses his sister Dorothy with moralising thoughts on the sins of the 'Minstrel'. As a whole, the poem speaks more to the growing vogue for Burns tourism than the other two poems discussed, which examine the poet's reputation and legacy in greater detail. Wordsworth's other major work on Burns is his *Letter to a Friend of Burns* (1816), which was addressed to James Gray, who was also a friend of James Hogg. This prose work examines Wordsworth's reactions to various reviews of editions/biographies that had appeared, such as those of Francis Jeffrey and Alexander Peterkin. For more on the critical reception of Burns during the early nineteenth century, see chapter four of the present work.

[23] For a thoroughgoing critique of Wordsworth's abstemiousness compared to Burns's conviviality, see the excerpt from William Hazlitt's lecture 'On Burns, and the Old English Ballads' reprinted in Low (1974: 301-02).

[24] Wordsworth returned to the cautionary figure of Burns again in 'Resolution and Independence', where he linked him with Thomas Chatterton as prime examples of inspired yet aberrant poets of *genius*: 'I thought of Chatterton, the marvellous Boy, / The sleepless Soul that perished in his Pride / Of Him who walked in glory and in joy / Following his plough, along the mountain-side' (152, 43-46). Establishing kinship with two such poets leads Wordsworth to his well-known apothegm: 'By our own spirits are we deified:

/ We Poets in our youth begin in gladness; / But thereof come in the end despondency and madness' (47-49).

[25] These lines refer to Wordsworth's definition of the poet in the 'Preface'.

[26] Keats's decision to represent Burns in this way is intriguing, to say the least. It is a decided *non sequitur* that Burns would have been drunk in his birthplace, for he left the cottage with his family at the age of seven to live in Mount Oliphant.

[27] For his part, Keats was very dismissive of this sonnet; in a letter to his brother, he writes that 'I was determined to write a sonnet in the cottage: I did, but it is so bad I cannot venture it here' (297-98). He was thought to have destroyed it, but it was found by his early editor Lord Houghton who preserved it. Dante Gabriel Rossetti was said to have considered this sonnet 'a fine thing. The "local colour" is strong in it: it might have been written where "Willie brewed a peck o' maut", and its geniality would have delighted the object of its admiration' (298).

[28] p. 126.

[29] *Poems*, p. 75, ll. 1, 5, 6. Further citations will be noted in-text by line numbers.

[30] For more on Rushton's politics (especially his ties to William Roscoe and James Currie), see Michael Royden, 'Edward Rushton (1756-1814)', in *DNB*.

[31] For more on Roscoe, see Donald A. Macnaughton, 'William Roscoe (1753-1831)', in *DNB*.

[32] p. 51, ll. 8, 11. Further citations will be noted in-text by line numbers.

[33] Roscoe's use of the word 'guerdon' in this elegy reveals the polemical nature of his representation of Burns, for 'guerdon' implies not only reward but also recompensation. In Scots law, 'recompensation' has an interesting meaning as well; in an action for debt, the term specifies a plaintiff's plea of a counterclaim made in response to a defendant's counterclaim. In this light, in Roscoe's court of law, only by establishing Burns's 'deathless name' (and thus settling the counterclaim for recompensation) can Scotland repay its debt to the dead poet. For more on 'recompensation', see *OED*, 'recompensation', def. 2.

[34] Roscoe's elegy was included in many early nineteenth-century reprints of Currie's edition of Burns's *Works*, as well as in Allan Cunningham's edition from 1846, among other editions. Since the editions of Currie and Cunningham were among the century's most popular editions, Roscoe's second elegy reached a major audience of Burns's readers.

[35] p. 12, ll. 1-2. Further citations will be noted in-text by line numbers.

[36] For the reference to 'Duessa', see Edmund Spenser, *The Faerie Queene*, I. 2. 34.

[37] Roscoe's phrase 'rend the welkin' in this context is deliberately archaic, referring to the sound of thunder. Jonathan Swift had used the expression

ironically in his 'Description of a City Shower', but it can also be found in rather straightforward symbolic fashion in James Thomson's *Castle of Indolence* (1748). For more on this term's literary applications, see *OED*, 'welkin', def. c.

[38] For more on Drummond, see R. K. Webb, 'William Hamilton Drummond (1778-1865)', in *DNB*. For Burns's influence in the Ulster community of Belfast, see Ferguson and Holmes, eds., *Revising Robert Burns and Ulster: Literature, Religion and Politics, c. 1770-1920* (Dublin: Four Courts Press, 2009) .

[39] For more on these related yet distinct associations of *genius*, see chapter one of the present work.

[40] p. 21, ll. 1-2. Further citations will be noted by line numbers in-text.

[41] For information on the publication of such elegies, see Gibson, pp. 116-26. Among many such examples, *The Scots Magazine* 59 (1797) published five elegies in a single issue.

[42] For an extensive assessment of the elegy genre, see Karen Weisman, ed., *The Oxford Handbook of the Elegy* (Oxford: Oxford University Press, 2010).

[43] Emanuel (1996: 217).

[44] 'Monody', p. 337, ll. 7-8. Further citations will be noted by line numbers in-text.

[45] For more on Burns's religious critics, see McGinty (2003: 235-38).

[46] For more on Reid as publisher, see G. Ross Roy, 'Robert Burns and the Brash and Reid Chapbooks of Glasgow', in Horst W. Drescher, ed., *Scottish Studies: Publications of the Scottish Studies Centre of the Johannes Gutenberg Universtät Mainz in Germershim* (Frankfurt am Main: Peter Lang, 1992), pp. 53-69.

[47] Reid's use of this phrase ('now he's dead') is a common facet of the Scots 'mock elegy'. As such, it deliberately echoes Burns's 'Tam Samson's Elegy' and 'Poor Mailie's Elegy'; Allan Ramsay's 'Elegy on John Cowper', 'Elegy on Lucky Wood', and 'Elegy on Maggy Johnstoun'; and 'The Life and Death of the Piper of Kilbarchan' by Robert Sempill of Beltrees.

[48] 'Pith' is both a Scots and English word; in Scots, it can refer to 'sexual potency' as well as 'strength, vigour or toughness'. Both qualities may be implied in Reid's usage. All Scots definitions refer to *The Concise Scots Dictionary*, ed. by Robinson.

[49] See Benjamin Walter, 'The Work of Art in the Age of Mechanical Reproduction', in Hannah Arendt, ed., *Illuminations*, trans. by Harry Zohn (New York: Schocken, 1969), pp. 217-52.

[50] For more on Reid's success in this endeavour, see Roy (1992: 53-69).

[51] See T. W. Bayne, 'John Struthers (1776-1853)', rev. by Douglas Brown, in *DNB*.

[52] p. 76, ll. 1-4. Further citations will be noted by line numbers in-text.

[53] For more on Burns's perceived 'failings of genius', see chapter four of the present work.

[54] See Andrew Tod, 'Anne Grant [née MacVicar] (1755-1838)', in *DNB*.

[55] p. 259. Further citations will be noted by page and line numbers in-text.

[56] She writes, 'What a fatal delusion, to lean for happiness on the bosom of the gay and fortunate, because they make us companions of their pleasure!' (259). The class register here is unmistakable, especially concerning the end of such convivial camaraderie: 'When the day of affliction comes, we are left to pine neglected, or perhaps have our sorrows embittered by the sneer of wanton insult' (259).

[57] *Hamartia* derives from Aristotle's *Poetics*, and its definition has been a source of critical contention. For more on the concept, see *OED*.

[58] For more on Chalmers, see Isobel Grundy, 'Margaret Chalmers (b. 1758)', in *DNB*.

[59] p. 44. Further citations will be noted by page and line numbers in-text.

[60] For more on Lapraik, see chapter two of the present work.

[61] Burns described Coila as a 'tight, outlandish hizzie' in line 41 of 'The Vision' (*Poems and Songs of Robert Burns*, I, poem 62). For more on Coila's representation in this fashion, see Sterling, pp. 32-33, and chapter one of the present work.

[62] For more on the growing vogue for 'Burnsiana' in the nineteenth century, see Andrews (2010: 97-115).

[63] See William Donaldson, 'Robert Tannahill (1774-1810)', in *DNB*.

[64] Tannahill wrote three birthday odes to the poet: 'Ode, Written for, and read at the Celebration of Robert Burns' Birthday, 1805'; 'Ode, Written for, and read at the Celebration of Robert Burns' Birthday, 1807'; and 'Ode, recited by the President of the Burns' Anniversary Society, Paisley'. The first two odes were published in his *Poems and Songs, Chiefly in the Scottish Dialect* (1817). In addition to the birthday odes, Tannahill also wrote an elegy entitled 'Dirge, Written on Reading an Account of Robert Burns's Funeral'.

[65] For more on Burns's club verse and its nationalist function, see Andrews (2004: 215-358).

[66] Andrew Tannahill, *Poems and Songs, Chiefly in the Scottish Dialect*, 4th edn (London: Cowie, 1817), p. 103, ll. 1-3. Further references to this edition will be noted by line numbers in-text.

[67] For more on the use of this terminology to describe and define Burns, see chapter two of the present work.

[68] Tannahill's other two odes explore similar territory, expressing reservations about his own fitness as a Scottish poet writing in Burns's shadow: for instance, 'And I, the meanest of the muses train, / Shall join my feeble aid to swell the strain', in 'Ode, recited by the President of the Burns' Anniversary Society, Paisley', p. 127, ll. 25-26.

---

[69] For more on Macaulay, see chapter two of the present work.

[70] See Hogg, *The Spy* (2000), pp. 557-58. I would like to thank Patrick Scott and Gillian Hughes for their help providing additional information on James Aikman.

[71] Burns's reference to Fergusson as his 'elder brother in the Muse' appears in 'Lines under the Portrait of Fergusson' (Kinsley, Vol I [1968: poem 143]). For more on the relationship between Burns and his 'elder brother', see James Connor, 'Elder Brother in the Muse', *Studies in Scottish Literature*, 30 (1998), 59-66.

[72] p. 86, ll. 1-4. Further citations will be noted in-text by page and line numbers.

[73] His 'Ode to the Memory of Burns' in the same volume also concludes in the same manner: 'And while a Scottish heart remains, / His song shall never die! — / While extacy can swell the veins, / Or rapture fill the eye: — / Tho' deaf his ear to praise or fame, / We'll cherish yet the honour'd name, / Which his admiring country mourns: — / In silence we the pledge shall take, / And drain the cup which tends to wake / THE MEMORY OF BURNS!' (104, 101-10).

[74] For more on Paul, see J. R. MacDonald, 'Hamilton Paul (1773-1854)', rev. by Douglas Brown, in *DNB*.

[75] p. 322.

[76] p. x, ll. 1-9. Paul's edition is hereafter cited in-text by page and line numbers.

[77] Low (1974: 249-50).

[78] For more on Peebles's critique of 'Burnomania, see Andrews (2010: 97-115).

Conclusion

The 'Only Worthy Successor': The Career of James Hogg, 1801-1834

1. The 'Great Dead Poet' and the 'Gifted Living': The Influence of Burns's Poetic Legacy upon James Hogg

In an article entitled 'Some Observations on the Poetry of the Agricultural and that of the Pastoral District of Scotland, illustrated by a Comparative View of the Genius of Burns and the Ettrick Shepherd' (printed in *Blackwood's Edinburgh Magazine* in February 1819), John Wilson presents a 'comparative view' of Robert Burns and James Hogg that proved to be quite influential in the reception history of both poets. Viewing Burns as representative of 'agricultural' verse and Hogg of 'pastoral' due to their respective biographies, Wilson analyses the sources of their *genius* as expressed primarily in their writing. He contends that such an approach does not diminish their accomplishments, but merely highlights their particular differences as Scottish poets in their own 'native dominions': he writes, 'There can be nothing more delightful than to see these two genuine children of Nature following the voice of her inspiration in such different haunts, each happy in his own native dominions, and powerful in his own legitimate rule'.[1]

This leads Wilson to remark upon the poets' common class status, which is categorised as 'peasant'. Of this unlikely source of distinction, Wilson observes that 'most philosophical Englishmen acknowledge that there is a depth of moral and religious feeling in the peasantry of Scotland, not to be found among the best part of their population' (309). Such linking of class and nation in the verse of Burns and Hogg leads Wilson to speculate upon the distinct character of the Scottish 'peasantry', a subject first addressed in the posthumous assessment of Burns by James Currie, his first editor.[2] Wilson boldly asserts that 'we do not feel any consciousness of national prejudice, when we say, that a great poet could not be born among the English peasantry' (309). Among the Scottish peasantry, it is altogether different; Wilson describes their exceptionality in depth, finding a 'difference of poetical feeling and genius in an agricultural and pastoral state of life' (310). This 'difference' between English and Scottish peasants is further clarified, for Wilson finds that it is 'exemplified as that difference [which] appears to be in the poetry of Burns, and *his only worthy successor*, the Ettrick Shepherd' (310, emphasis mine).

Thus, as in many other comparisons of the two poets, Burns and Hogg are indissolubly linked as 'peasants'. However, they are very different types of 'peasant', enjoined in a decidedly competitive relationship. As Douglas Mack observes, the goal to 'succeed' Burns was central to Hogg's literary career, which was 'defined and shaped by his intense desire, as shepherd-poet, to become the successor of the great ploughman-poet, Robert Burns'.[3] The nature of this kinship is expressed pithily by Hogg's assumption (and endorsement) of his own persona, the 'Ettrick Shepherd'; unlike Burns, Hogg never attempted to disavow this persona in his personal or professional lives. Hogg displayed little (if any) ambivalence about his status as the 'Ettrick Shepherd', seeing the title as an honorific that signified his aspiration to be recognised as Burns's 'only worthy successor'.[4]

Hogg's designation as the 'only worthy successor' to Burns is supported in some depth in the 'comparative view' of Wilson, whose support of Hogg would be sporadic and ambivalent throughout the Ettrick Shepherd's career. Wilson characterises Burns's verse as defined by struggle endemic to his life as an agricultural labourer, stating that 'when we consider the genius of Burns, we see it manifestly moulded and coloured by his agricultural life' (312). This 'moulding' is expressed by the poet's works, for Wilson claims that 'we see in all his earliest poems – and they are by far his finest – a noble soul struggling – labouring with a hard and oppressive fate' (312). In Wilson's account, Burns's 'hard and oppressive fate' derives from both his class position and his locale in an agricultural district of rural Scotland. Although such factors doomed Burns from the beginning, they also provided the greatest proof of his *genius*, when viewed in sharp relief: 'The calamities of a life of hardship, that bows down ordinary spirits to the earth, elevated and sublimed the genius and character of our immortal poet' (312).

Wilson argues that Burns's achievements were staggering in light of his 'life of hardship', leaving his successors some room for advancement but many 'monuments' in their path:

The crown that he has worn can never be removed from his head. Much is left for other poets, even among that life where the spirit of Burns delighted to work; – but he has built monuments on all the high places, and they who follow can only hope to leave behind them some far humbler memorials. (314)

Such 'monuments' obscure the view of those poets imbued with 'the spirit of Burns', leaving them very limited space upon which to construct their own 'far humbler memorials'. It is worth noting that this view was advanced in 1819, only twenty-three years after Burns's death. Wilson's gloomy vision of the future of Scottish poetry after Burns would be echoed by many other critics throughout the century, leading to the thesis that Burns was both apogee and terminus of national vernacular verse.[5]

After admitting that Burns 'might have done far more good than he has done' (316), Wilson introduces the Ettrick Shepherd by deeming him a 'living genius' who has the 'spirit' of his predecessor. However, Wilson expresses some trepidation about naming Hogg the 'only worthy successor'; indeed, this search would occupy many critics in the years following Burns's death, not all agreeing with the choice of the Ettrick Shepherd for such an important role. Others would also question Hogg's fitness as Burns's successor. Wilson is cautionary from the very start, stating that

We should be afraid of turning from so great a national poet as Burns, to a living genius, also born like him in the lower ranks of life, were we not assured that there is a freshness and originality in the mind of the Ettrick Shepherd, well entitling him to take his place. (317)

Hogg's 'freshness and originality' link him to other self-taught poets in the Scottish tradition; as Valentina Bold has attested, 'it was with James Hogg that the autodidactic tradition [...] reached its fullest development and attained its highest achievements'.[6]

However, as Gillian Hughes remarks, the nature of Hogg's *genius* led it to be diminished in the literary marketplace, for his 'original genius' not only 'implies closeness to nature and inspiration but it also indicates distance from the learning, writing, and publishing of the early nineteenth century'.[7] The disadvantages of the publicity surrounding 'original genius' did not prevent the continuing emergence of its gifted practitioners among the labouring classes, for 'Burns's "divinity of genius" was liberally accorded to peasant poets thereafter'.[8] The figure of Hogg is foremost when examining the concept of poetic inheritance as well as the ambiguous nature of Burns's legacy for labouring-class Scottish poets in the early nineteenth century. Fiona Wilson describes the complications of assuming Burns's mantle faced by such a poet as Hogg, noting that 'Burns offered Hogg a powerfully enabling example of what could be done at the interface of oral and written poetry – as well as a warning […] of the risks of being typecast as a "natural" or "peasant poet"'.[9]

For an early critic like John Wilson, comparing the poets was much less complicated, despite their differing *genius*. Stating that 'the genius of the two poets is as different as their life' (320), he stresses Hogg's debt to the landscape of his birth and his profession as a shepherd. Contrary to Burns's struggles in agricultural Ayrshire, Hogg's life in 'the pastoral vallies of the south of Scotland' nurtured his verse, for Wilson contends that it is there 'that the poetical genius of our country has been most beautifully displayed' (311). Wilson does not examine pastoral as a genre, but instead views it as an expression of Hogg's facility in descriptive verse focusing on the landscape. For this reason, Hogg is to be preferred over Burns:

Open a volume of Burns – and then one of the Ettrick Shepherd – and we shall see how seldom the mind of the one was visited by those images of external nature which in that of the other find a constant and chosen dwelling-place. (318)

This feature of Hogg's poetry is one of its key distinctions from the work of his predecessor, whom Wilson finds to have been sorely lacking in the ability to depict 'external nature'.

In addition to his talent in representing 'external nature', Hogg also bests Burns in the attempt to preserve vanishing aspects of Scottish culture, associated in Wilson's mind with 'the dead': 'His genius loves better to lift up the veil which forgetfulness has been slowly drawing over the forms, the scenes, the actions, and the characters of the dead, than to gaze on the motions of the living' (319). Although Burns certainly sought to record 'the forms, the scenes, the actions, and the characters' of his time and place, he cannot vie with the Ettrick Shepherd in this arena, for which Hogg is crowned as 'the poet laureate of the Court of Faery' (320). Wilson's praise of Hogg is tempered in comparison to Burns's continuing appeal to Scots of all ranks, for Hogg 'can never become so popular a poet, nor does he deserve to be so' (318). Nevertheless, Wilson argues that Hogg must be embraced by Scots and allowed to cultivate his talents.

The posthumous valorisation of Burns at the expense of 'gifted' living poets like Hogg is represented as severely detrimental to the future development of Scotland's *genius*:

It would be indeed strange if they who hold annual or triennial festivals in commemoration of their great dead poet should be cold to the claims of the gifted living. It cannot but be deeply interesting to all lovers of genius – and more especially to all proud lovers of *the genius of their own Scotland*, to see this true poet assisting at the honours paid to the memory of his illustrious predecessor. He must ever be, on such high occasions, a conspicuous and honoured guest; and we all know, that it is impossible better to prove our admiration and love of the character and genius of Burns, than by the generous exhibition of similar sentiments towards the Ettrick Shepherd. (321, emphasis mine)

Hogg's efforts in this national duty of veneration were conspicuous throughout his career, revealing a constant strategy to gain recognition as Burns's 'only worthy successor'. As this conclusion will demonstrate, however, Hogg met with considerable challenges in this enterprise, forcing him to reassess his strategy by exploring other creative outlets than poetry alone in the literary marketplace. Although he would serve as 'a conspicuous and honoured guest' at many festivals, Hogg would find his efforts to assume Burns's mantle difficult indeed, as critics and readers were reluctant to grant 'honours paid to the memory of his illustrious predecessor' upon one of the 'gifted living'.

2. Following in 'the Steps of Burns': Hogg's Self-Construction as Poet in the *Memoirs*

By 1819, the year of Wilson's article, Hogg had already endured many difficulties in his career as 'the Ettrick Shepherd'. These challenges would continue throughout the rest of his life, as even former champions like Wilson changed their views of the 'next Burns'. Wilson would lampoon Hogg mercilessly as the foolish, dim-witted Shepherd in the 'Noctes Ambrosianae' section of *Blackwood's Edinburgh Magazine* from 1822 to 1835.[10] Hogg had encountered such abuse from the early stages of his career as well. Bold notes that 'as "The Ettrick Shepherd" Hogg was depicted in an often offensive way: as coarse but poetic and as unrefined genius personified' (69). However, Bold also rightly notes that 'peasant poets' like Hogg 'were often willing collaborators in their typecasting or role-playing' (15). In much the same fashion that Burns had employed the 'heaven-taught ploughman' persona when it served his interests, Hogg actively collaborated in the process of constructing the 'Ettrick Shepherd'. As already noted, he believed this persona was central to his eventual success in claiming Burns's mantle as Scotland's national poet. He even went so far as to claim that he shared a birthday with Burns, although this was later proven to be false. Douglas Mack observes that 'in his own time he was generally regarded as a poet rather than a novelist', further stating that 'Hogg aspired to be regarded as Burns's successor in the role of poet to the Scottish nation'.[11]

While Bold rightly claims that 'Hogg was well qualified for the role of national peasant poet' (63), Hogg's own memoirs of his life reveal the constant struggle that he faced as he sought to claim this title. Indeed, he wrote extensively about his own life, claiming rather tongue-in-cheek that 'I like to write about myself: in fact, there are few things which I like better'.[12] He wrote three separate 'Memoirs of the Author's Life', which prefaced two editions of *The Mountain Bard* and that of *Altrive Tales*; in each version, he modified the narrative of his decision to write verse.[13] Significantly, the first two versions of the 'Memoirs' (included in *The Mountain Bard* first published in 1807 and reprinted in 1821) do not mention Burns at all in this process. Rather, Hogg recounts his turn to poetry as a wholly individual choice; he is eager to reveal that his literacy was achieved only with great effort on his part. As Suzanne Gilbert notes, Hogg was eager to represent the challenges he faced in not only becoming accepted in the literary marketplace but also in becoming literate: 'in the "Memoir" [...] Hogg undertakes a strategic effort to authenticate his roots and narrate his career in terms of an overcoming of early adversity'.[14]

Unlike Burns, Hogg's education during his youth was exceedingly scanty, consisting of very brief encounters with tutors. He describes this period of his life with curt brevity: 'All this while, I neither read nor wrote, nor had I access to any books, saving the Bible'.[15] His exposure to other books than the Bible came with the fortuitous generosity of his employer's son William Laidlaw, who lent him Allan Ramsay's 'The Gentle Shepherd' and Blind Harry's 'The Life of Sir William Wallace'.[16] Where Burns had recounted the story of first reading 'Wallace' with great verve in his autobiographical letter to Dr. John Moore, Hogg is much less enthusiastic about his initial encounter with verse as a literary genre. Speaking of these two books of poetry, Hogg states that 'though immoderately fond of them, yet (what you will think remarkable in one who hath since dabbled so much in verse) I could not help regretting deeply that they were not in prose, that every body might have understood them' (10).

The reason for his reservations is simple and surprising, given his later aspirations to succeed Burns as a national poet: 'The truth is, I made exceedingly slow progress in reading them; the little reading I had learned, I had nearly lost, and the Scottish dialect quite confounded me' (10). However, despite his troubles reading, he began to compose verse, becoming known as 'Jamie the Poeter' in the local community of the Ettrick and Yarrow Valleys. The first example of his efforts in verse underscores his class status: he writes, 'The first thing that ever I composed that was really my own, was a rhyme, entitled An Address to the Duke of Buccleuch, in beha'f o' mysel', an' ither poor fo'k' (12). His desire to establish himself as a 'worthy successor' to Burns is foregrounded by his awareness of his identity as one of Scotland's 'poor fo'k', those who write mainly to represent and preserve their experiences. Becoming literate is the first stage of this process, to be followed by a firm sense of purpose in writing.[17]

For Hogg, this sense of purpose derived from reading popular verse in the Scottish literary marketplace and seeking to imitate it in order to gain initial acceptance. In his 'Memoirs' (1807), he describes the experience of reading Walter Scott's *Minstrelsy of the Scottish Border* (1802-03), which led him to start writing verse with a clear purpose:

In 1802, *The Minstrelsy of the Scottish Border* came into my hands; and, though I was even astonished to find such exact copies of many old songs, which I had heard sung by people who never could read a song, but had them handed down by tradition [...] yet, I confess, that I was not satisfied with many of the imitations of the ancients. I immediately chose a number of traditional facts, and set about imitating the different manners of the ancients myself. (15-16)

Hogg's initiation into the literary marketplace is marked by such experiences, where his dissatisfaction with popular productions like Scott's *Minstrelsy* is expressed through direct imitation. In the example above, Hogg's imitations question the legitimacy of Scott's project; as he would experience throughout his career, Hogg would be forced to contend repeatedly with his more illustrious contemporary

Scott.[18] Because Hogg shared a reputation of Scottish folk authenticity with Burns due to their status as 'peasants', he felt that he could interrogate the validity of Scott's song-collecting endeavours and produce his own more 'genuine' efforts. As a result, *The Mountain Bard* was Hogg's answer to Scott's *Minstrelsy*, competing directly with it in the literary marketplace.

Later works like *The Poetic Mirror* (1816) continue this process, expressing Hogg's desire to compete with renowned English and Scottish poets like Wordsworth, Byron, and Southey. Fiona Wilson states in this respect that Hogg's poetry 'is often marked by a sense of struggle. This struggle shows up in his competitive relations with other writers and in his simultaneous embrace and distrust of Romanticism as an ideology' (16). In fact, *The Poetic Mirror* derived from Hogg's dissatisfaction with the valorisation of acclaimed Romantic poets at the expense of his own work; as he himself would later be parodied by Wilson in *Blackwood's*, Hogg seeks to subvert his poetic rivals through parodic imitation. In his 'Memoirs' (1821), Hogg proudly describes his process of writing such imitative works: 'The Poetic Mirror was completely an off-hand production. I wrote it all in three weeks, except a very small proportion; and in less than three months it was submitted to the public'. Despite its slapdash composition, Hogg boasted that 'I have been told, that in England, one of the imitations of Wordsworth's Excursion has been deemed excellent'.[19] Douglas Gifford states that such imitations were valuable elements of Hogg's poetic growth, writing that he had 'the astonishing gift of poetic parody which produced the best imitations we have of Scott, Wordsworth, Southey and the like in his *Poetic Mirror*'.[20]

The Poetic Mirror was a highly successful work in its first edition, which was issued anonymously and sold well. However, when the second edition appeared in 1817 and Hogg was identified as its author, the book's sales plummeted, leaving many unsold copies of the second edition up to 1821.[21] As would be the case throughout his career, Hogg's recognition as a serious contender in the literary marketplace was highly conditional, fluctuating with his varying efforts in prose and verse that sought to establish and consolidate his reputation. In addition to the vagaries of publishing, Gilbert describes the political in-fighting that Hogg experienced at this time from his erstwhile supporters William Blackwood and John Wilson: 'during this period [Hogg] also fell out with William Blackwood, mostly over the publication in *Blackwood's Edinburgh Magazine* of a vitriolic response to the "Memoir" by John Wilson' (41).

Hogg's 'Memoirs' preceding *Altrive Tales* (1832) depicts the serious challenges he faced in being considered Burns's 'only worthy successor' in much greater detail than his previous versions. Douglas Mack claims that the 1832 'Memoirs' is 'a piece of Romantic myth-making, in which Hogg stakes a claim to be recognised as Burns's successor in the role of spokesman for, and poet of, the Scottish people'.[22] Written three years before his death, this final version is the first to mention Burns as a source of inspiration for writing poetry; indeed, his description of this 'first encounter' with Burns's verse in this memoir has been regarded with considerable critical suspicion. Given the absence of such an encounter in the previous 'Memoirs', it is most likely that Hogg's description of this experience is entirely a work of imagination, allowing him to construct an 'authentic' line of inheritance with his predecessor through class-based kinship.

All previous discussion of Hogg's poetic inheritance in the first two versions of the 'Memoir' in *The Mountain Bard* is dwarfed in comparison to his first exposure to Burns in the account given in *Altrive Tales*. In this 'Memoir', Hogg represents the encounter as an epochal moment, one owing only to a chance meeting with a 'half daft' man named John Scott:

The first time I ever heard of Burns was in 1797, the year after he died. One day during that summer a half daft man, named John Scott, came to me on the hill, and to amuse me repeated Tam O'Shanter. I was delighted! I was far more than delighted – I was ravished![23]

Hogg finds himself at a loss for words at this point – 'I cannot describe my feelings' – but claims that 'before Jock Scott left me, I could recite the poem from beginning to end, and it has been my favourite poem ever since' (xvi). Hogg learns from Scott that the poem 'was made by one Robert Burns, the sweetest poet that ever was born; but that he was now dead, and his place would never be supplied' (xvi). Scott further informs Hogg that Burns 'was born on the 25th of January [and] bred a ploughman [...] and that he had died last harvest, on the 21st of August' (xvi).

This leads Hogg to reflect on the meaning of this chance encounter, an experience that would shape his own career and identity as a Scottish poet:

This formed a new epoch of my life. Every day I pondered on the genius and fate of Burns. I wept, and always thought with myself – what is to hinder me from succeeding Burns? I too was born on the 25th of January, and I have much more time to read and compose than any ploughman could have, and can sing more old songs than ever ploughman could in the world. But then I wept again because I could not write. However, I resolved to be a poet, and to follow in the steps of Burns. (xvi-xvii)

Hughes highlights the retrospective valuation that Hogg employs in this passage to describe this life-changing moment, noting that 'his discovery of Burns came to be viewed as an almost religious revelation'.[24]

Despite such testimony to the revelatory power of Burns's example, Hogg deliberately misconstrued the facts of his own life here to create a better story. Mack points out that 'although [Hogg] had been a semi-literate shepherd in his late teens, by 1797 he was in his late twenties and could write perfectly well. Indeed, he was already a published poet'.[25] Given such obvious and verifiable evidence, it is highly unlikely that such an encounter between Scott and Hogg ever occurred, at least in the symbolic fashion in which it is narrated in the 1832 'Memoir'. Burns's continuing widespread celebrity in 1797, particularly given the spate of elegies published in Scottish periodicals and newspapers after the poet's death the previous year, makes Hogg's assertion that he had never heard of Burns until this meeting quite dubious.[26] It is not enough to simply catch Hogg in a lie, though, for his reconstruction of his initial relationship with Burns speaks to a lifetime of trying to succeed his famous predecessor, an epic struggle which was drawing to a close for the Ettrick Shepherd.

Despite its questionable authenticity, this 'first encounter' with Burns presents a highly self-conscious, retrospective appraisal of the elder poet's influence upon Hogg's literary career. Mack rightly observes that 'clearly this passage in the "Memoir" is important for any assessment of Hogg's own understanding of his literary career'.[27] In addition, the passage is written from the perspective of a poet nearing the end of his career, encapsulating much of the mythology surrounding Hogg as Burns's 'only worthy successor'. As he clearly states, Hogg is determined not only to 'follow in the steps of Burns' but also to outdo his predecessor by singing more songs 'than ever ploughman could in the world'. Hogg's actual achievements in this respect are worth close scrutiny, for his limited success in this endeavour derived as much from his own efforts as from the literary marketplace in which he competed with his rivals.

3. 'Not Altogether Void of Native Genius': Hogg's Adoption of the 'Ettrick Shepherd' Persona

Four years after purportedly first learning of Burns from John Scott, Hogg set out to publish his first book of verse, entitled *Scottish Pastorals* (1801). Hogg's account of the publication of this short book (numbering seven poems in all) can be found in his 1832 'Memoir', in which his attitude about the whole affair is dismissive and self-depre-catory. He states that 'in 1801, believing that I was then become a grand poet, I most sapiently determined on publishing a pamphlet, and appealing to the world at once' (xxiii) He continues by noting that 'this noble resolution was no sooner taken than executed; a proceeding much of a piece with many of my subsequent transactions' (xxiii).

His initiative resulted from a short stay in Edinburgh, where he had gone to sell sheep; during his spare time, he wrote out poems that he had already composed in his mind and took them to a printer. He remarks that

I knew no more about publishing than the man of the moon; and the only motive that influenced me was, the gratification of my vanity by seeing my works in print. But, no sooner did the first copy come to hand, than my eyes were open to the folly of my conduct. (xxiv)

Like Burns, who had written of the gratification of seeing his works in 'guid black prent', Hogg also admits being motivated by the desire (coded here as 'vanity') for the legitimacy of print.[28] David Macbeth Moir states that Hogg at this time 'resolved on the desperate enterprise of settling in Edinburgh – and as what? A literary adventurer'.[29]

Despite Hogg's later embarrassment over *Scottish Pastorals*, the occasion affords comic reflection in the 1832 'Memoir', in which Hogg speaks with an authority conferred by a long career of publica-tions in an array of genres and venues. Seeing *Scottish Pastorals* as the work of folly, Hogg explains his reaction as a confused, anxious author upon seeing his first works in print. He writes with dismay over the poems within the poorly-edited printed copy:

Indeed, all of them were sad stuff, although I judged them to be exceedingly good. The truth was, that, notwithstanding my pride of authorship, in a few days I had discernment enough left to wish my publication heartily at the devil, and I had hopes that long ago it had been consigned to eternal oblivion. (xxiv)

He complains of later critics using *Scottish Pastorals* to discredit his current works, as if the slim volume were all the proof needed of the Ettrick Shepherd's illegitimacy in the literary marketplace. However, as Hughes has argued, 'the seven poems of *Scottish Pastorals* show the influence of Hogg's reading in the eighteenth-century British classics of poetry as clearly as his folklore background'.[30] This allusiveness links Hogg's poetic practice with Burns's, for in both there is a deliberately intertextual approach to 'folk' and 'mainstream' verse.[31] Such strategies indicate Hogg's serious intentions to be legitimated as a poet in the literary marketplace within (and beyond) Scotland.

As in the previous versions of his 'Memoir', the 1832 version alludes to the influence of Scott's *Minstrelsy of the Scottish Border* upon Hogg's poetic development. Although Burns's influence is first addressed in the 1832 'Memoir', it is actually the figure of Scott who is seen to have had the most direct impact upon Hogg's literary productions. This is due in large part to Scott's major contributions to popularising ballad collections and verse narratives associated with Scottish folk culture.[32] The type of poetry associated with Burns in the early nineteenth century – the lyric in particular – did not find a niche in a literary marketplace that would increasingly become driven by the appetite for Scott's fiction.[33] Hogg describes his first encounter with Scott's *Minstrelsy of the Scottish Border* in nearly identical fashion as in the previous iterations of the 'Memoir'. However, the variation in the 1832 version is telling:

On the appearance of 'The Minstrelsy of the Scottish Border,' I was much dissatisfied with the imitations of the ancient ballads contained in it, and immediately set about imitating the ancient ballads myself – selected a number of traditionary stories, and put them in metre by chanting them to certain old tunes. In these I was more successful in any thing I had hitherto tried, although they were still but rude pieces of composition. (xxv)

Writing again from the vantage point of both age and authority, Hogg is capable of simultaneously praising and dismissing his efforts in imitation due to 'much dissatisfaction' with Scott's versions of the 'ancient ballads'. Thus he signals his own poetic growth from such 'rude pieces of composition', while diminishing Scott's achievement in the same breath.

Bold argues that 'Hogg's relationship with Walter Scott played a crucial role in his adoption of the Ettrick Shepherd image' (66). Scott's influence also directly affected Hogg's later writings, for he felt that Scott's remarkably successful turn to fiction played a considerable role in devaluing the popularity of verse in the literary marketplace. This was especially frustrating for Hogg, whose steady poetic output in the 1810s included *The Forest Minstrel* (1810), *The Queen's Wake* (1813), *The Pilgrims of the Sun* (1815), *Mador of the Moor* (1816), and the weighty two volume *Jacobite Relics* (1819). In *Familiar Anecdotes of Sir Walter Scott*, Hogg writes that 'as long as Sir Walter Scott wrote poetry there was neither man nor woman ever thought of either reading or writing any thing but poetry. But the instant that he gave over writing poetry, there was neither man nor woman ever read it more!'; he further claims that 'I was obliged from the irresistible current that followed him to forego the talent which God gave me at my birth and enter into a new sphere with which I had no acquaintance'.[34]

Hogg's next major book of poems, *The Mountain Bard* (1807), provides evidence of his attempts to adapt to changing tastes in the literary marketplace. In this work he also began to assume the 'Ettrick Shepherd' persona more conspicuously as a promotional tool. Gilbert remarks that 'Hogg's arrival on the literary scene was modest and self-promoted; coming from obscurity, he had to seek ways of putting himself before the public' (39). One of his key strategies to do so involved maximising the appeal of the 'Ettrick Shepherd' persona, particularly its 'pastoral' associations. In this regard, he met with much greater success with the publication of *The Mountain Bard*, which was printed by one of the leading publishers in Edinburgh, Archibald Constable, and is considered 'Hogg's first important collection of poetry'.[35]

Dedicated to Walter Scott (who is called the 'sheriff of Ettrick forest, and Minstrel of the Scottish Border'), *The Mountain Bard* is prefaced with Hogg's first version of the 'Memoirs of the Author's Life'. The collection begins with a section of 'Ballads, in Imitation of the Antients', in which the presence of Burns is strongly felt (despite Hogg's admitted debt to the oral tradition of Scottish ballads).[36] As in Burns's 'Halloween' and *Notes on Scottish Song*, Hogg presents his ballads with multiple paratexts, including extensive, quasi-anthro-pological footnotes.[37] The songs themselves are written in dense Scots, with no glossary appended; this speaks as much to Hogg's differences from Burns (whose works routinely appeared with glossaries throughout the nineteenth century) as to his cultural mo-ment, when popular interest in balladry was pervasive. Hogg's canny awareness of literary trends is thus revealed at the start of his poetic career, reflecting an astute author who understood how to position his works in the literary marketplace.

However, critical reviews of *The Mountain Bard* and its follow-up volume, a collection of songs entitled *The Forest Minstrel* (1810), were mixed, reflecting Hogg's still uncertain status as Burns's 'only worthy successor'. As Gilbert states, 'early reviews generally approve of Hogg's efforts, though the tone is inevitably patronising. Most assume "self-taught poets" lack originality' (38). For instance, when the reviewer for *The Critical Review* assessed *The Forest Minstrel* in 1811, he wrote that 'it is very evident that Burns is the model of imitation with most of these poets of the mountains.' The reviewer did find that Hogg was 'not altogether void of native genius' and was 'more worthy to be compared with his original' than other 'geniusses of modern times'.[38] *The Oxford Review* of *The Mountain Bard* had been more complimentary, its reviewer deeming Hogg to be 'a poet of nature's own creation, and worthy to rank among the most distinguished of the Caledonian Bards'.[39] However, even given such praise, the reviewer for *The Poetical Register* expressed irritation with Hogg's efforts in *The Mountain Bard*, finding that 'the labouring class of society has, of late years, teemed with poets and would-be poets'.[40] Likewise, in another review of *The Mountain Bard*, the critic writing for *Annual Review* claimed that 'few classes of writer have, generally speaking, less claim to originality than these self-taught poets'.[41] The reviewer writing in *The Critical Review* was more charitable in assessing the 'originality' of *The Mountain Bard*, conceding that some of Hogg's poems are 'worthy of Burns, without copying him' and lamenting 'England's inferiority' to Scotland in producing 'men of rising genius'.[42]

While *The Mountain Bard* began the process of establishing Hogg's reputation as a possible successor to Burns, Hughes states that 'real success came to Hogg with the publication of *The Queen's Wake* in January 1813'.[43] This ambitious work was dedicated to Princess

Charlotte of Wales by 'a shepherd among the mountains of Scotland';
the poem recounts an epic storytelling contest in the manner of
Canterbury Tales, where various narrators present stand-alone tales
for the amusement of the court. Among these tales are Hogg's well-
known verse narratives 'The Witch of Fife' and 'Kilmeny', the latter
which was frequently singled out for praise by Hogg's nineteenth-
century critics. The collection as a whole sold well and was positively
received by reviewers; David Moir described *The Queen's Wake* as 'a
poem of distinguished excellence [...] wonderfully free from those
blemishes of coarseness and indifferent taste, which had unfortunately
– but not miraculously – disfigured Hogg's former writings'.[44] An
anonymous reviewer for *Scots Magazine* found the collection to be
proof that 'Mr. Hogg seems at present to hold, in this country, the first
rank among men of self-taught genius'.[45] Hogg's renown for *The
Queen's Wake* reached across the Atlantic, where a reviewer for *The
Analectic Magazine* in Philadelphia wrote admiringly of 'shepherds
and ploughmen writing poetry' in Scotland.[46]

Concerning the long-term utility of the 'Ettrick Shepherd'
persona, Hughes asserts that 'the marketing value of his Ettrick
Shepherd pseudonym was clearly welcome to Hogg but he often tried
to liberate himself from the restrictions it imposed'.[47] Part of his
strategy of 'liberation' involved repositioning himself as a 'bard'
rather than only as a shepherd, in much the same fashion as Burns
himself had tried to wrest his image away from the 'heaven-taught
ploughman' persona toward 'Scotch Bard'.[48] Fiona Wilson discusses
Hogg's development as a poet during this period by arguing that he
'further developed his self-presentation: the pastoral poet was
beginning to be replaced by the more culturally prestigious figure of
the bard' (97).

The next stage of Hogg's career, however, would find him
struggling mightily against a caricature of himself penned by his
former supporter, John Wilson. As the 'Shepherd', Hogg would
appear in Wilson's 'Noctes Ambrosianae' columns in *Blackwood's
Edinburgh Magazine* beginning in 1822 and lasting for the next
thirteen years. These were critical years for Hogg, coinciding with his
initial success as a poet and his marked turn to writing fiction in the
latter stages of his career. Hughes notes that this series of columns
'was to have a lasting effect on [Hogg's] reputation'.[49] In many
respects, the hard work Hogg had done to establish and authenticate

his *genius* as Burns's poetic successor would be scuttled once he found himself reconstructed in the pages of *Blackwood's*.

4. The Lasting Negative Influence of Hogg's 'Noctean Shepherd' Persona

Hogg's ambiguous dealings with *Blackwood's Edinburgh Magazine* and its editorial staff are well-documented, and it has been suggested that he paid a high price for being a fixture in Wilson's column.[50] Hughes observes that 'Hogg in his lifetime was repeatedly told by the literary coterie of *Blackwood's Edinburgh Magazine* and others that the cobbler should stick to his last and that the business of a peasant poet was to write lyric poetry'.[51] Writing as 'Christopher North', Wilson sought to enforce this restrictive representation of the 'Ettrick Shepherd' by recourse to deliberate exaggeration, creating a caricature of Hogg replete with class-based stereotyping. Bold argues that despite being viewed as an 'untaught genius' in the 'Noctes Ambrosianae' series, 'Hogg as caricature is irrational, lacking erudition, and prone to malapropisms and misunderstandings' (70-71). Thus, he is a comic figure in the same vein as the eighteenth-century stage Scot, speaking in broad Scots and exhibiting Falstaffian buffoonery.[52] After having heralded Hogg as Burns's 'only worthy successor', Wilson sought to restrain the Ettrick Shepherd from developing his *genius* in other literary genres than poetry.

The 'Noctes Ambrosianae' series conceit was delivered in dialogue among various characters, who discussed issues of the day while enjoying nightly convivial pleasures at Ambrose's tavern. Though a stereotypical Irish character (Morgan Odoherty) was featured in the column, the semi-fictional character of 'The Shepherd' based on Hogg proved to be very popular; in fact, the series was widely-imitated in competing periodicals of the day.[53] Hughes notes that the circulation of *Blackwood's* was so extensive during the 1820s (even in British colonies abroad) that 'the Noctean Shepherd became rather better known than his prototype James Hogg'. Wilson's flair for caricature belied his initial advocacy for Hogg, whom he had met in 1813 as a young poet himself; at that time, the Ettrick Shepherd was 'a far more successful poet than he was himself, and in many respects

[he] behaved as Hogg's protégé during the early stages of their rela-
tionship'.[54]

However, Wilson may have tired of this role, for he authored a
'vicious attack' on Hogg's 'Memoir of the Author's Life' prefacing
the new edition of *The Mountain Bard* (1821), a negative review so
hostile to Hogg personally that he believed it to have been written by
rival publisher George Goldie.[55] In a letter to Blackwood (19-20
August 1821), Hogg wrote that Goldie's article 'shows a disposition'
to 'crush me to pieces in all respects at once'; he further advised
Blackwood that 'you should not let such creatures as Goldie [...] in-
fluence you against an old friend'.[56] Blackwood refused initially to
divulge Wilson's authorship of the review, but Hogg eventually
learned it had been written by his former protégé, now firmly en-
trenched at *Blackwood's* and exerting much critical authority as a
reviewer. Gilbert notes that the impetus for Wilson's attack derived
from Hogg's decision in the revised 'Memoir' to include
'controversial remarks about Scott' as well as 'airing his disagree-
ments with reviewers and publishers' (41). For being so impudent to
publish such criticisms, Hogg found himself increasingly attacked and
marginalised in the literary marketplace.

That Wilson would pen such an angry response to the 'Memoir'
was deeply distressing to Hogg; it had been only a year since Wilson
had championed the Ettrick Shepherd as a 'living genius' who was the
'only worthy successor' to Burns. Although Hogg had formerly con-
sidered Wilson to be somewhat 'rash and thoughtless', he had never
believed him to be a person in 'whose heart [...] any malice or evil
dwelt', vowing that 'I never will forgive him'.[57] Hogg may have had
good reason to feel betrayed by Wilson; as Bold observes, the long-
term effect of the 'Noctes Ambrosianae' columns 'did incalculable
damage to Hogg's reputation, personal and poetic' (70). In the 1820s
and 1830s, Hogg would need to find new avenues for expression,
turning to fiction and seeking to reinvent himself once again. His suc-
cess in doing so reveals the changing tastes of the literary marketplace
as well as Hogg's great ingenuity as a competitor therein, forced to
adapt to popular tastes and reimagine his persona as the Ettrick Shep-
herd.

5. 'The Splendid Meteor of Our Admiration': Hogg's *Memoir of Burns*

By the 1830s, Hogg was still working steadily in the literary marketplace, producing many works of fiction – such as *The Private Memoirs and Confessions of a Justified Sinner* (1824) – for which he is remembered today. His poetic output had slowed considerably over this time, but he continued to think of himself primarily as a poet.[58] It was in this guise that he was asked by the Glasgow publisher Archibald Fullarton to write a memoir of Burns in a new edition of Burns's works and serve as its editor, for which he would receive a minimum of £100.[59] Fullarton gave Hogg a rather short deadline, which he met despite considerable distraction in his personal life at the time; once he delivered the *Memoir of Burns*, however, he quickly learned that it was not satisfactory to the publisher. Hogg tried to mollify Fullarton by admitting in a letter that 'I thought I had given you liberty to modify any part of my M.S. as I am a rash and careless writer'.[60] The need for such editorial changes occasioned a major delay in the work's publication, which was detrimental to the success of the edition as a whole.[61] Although started in 1832, it would not be published as a whole until 1836, a year after Hogg's death.[62]

As Patrick Scott has noted, 'Hogg's *Memoir* has been overshadowed by other early Burns biographies that offered more in the way of new information or fresh documents. In particular, for Burnsians, Hogg's *Memoir* has suffered from the inevitable comparison with Allan Cunningham's nearly-simultaneous 8-volume edition' (1). In a letter to John Gibson Lockhart, Hogg wrote that 'I have undertaken to write a memoir and criticism on Burns [...]. Pray do you know of any unexhausted sources? I must at all events produce something original and queer'.[63] His difficulty in producing 'something original and queer' led to a much-maligned and misunderstood memoir, deemed by Franklin Snyder to be 'a most astonishing document – perhaps the worst life of Burns written before the twentieth century'.[64] Hogg's contemporary critics were no less charitable in their opinions of both the *Memoir* and the notes Hogg supplied throughout the edition with his co-editor, William Motherwell. Some critics believed that Hogg was involved in the project only for his own self-aggrandisement; for example, William Maginn's review in the popular *Fraser's Magazine* suggested that

'Hogg has a complete contempt for Burns; and [...] as lofty an opinion of the Ettrick Shepherd as even our own warm partiality could have wished to see him expressing on such an occasion'.[65]

Conceiving the *Memoir of Burns* as a work of self-promoting vanity has led to its near absence in criticism of both Hogg and Burns. Douglas Mack has argued that 'the *Memoir of Burns* seeks to provide a sympathetic but unsentimentalised and clear-eyed account of Burns', further claiming that 'this did not endear Hogg's text to a readership that would have responded more warmly to a contribution to the literature of the Burns cult'.[66] Bold disagrees, stating that '[Hogg's] *Memoir* is of interest less for its insights into Burns's experiences than for the light it shed on Hogg's ideas of the peasant poet' (54). My own position is somewhere between the two; in my view, Hogg's *Memoir of Burns* provides considerable, if not overly critical insight into Hogg's evolving views of his illustrious predecessor. It also offers interesting analysis of his own status as Burns's successor as Hogg neared the end of his career. As Patrick Scott remarks, Hogg's *Memoir of Burns* represents 'the culmination of a lifelong interest in Burns's poetry and life' (3).

The *Memoir of Burns* begins with a personal aside, delivered with the assurance of a writer who has both experience and authority in the literary marketplace:

So I am set down to write a memoir of the life of ROBERT BURNS. I wish from my soul that as many lives of that singular man had been written during his lifetime as have been of myself, and then we should have known all of the bard and the man that behoved us to know; for really this everlasting raking up of the ashes of the illustrious dead, in search of collateral evidence relating to things about which we have no concern and ought not to know, is too bad.[67]

Hogg's defensiveness perhaps belies the lack of 'collateral evidence' in his *Memoir*, but more importantly, it establishes clear kinship between 'singular men' (Burns and himself) whose lives have already been written. Hogg seeks to protect the 'ashes of the illustrious dead' by refusing to concern himself (and by extension, his readers) with 'things about which we ought not to know'. He defends his method by choosing only to focus on Burns's 'public' character, writing that 'for what [Burns] has produced under the sanction of his name to the public, his character is answerable, both to the existing public and posterity; but no farther' (1-2).

However, Hogg is not above alluding to 'things we ought not to know', remarking of Burns that 'he who of all men [was] the most exposed to erratic wanderings, but without whose strong passions and ardent feelings, he could never have been the splendid meteor of our admiration, or the being of our high concern' (1). Nevertheless, as editor and biographer, he asserts the primacy of the need for discretion when treating Burns's personal life, insisting that his readers recognise the inherent intrusiveness brought about by public fame: 'Let any man consider how he would like to have all his private amours, follies, political and selfish intrigues, raked together and exposed to public view […]. The very thought is awful' (2). In a refreshingly tonic assertion, Hogg claims that the public is 'agreed about the character and genius of Burns. None but the most narrow-minded bigots think of his errors and frailties but with sympathy and indulgence; none but the blindest enthusiasts can deny their existence' (8). At a time when the idolatry of Burns was gaining momentum, Hogg's demystification of the poet's 'character and genius' signals an important deviation from other competing biographies and editions which generally tended to venerate or calumniate their subject.[68]

Hogg attempts to differentiate his *Memoir of Burns* by writing a 'sympathetic but unsentimentalised' account, one that seeks to depict Burns as a gifted (but decidedly human) fellow poet. To discover the 'truth' about Burns, Hogg advises that we have only to read Burns ourselves: 'There is no need for any one now-a-days to say what Burns was, or what he was not. This he has himself told us a hundred times in immortal language' (8). However, Hogg does not furnish evidence of Burns's self-definitions in verse and in fact, neglects his own advice by offering to 'say what Burns was'. He evaluates the current state of Burns criticism, focusing in particular on the biographies and editions that have preceded his efforts, in order to distinguish his own efforts. Considering Currie's 1800 edition, Hogg has little critical commentary, stating that 'for Dr. Currie I have the highest veneration' (3). He defends Currie's biography and edition *in toto*, stating that he has been unable to 'discover, for all the blame attached to him by whole herds of reviewers and self-important biographers, that any one sentence which [Currie] has published has yet been disproved' (3-4).

He is more critical of Hamilton Paul's edition, which had received censure for its spirited defense of Burns's moral character by a member of the clergy.[69] To Hogg, Paul errs by admiring his subject too much:

> There is a hero for you. Any man will stand up for a friend, who, while he is manifestly in the right, is suffering injuries from the envy or malice of others; but how few like Mr. Paul have the courage to step forward and defend a friend whether he is right or wrong; and even to show his determination, when he feels that the bard is farthest wrong, to persist that there he was most mainly right. (9)

Such obtuse 'hero-worship' infuriates Hogg, although he admits that 'when Mr. Paul's work appeared, I could not help admiring it greatly, not for its internal merits, but for the spirit in which it was executed' (9).

Despite Hogg's implicit need to distinguish his own *Memoir of Burns* from the works of his competitors, his biography of the poet blends disparate sources such as Currie, Thomas Carlyle, and John Gibson Lockhart in constructing its own representation of the 'illustrious dead'. Not much 'raking of the ashes' takes place in Hogg's *Memoir*, although he promises that 'wherever I can procure any thing highly original or deeply interesting, and better than I could express it myself, respecting our bard, I deem it my duty to interweave such in this edition' (10). What emerges in his portrayal of Burns is a composite of Hogg's sources, rendering the poet's character and significance through judicious sifting of available commentary. Hogg's *Memoir of Burns* is really a hybrid of nineteenth-century biographical and literary criticism, evaluating the importance of its subject by means of his cultural and national legacy for Scottish readers and writers. Concerning Burns's character, Hogg states that 'for all that has been said and written about the character of Burns, I have very few faults to find with it' (185). He admits that his subject 'had an incontrollable passion for the other sex', but he claims that 'a man cannot help having the bump of amativeness, and when he has it, he cannot get quit of it' (186). Hogg sums up his thoughts on Burns's 'general character' by declaring that 'Burns was framed with impetuous passions, which he deeply deplored; but I shall always regard him, as not only a great, but a good man' (186).

Despite much adverse criticism, Hogg's *Memoir* had its supporters throughout the mid- to late-nineteenth century. Writing in *The Peasant Poets of Scotland* (1881), Henry Shanks claimed that Hogg's 'Life of Burns is on the whole a just and vigorous defence of his great prototype; in it he manfully combats the prevailing notion that Burns while in Dumfries had sunk to an utterly low and degraded state through drink'. Concerning Burns's 'poetical powers', Shanks adds that 'the Shepherd forms a high estimate of the poetical powers of Burns; but is severe upon him for his too close imitation of, if not actual plagiarism from the poet Ferguson [sic], whom the Shepherd wishes Burns had never known'.[70] Despite such marks of approbation from later readers, Hogg's *Memoir of Burns* was a dispiriting production for its author, due largely to the lag time in publication and mainly negative reviews.[71] Rather than serving to crown his accomplishments as the poet's 'only worthy successor', Hogg's *Memoir of Burns* met a fate similar to his first published work *Scottish Pastorals* by apparently being 'consigned to eternal oblivion'.

6. 'There's Nae Bard o' Nature sin' Robin's Awa': The Fate of Scottish Poetry after Hogg

Although his later literary career as a poet was overshadowed by his fiction and essays, Hogg would receive extensive public (and national) recognition as Burns's successor in a series of Burns Dinners beginning in 1815 and concluding in 1834, the year before his death. These events were widely covered in the press, with Hogg's presence considered a major factor in their popularity and publicity. Patrick Scott observes that 'as early as 1816, it had been a matter of public comment when Hogg did not appear at a Burns Night dinner' (4), and Bold concurs that 'Burnsian dinners became a natural way, in the popular imagination, to celebrate Hogg' (79). The first major Burns event that Hogg attended occurred in Edinburgh in 1815, where he served as the host for the evening to much popular acclaim. Hughes states that 'he was the life and soul of the Burns Dinner at Oman's Tavern, filling and refilling Burns's marble bowl with whisky punch until the approach of morning'.[72] His attendance at various Burns Dinners continued regularly thereafter, where Hogg became increasingly as much the object of attention as Burns himself. Kirsteen McCue has argued that the coupling of Hogg and Burns in this fashion derived from their traditional roles as Scottish bards who sought to record and express their nation's folk culture. She states that their 'ability to capture and recreate what was, and still is, most readily regarded as "the tradition" was precisely what Burns and Hogg went on to emulate – having the personal credentials par excellence'.[73]

This perception of Hogg became standard during the 1810s and 1820s, when he was invited to countless Burns Dinners throughout Britain. Hughes provides a detailed account of Hogg's acculturation at such events, noting that his assumption of Burns's mantle was part of a deliberate process sustained by public interest in Hogg:

Hogg actively commemorated Burns as his predecessor during these years, and graced numerous dinners on 25 January to honour Burns in that role [...]. Although in later years Hogg was to feature at Burns dinners in the Burns heartland of Dumfries (1822), as well as in London (1832), the most spectacular and best-recorded occasion was probably the triennial Burns dinner held on 22 February 1819 at the Assembly Rooms on Edinburgh's George Street. Some three hundred and twenty gentlemen attended, prominent whigs such as Francis Jeffrey and Henry Cockburn among them as well as Hogg's Blackwoodian cronies Lockhart and Wilson, and surviving friends of Burns.[74]

The 1819 Dinner served to establish Hogg's role as Burns's 'only worthy successor' in the public eye; as Bold notes, 'the habit, drawn from Burns customs, of celebrating Hogg's genius with a meal, began at [this] Burns Supper' (79).

Such popular acclaim was not without its drawbacks. Similar to his later fame as 'The Shepherd' in the pages of *Blackwood's*, Hogg found himself at the mercy of public reconstructions of his identity. Soon after the dust had settled following the 1819 Burns Dinner, Hogg was parodied in John Gibson Lockhart's *Peter's Letters to his Kinsfolk* (1819), where his status as a foolish peasant poet is represented as his foremost character trait. Hughes highlights Lockhart's political strategy in depicting Hogg – and Burns – in this way: 'Hogg, like Burns, is shifted from national poet to Tory icon of an appropriately naïve if gifted peasantry that is maligned and misunderstood by Enlightenment whiggery'.[75] By the time of his last major Burns Dinner event in 1832, Hogg's reputation had endured the caricatures of both Lockhart and Wilson. He was about to embark on his *Memoir of Burns* as well, lending a sense of urgency to this period of his life and his role as Burns's successor.

The Burns Dinner held at the Freemason's Tavern in London on 25 January 1832 was a particularly prestigious event for Hogg, with over two hundred people expected to attend. However, Hughes records that actually 'between four and five hundred gentlemen attended, crowding the premises and causing some problems for the promoters and caterers, since insufficient food for the number had been provided'.[76] Among those attending were two of Burns's sons, for whom Hogg brewed punch in their father's punch bowl.[77] Despite the obvious homage to his predecessor, Hogg claimed that the event was really about promoting himself and his works, even at this late stage in his career. He stated that 'though the name of Burns is necessarily coupled with mine, the dinner has been set on foot solely to bring me forward and give me éclat in the eyes of the public, thereby to inspire an extensive sale of my forthcoming work'.[78] The éclat he sought from the public on that night he duly received from female as well as male admirers; Hughes notes that 'the galleries of the hall were crowded right up to the close of the meeting at half-past twelve with ladies eager to see Hogg'.[79]

As had become the established custom, Hogg's *genius* was toasted, and his elegy for Burns was recited after a 'moment of silence'. The song was composed for the occasion and set to the Jacobite tune 'There'll never be peace till Jamie comes home'.[80] In the elegy, Hogg expresses discontent with the present state of poetry, which is foundering after the death of 'Robin':

The bards o' our country, now sing as they may,
The best o' their ditties but maks my heart wae;
For at the blithe strain there was ane beat them a', –
O there's nae bard o' nature sin' Robin's awa![81]

In spite of his accolades and self-regard, Hogg expresses little bravado in this elegy written for his 'coming-out'. Indeed, there is a pall cast on living Scottish poets – those would-be 'bards o' nature' – who write in Burns's shadow, seeking to succeed and surpass him in the present.

Hogg ends his elegy with little hope that he would indeed live to be considered Burns's equal in the eyes of posterity; however, only three years after this epochal Burns Dinner, Hogg died with little public fanfare and few posthumous remembrances of his claim to be Burns's 'only worthy successor'. He writes,

If he had some fauts I cou'd never them see,
They're nae to be sung by sic gilpies as me,
He likit us weel, an' we likit him a', –
O there's nae sickan callan sin' Robin's awa!
Whene'er I sing late at the milkin my kye,

I look up to heaven an' say with a sigh,
Although he's now gane, he was king o' them a,' –
Ah! there's nae bard o' nature sin' Robin's awa! (25-30)

Hogg's pessimism extends beyond the parameters of the elegiac mode, expressing a lifetime of frustration in his attempts to be a 'bard o' nature' like Burns and gain lasting public recognition as his successor.

That Hogg failed to assume Burns's mantle speaks more to the dead poet's ongoing popular appeal and influence, as well as the ever-changing reconstruction of his iconic persona as the 'genius of Scotland'. Those like Hogg who wrote in his shadow faced obstacles over which they had little control, such as the parameters of literary success which were in a constant state of change in the literary marketplace. The 'cultural production' of Burns during this period attests to his ongoing relevance for readers and writers, in Scotland and beyond; their perceptions depended largely upon the competing versions of the poet's life and legacy that were promulgated by fellow poets, critics, biographers, and editors. As this book hopes to have proven, these competing versions – based in some cases on outright falsehoods – exerted a powerful influence in nineteenth-century Scotland. The challenges of poetic succession were vividly negotiated by James Hogg, whose 'Ettrick Shepherd' persona relied greatly on Burns's own 'heaven-taught ploughman' persona. Hogg's creative choices – particularly his decision to explore other literary genres and modes than poetry – speak to the difficulty of being Burns's 'only worthy successor'.

Learning to adapt to the changing literary marketplace meant reimagining the creative possibilities available to a self-taught 'living genius'. In doing so, Hogg reveals that being the successor to Burns could not be dictated (or achieved) through his own agency; succession instead greatly depended upon understanding and conforming to the current standards and criteria for recognition in the literary marketplace. As Hogg learned at the end of his life, when his enthusiasm for being the 'next Burns' was still guiding his creative decisions and public appearances, he could not achieve 'consecration' as the 'only worthy successor' on his merits alone.

Adapting to the various permutations that shaped the 'cultural production' of his idol was not enough to enable him to gain the esteem and recognition of his fellow Scots as Burns had done. Perhaps it ultimately seemed to Hogg in his last years that becoming the next 'Genius of Scotland' was a futile venture, but it is to his credit that he continued to write, publish, and maintain a public image until his death in 1835. It would not be until Hugh MacDiarmid's public (and quite hostile) battles with Burns's legacy that Scottish verse emerged from the dead poet's shadow. Though Hogg had believed he had sufficient *genius* to compete with his predecessor, writing in the 'great shadow' of Burns proved to be a dark enterprise indeed, one which pointed to a grim future for Scottish poets who sought to gain their own recognition and consecration in the literary marketplace.

---

[1] Low (1974: 317). All citations of this article refer to this edition and will be noted in-text by page numbers.

[2] For more on Currie's views of the Scottish 'peasantry', see chapter four of the present work.

[3] Douglas S. Mack, 'James Hogg's First Encounter with Burns's Poetry', in Patrick Scott and Kenneth Simpson, eds, *Burns and Friends: Essays by W. Ormiston Roy Fellows Presented to G. Ross Roy* (Columbia: University of South Carolina Press, 2012), pp. 122-30:126

[4] For more on Hogg's designation as the 'Ettrick Shepherd', see Gillian Hughes, *James Hogg: A Life* (Edinburgh: Edinburgh University Press, 2012), pp. 114-45.

[5] For more on this critical tradition, see *Scottish Literature*, ed. by Gifford, Dunnigan, and MacGillivray (Edinburgh: University of Edinburgh Press, 2002), pp. 315-17.

[6] Valentina Bold, *James Hogg: A Bard of Nature's Making* (Oxford: Peter Land, 2007), p. 58.

[7] Gillian Hughes, '"I think I shall soon be qualified to be my own editor": Peasant Poets and the Control of Literary Production', *John Clare Society Journal*, 22 (2003), pp. 6-16:7.

[8] Bold (2007: 42). Further references to this edition are given after quotations in the text.

[9] p. 97. Further references to this article are given after quotations in the text.

[10] For more on the drawbacks of the 'Noctes' Shepherd persona, see Thomas C. Richardson, 'James Hogg and *Blackwood's Edinburgh Magazine*: Buying and Selling the Ettrick Shepherd' in Sharon Alker and Holly Faith Nelson, eds, *James Hogg and the Literary Marketplace* (Farnham: Ashgate, 2009), pp. 185-200. See also Hughes, 'Magazines, Annuals, and the Press', in Ian Duncan and Douglas S. Mack, eds, *The Edinburgh Companion to James Hogg* (Edinburgh: Edinburgh University Press, 2012), pp. 31-37, 34-35.

[11] Douglas S. Mack, 'Hogg as Poet: A successor to Burns?' in Kenneth Simpson, ed., *Love and Liberty, Robert Burns: A Bicentenary Celebration* (East Linton: Tuckwell, 1997), p. 119.

[12] James Hogg, *Altrive Tales: Collected among the Peasantry of Scotland and from Foreign Adventurers*, ed. by Gillian Hughes, Stirling/South Carolina Research Edition of the Collected Works of James Hogg, 13 (Edinburgh: Edinburgh University Press, 2005), p. 11.

[13] See Hogg, *The Mountain Bard* (2007), for both versions of the 'Memoir'. See also Hogg, *Altrive Tales* (2005) for its version of the 'Memoir'.

[14] p. 39. Further references to this article are given after quotations in the text.

[15] *The Mountain Bard* (2007), p. 9. All further citations of Hogg's 1807 'Memoir' refer to this edition and will be noted in-text by page numbers.

[16] See Douglas S. Mack, 'James Hogg (bap. 1770, d. 1835)', in *DNB*.

[17] On this facet of labouring-class verse, see Prandi (2008: 80-87).

[18] For more on this relationship, see Valentina Bold, *James Hogg: A Bard of Nature's Making* (Oxford: Peter Lang, 2007), pp. 66-67.

[19] *The Mountain Bard* (2007), p. 222.

[20] *James Hogg*, p. 33.

[21] See Hughes (2012: 12).

[22] Douglas S. Mack, 'James Hogg's First Encounter with Burns's Poetry', in Patrick Scott and Kenneth Simpson, eds, *Burns and Friends: Essays by W. Ormiston Roy Fellows Presented to G. Ross Roy* (Columbia: University of South Carolina Press, 2012), pp. 122-30, 26.

[23] *Altrive Tales* (2005: xvi). All further citations of the 1832 'Memoir' refer to this edition and will be noted in-text by page numbers.

[24] *A Life*, p. 32.

[25] Mack (1997: 119).

[26] For more on the high volume of elegies during this period, see chapters three and four of the present work.

[27] 'James Hogg's First Encounter', p. 122.

[28] For more on Burns's desire to see his works in 'guid black prent', see Rhona Brown (2012: 71-86).

[29] p. 104.

[30] *A Life*, p. 40.

[31] For more on this practice, see Andrews (2006: 59-79).

[32] See Newman (2007: 97-135).

[33] For more on the changing taste for fiction at this time, see Peter Garside, 'Hogg and Scott's "First Meeting" and the Politics of Literary Friendship' in Alker and Nelson (2009: 21-42).

[34] James Hogg, *Memoir of the Author's Life and Familiar Anecdotes of Sir Walter Scott*, ed. by Douglas S. Mack (New York: Barnes and Kennethe, 1972), p. 124.

[35] Hughes (2003: 8).

[36] For the influences of Burns and the ballads, see Gilbert's introduction to Hogg, *The Mountain Bard* (2007), pp. xi-lxiii.

[37] For a discussion of the paratexts in Burns's 'Halloween', see Andrews, 'Footnoted Folklore: Robert Burns's "Halloween"'. For the *Notes on Scottish Song*, see Andrews (2009: 110-24).

[38] [Review of *The Forest Minstrel*], pp. 140, 141.

[39] [Review of *The Mountain Bard*], p. 541.

[40] [Review of *The Mountain Bard*], p. 548.

[41] [Review of *The Mountain Bard*], p. 555.

[42] pp. 237, 241, 244. For more on the critical reception of *The Mountain Bard*, see Gilbert's introduction to Hogg, *The Mountain Bard* (2007), pp. xli-xlvii.

[43] Hughes (2003: 9).

[44] p. 105.

[45] [Review of *The Queen's Wake*], p. 126.

[46] [Review of *The Queen's Wake*], p. 104.

[47] Hughes (2003: 12).

[48] For more on this strategy employed by Burns, see chapter two of the present work.

[49] *A Life*, p. 183.

[50] For more on this, see Richardson, 'James Hogg and *Blackwood's Edinburgh Magazine*: Buying and Selling the Ettrick Shepherd'.

[51] 'Peasant Poets', p. 14.

[52] For more on Scots in eighteenth-century drama, see the introduction to *Twentieth-Century Scottish Drama*, ed. by Stevenson and Craig, pp. vii-xiv.

[53] For more on this aspect of the 'Noctes Ambrosianae' series, see Hughes, *A Life*, p. 183.

[54] Hughes, *A Life*, pp. 183, 117.

[55] Hughes, *A Life*, p. 178.

[56] *The Collected Letters of James Hogg*, ed. by Hughes, II, 105.

[57] Hughes, *A Life*, p. 179.

[58] From 1820 to his death in 1835, Hogg published eight works of fiction but only three collections of verse.

[59] See Hughes, *A Life*, p. 266.

[60] Qtd. in Patrick Scott, p. 9. I would like to thank Dr. Scott for allowing me to see this forthcoming work.

[61] See Hughes (2007: 268-69).

[62] See Patrick Scott (Forthcoming: 3). Further references to this introduction are given after quotations in the text.

[63] Qtd. in Patrick Scott, p. 6.

[64] p. 490.

[65] p. 10. See also Hughes (2007: 286).

[66] Mack (2012: 126).

[67] *The Works of Robert Burns*, ed. by the Ettrick Shepherd and Motherwell, V, 1. All citations of the *Memoir* refer to this edition/volume and will be noted in-text by page numbers.

[68] For more on this element of Burns's early nineteenth-century reception, see chapter four of the present work.

[69] For discussion of Hamilton Paul's edition, see chapter five of the present work.

[70] p. 86.

[71] For the publication details of the *Memoirs of Burns* and the Motherwell-Hogg edition, see Patrick Scott, pp. 8-10.

[72] Hughes (2007: 133).

[73] p. 128.

[74] Hughes (2007: 160).

[75] Ibid., p. 160.

[76] *Ibid.,* p. 246.

[77] See Bold (2007: 79).

[78] See Hughes (2007: 245).

[79] Ibid., p. 246.

[80] Ibid., p. 247.

[81] 'Robin's Awa', p. 91, ll. 5-8. Hereafter cited in-text by line numbers.

Bibliography

Abizadeh, Arash, 'Liberal Nationalist versus Postnational Social Integration: On the Nation's Ethno-Cultural Particularity and "Concreteness"', *Nations and Nationalism*, 10.3 (2004), 231-50

Affleck, Colin, 'Windows of Opportunity: The Scottish-English Career of Robert Kellie Douglas', *The Drouth*, 38 (2010-11), 37-49

Aikman, James, *Poems: Chiefly Lyrical, Partly in the Scottish Dialect* (Edinburgh: Macredie, Skelly, and Muckersy, 1816)

Ainslie, Hew, *A Pilgrimage to the Land of Burns* (Deptford: the author, 1822)

Alker, Sharon, and Holly Faith Nelson, 'Transatlanticism and Beyond: Robert Burns and the World Wide Web', in Sharon Alker, Leith Davis, and Holly Faith Nelson, eds, *Robert Burns and Transatlantic Culture* (Farnham: Ashgate, 2012), pp. 247-60

Anderson, Benedict, *Imagined Communities: Reflections on the Origin and Spread of Nationalism* (London: Verso, 1991)

Andrews, Corey E., '"Almost the Same, but Not Quite": English Poetry by Eighteenth-Century Scots', *Eighteenth Century: Theory and Interpretation*, 47.1 (2006), 59-79

—— 'Burns the Critic', in Gerald Carruthers, ed., *The Edinburgh Companion to Robert Burns* (Edinburgh: Edinburgh University Press, 2009), pp. 110-24

—— 'Footnoted Folklore: Robert Burns's "Halloween"', in Patrick Scott and Kenneth Simpson, eds, *Robert Burns and Friends: Essays by W. Ormiston Roy Fellows Presented to G. Ross Roy* (Columbia: University of South Carolina Press, 2012), pp. 24-37

—— 'The Genius of Scotland: Robert Burns and his Critics', *International Journal of Scottish Literature*, 6 (2010), 1-16

—— *Literary Nationalism in Eighteenth-Century Scottish Club Poetry* (Lewiston: Mellen, 2004)

—— 'Venders, Purchasers, Admirers: Burnsian "Men of Action" from the Nineteenth to the Twenty-First Century', *Scottish Literary Review*, 2.1 (2010), 97-115

—— '"Work Poems": Assessing the Georgic Mode of Eighteenth-Century Working-Class Poetry', in Sandro Jung, ed., *Experiments in Genre in Eighteenth-Century Literature* (Ghent: Academic Scientific, 2011), pp. 105-33

Axelsson, Karl, *The Sublime: Precursors and British Eighteenth-Century Conceptions* (Bern: Peter Lang, 2007)

Balfour, Alexander, *Contemplation* (Edinburgh: Watson, 1820)

—— 'Elegy to the Memory of Robert Burns', *Edinburgh Magazine or Literary Miscellany*, 8 (1796), 465-67

Ball, Margaret, *Sir Walter Scott as a Critic of Literature* (New York: Columbia University Press, 1907)

Basker, James, 'Scotticisms and the Problem of Cultural Identity in Eighteenth-Century Britain', in John Dwyer and Richard B. Sher, eds, *Sociability and Society in Eighteenth-Century Scotland* (Edinburgh: Edinburgh University Press, 1993), pp. 82-95

Beattie, James, *Essays on Poetry and Music*, 3rd edn (London: Creech, 1779)

——— *The Minstrel; or, The Progress of Genius*, 8th edn (London: Dilly and Creech, 1784)

——— *Scotticisms Arranged in Alphabetical Order, Designed to Correct Improprieties of Speech and Writing* (Edinburgh: Creech, 1787)

Benjamin, Walter, 'The Work of Art in the Age of Mechanical Reproduction', in Hannah Arendt, ed., *Illuminations*, trans. by Harry Zohn (New York: Schocken, 1969), pp. 217-52

Bentman, Raymond, 'Robert Burns's Declining Fame', *Studies in Romanticism*, 2 (1975), 207-25

Biester, James, 'Gender and Style in Seventeenth-Century Commendatory Verse', *SEL: Studies in English Literature, 1500-1900*, 33.3 (1993), 507-22

Billig, Michael, *Banal Nationalism* (London: Sage, 1995)

Blair, Hugh, *A Critical Dissertation on the Poems of Ossian the Son of Fingal* (London: Becket and De Hondt, 1763)

——— *Lectures on Rhetoric and Belles-Lettres*, 2 vols (London: Strahan and Cadell, 1783)

Blind Harry, *Wallace*, trans. by William Hamilton of Gilbertfield (Glasgow: Duncan, 1722)

Bloom, Harold, *The Anxiety of Influence* (New York: Oxford University Press, 1973)

——— *Genius: A Mosaic of One Hundred Exemplary Creative Minds* (New York: Warner Books, 2002)

——— *A Map of Misreading* (New York: Oxford University Press, 1975)

Bold, Valentina, *James Hogg: A Bard of Nature's Making* (Oxford: Peter Lang, 2007)

——— 'Janet Little "The Scotch Milkmaid" and "Peasant Poetry"', *Scottish Literary Journal*, 20.2 (1993), 21-30

Bourdieu, Pierre, *Distinction: A Social Critique of the Judgement of Taste*, trans. by Richard Nice (Cambridge: Harvard University Press, 1984)

——— *The Field of Cultural Production: Essays on Art and Literature*, ed. by Randal Johnson (New York: Columbia University Press, 1993)

——— 'The Forms of Capital', in Hugh Lauder and others, eds, *Education, Globalisation and Social Change* (Oxford: Oxford University Press, 2006), pp. 105-19

——— *The Rules of Art: Genesis and Structure of the Literary Field*, trans. by Susan Emanuel (Stanford: Stanford University Press, 1996)

Brown, Marshall, *Preromanticism* (Stanford: Stanford University Press, 1991)

Brown, Rhona, 'Allan Ramsay, Robert Fergusson and Robert Burns', in Sergeant and Stafford, eds, *Burns and Other Poets*, pp. 23-38

——— '"Guid Black Prent": Robert Burns and the Contemporary Scottish and American Periodical Press', in Sharon Alker, Leith Davis, and Holly Faith Nelson, eds, *Robert Burns and Transatlantic Culture* (Farnham: Ashgate, 2012), pp. 71-86

——— *Robert Fergusson and the Scottish Periodical Press* (Farnham: Ashgate, 2012)

Buchan, James, *Crowded with Genius, The Scottish Enlightenment: Edinburgh's Moment of the Mind* (New York: Harper Collins, 2003)

Bunyan, John, *Pilgrim's Progress* (New York: Collier, 1909)

Burd, Henry Alfred, 'Joseph Ritson: A Critical Biography' (unpublished doctoral dissertation, University of Illinois, 1915)

Burke, Tim, 'Labour, Education and Genius', in Johnny Rodger and Gerard Carruthers, eds, *Fickle Man: Robert Burns in the 21st Century* (Dingwall: Sandstone, 2009), pp. 13-24

Burns, Robert, *Poems, Chiefly in the Scottish Dialect* (Kilmarnock: J. Wilson, 1786)

―――― *Poems, Chiefly in the Scottish Dialect*, rev. edn (Edinburgh: Creech, 1787)

―――― *Poems, Chiefly in the Scottish Dialect*, 2nd edn, 2 vols (Edinburgh: Creech, 1793)

Burns, Robert, and Robert Riddell, *Notes on Scottish Song*, ed. by James C. Dick (London: Frowde, 1908)

Butler, Marilyn, 'Burns and Politics', in Robert Crawford, ed., *Robert Burns and Cultural Authority* (Iowa City: University of Iowa Press, 1997), pp. 86-112

Campbell, Thomas, 'Ode to the Memory of Burns', *European Magazine and London Review*, 70 (July-December 1816), 7

―――― *Specimens of the British Poets* (London: Murray, 1819)

Carlyle, Thomas, *On Heroes and Hero-Worship* (New York: Harper, 1841)

Carnie, Robert Hay, 'Hugh MacDiarmid, Robert Burns and the Burns Federation', *Studies in Scottish Literature*, 30 (1998), 261-76

Carruthers, Gerard, 'Burns and the Scottish Critical Tradition', in Kenneth Simpson, ed., *Love and Liberty, Robert Burns: A Bicentenary Celebration* (East Linton: Tuckwell, 1997), pp. 239-47

―――― 'Introduction', in Gerard Carruthers, ed., *The Edinburgh Companion to Robert Burns*, (Edinburgh: Edinburgh University Press, 2009), pp. 1-5

―――― *Robert Burns* (Tavistock: Northcote House, 2006)

―――― 'Robert Burns's Scots Poetry Contemporaries', in Sergeant and Stafford, eds, *Burns and Other Poets*, pp. 39-52

―――― 'The Word on Burns', in Johnny Rodger and Gerard Carruthers, eds, *Fickle Man: Robert Burns in the 21st Century* (Dingwall: Sandstone, 2009), pp. 25-37

Chalmers, Margaret, *Poems* (Newcastle: Hodgson, 1813)

Chambers, Robert, *A Biographical Dictionary of Eminent Scotsmen*, 4 vols (Glasgow: Blackie, 1835)

Coleman, Patrick, *Anger, Gratitude, and the Enlightenment Writer* (Oxford: Oxford University Press, 2011)

Connell, Liam, 'Modes of Marginality: Scottish Literature and the Uses of Postcolonial Theory', *Comparative Studies of South Asia, Africa, and the Middle East*, 23.1-2 (2003), 41-53

―――― 'Scottish Nationalism and the Colonial Vision of Scotland', *Interventions: International Journal of Postcolonial Studies*, 6.2 (2004), 252-63

Conner, James, 'Elder Brother in the Muse', *Studies in Scottish Literature*, 30 (1998), 59-66

Corbett, John, *Language and Scottish Literature* (Edinburgh: Edinburgh University Press, 1997)

Cowan, Edward, 'The Philosopher, The Physician, The Fanatic, The Fraudster, and the First Secretary: The "Doonhame" Creation of Robert Burns', Lecture (Columbia: University of South Carolina, 2 April 2009)

Crawford, Robert, *The Bard: Robert Burns, a Biography* (Princeton: Princeton University Press, 2009)

―――― *Devolving English Literature*, 2nd edn (Edinburgh: Edinburgh University Press, 2001)

———— ed., *'Heaven-Taught Fergusson': Robert Burns's Favourite Scottish Poet* (East Linton: Tuckwell, 2003)

———— *Scotland's Books: A History of Scottish Literature* (Oxford: Oxford University Press, 2009)

———— ed., *The Scottish Invention of English Literature* (Cambridge: Cambridge University Press, 1998)

Crawford, Thomas, *Burns: A Study of the Poems and Songs* (Stanford: Stanford University Press, 1960)

———— 'Burns, Genius and Major Poetry', in Kenneth Simpson, ed., *Love and Liberty, Robert Burns: A Bicentenary Celebration* (East Linton: Tuckwell, 1997), pp. 341-53

Cromek, R. H., ed., *Reliques of Robert Burns* (London: M'Creery, 1808)

Crossley, Nick, 'Social Class', in Michael Grenfell, ed., *Pierre Bourdieu: Key Concepts* (Durham: Acumen, 2011), pp. 87-100

Curran, Stuart, ed., *The Poems of Charlotte Smith* (Oxford: Oxford University Press, 1993)

Currie, James, ed., *The Complete Works of Robert Burns* (Halifax: Milner, 1845)

———— ed., *The Works of Robert Burns* (Edinburgh: Nelson and Brown, 1835)

Daiches, David, *The Paradox of Scottish Culture: The Eighteenth-Century Experience* (London: Oxford University Press, 1964)

———— *Robert Burns* (New York: Macmillan, 1966)

Davis, Leith, *Acts of Union: Scotland and the Literary Negotiation of the British Nation, 1707-1830* (Stanford: Stanford University Press, 1999)

———— 'Gender and Nation in the Work of Janet Little and Robert Burns', *Studies in English Literature, 1500-1800*, 38.4 (1998), 621-45

———— 'James Currie's *Works of Robert Burns*: The Politics of Hypochondriasis', *Studies in Romanticism*, 36.1 (1997), 48-66

Devine, T. M., *Scotland and the Union, 1707-2007* (Edinburgh: Edinburgh University Press, 2008)

———— *The Scottish Nation: A History, 1700-2000* (New York: Viking, 1999)

Drummond, William Hamilton, *The Giant's Causeway: A Poem* (Belfast: Longman, Hurst, Rees, Orme, & Brown, 1811)

———— 'The Sighs of Genius: An Elegiac Ode, Occasioned by the Death of Robert Burns, The Ayrshire Poet', in *The Man of Age: A Poem*, 2nd edn (Glasgow: [n. pub.], 1798), pp. 21-24

Duff, William, *Critical Observations on the Writings of the Most Celebrated Original Geniuses in Poetry* (London: Becket and Hondt, 1770)

———— *An Essay on Original Genius* (London: Dilly and Dilly, 1767)

Duncan, Ian, *Scott's Shadow: The Novel in Romantic Edinburgh* (Princeton: Princeton University Press, 2007)

Dyce, Alexander, ed., *The Poetical Works of James Beattie, with a Memoir* (Boston: Osgood, 1871)

Egerer, J. W., *Bibliography of Robert Burns* (Carbondale: Southern Illinois University Press, 1964)

Eggers, Dave, *A Heartbreaking Work of Staggering Genius* (New York: Vintage, 2001)

Feldman, Paula R., ed., *British Women Poets of the Romantic Era: An Anthology* (Baltimore: Johns Hopkins University Press, 1997)

Ferguson, Adam, *An Essay on the History of Civil Society* (Dublin: Grierson, 1767)

Ferguson, Frank, and Andrew R. Holmes, eds, *Revising Robert Burns and Ulster: Literature, Religion and Politics, c. 1770-1920* (Dublin: Four Courts Press, 2009)

Ferguson, J. DeLancey, 'The Earliest Obituary of Burns: Its Authorship and Influence', *Modern Philology*, 32.2 (1934), 179-84

—— 'Maria Riddell's Sketch of Burns', *Philological Quarterly*, 13 (1934), 261-66

—— *Pride and Passion: Robert Burns, 1759-1796* (New York: Oxford University Press, 1939)

—— 'Robert Burns and Maria Riddell', *Modern Philology*, 28.2 (1930), 169-84

—— 'They Censored Burns', *Scotland's Magazine*, 51 (1955), 38-40

Ferguson, J. DeLancey, and G. Ross Roy, eds, *The Letters of Robert Burns*, 2 vols (Oxford: Clarendon, 1985)

Ferguson, Moira, *Eighteenth-Century Women Poets: Nation, Class, and Gender* (Albany: State University of New York Press, 1995)

—— 'Janet Little and Robert Burns: An Alliance with Reservations,' *Studies in Eighteenth-Century Culture*, 24 (1995), 155-74

Finlay, Richard J., 'The Burns Cult and Scottish Identity in the Nineteenth and Twentieth Centuries', in Kenneth Simpson, ed., *Love and Liberty, Robert Burns: A Bicentenary Celebration* (East Linton: Tuckwell, 1997), pp. 69-78

Finlayson, James, ed., *The Works of Hugh Blair*, 5 vols (London: Cadell and Davies, 1820), V

Flynn, Philip, *Francis Jeffrey* (Newark: University of Delaware Press, 1978)

Forbes, Margaret, *Beattie and his Friends* (Westminster: Constable, 1904)

Forbes, William, *An Account of the Life and Writings of James Beattie*, 2 vols (Edinburgh: Constable, 1806), I

Forbes of Disblair, William, *A Pill for Pork-Eaters; or, A Scots Lancet for an English Swelling* (Edinburgh: Watson, 1705)

—— *The True Scots Genius, Reviving* (Edinburgh: [n. pub.], 1704)

Forman, H. Buxton, ed., *The Poetical Works and Other Writings of John Keats*, 4 vols (London: Reeves & Turner, 1889), II

'Frontispiece. The Monument of Burns', *The European Magazine and London Review*, 70 (July-December 1816), 5-7

Garside, Peter, 'Hogg and Scott's "First Meeting" and the Politics of Literary Friendship', in Sharon Alker and Holly Faith Nelson, eds, *James Hogg and the Literary Marketplace* (Farnham: Ashgate, 2009), pp. 21-42

Gaskill, Howard, ed., *Ossian Revisited* (Edinburgh: Edinburgh University Press, 1991)

—— ed., *The Reception of Ossian in Europe* (London: Thoemmes, 2004)

Gerard, Alexander, *An Essay on Genius* (London: Strahan and Cadell, 1774)

Gibson, James, *The Bibliography of Robert Burns* (Kilmarnock: McKie, 1881; repr. New York: Kraus, 1969)

Gifford, Douglas, *James Hogg* (Edinburgh: Ramsay Head Press, 1976)

Gifford, Douglas, Sarah Dunnigan, and Allan MacGillivray, eds, *Scottish Literature in English and Scots* (Edinburgh: University of Edinburgh Press, 2002)

Gilbert, Suzanne, 'Hogg's Reception and Reputation', in Ian Duncan and Douglas S. Mack, eds, *The Edinburgh Companion to James Hogg* (Edinburgh: Edinburgh University Press, 2012), pp. 37-45

Gill, Stephen, 'Wordsworth and Burns', in Sergeant and Stafford, eds, *Burns and Other Poets*, pp. 156-67

Gombrich, E. H., *The Preference for the Primitive: Episodes in the History of Western Taste and Art* (London: Phaidon, 2002)

Gorji, Mina, 'Burns's Sentiments: Gray, Milton and "To A Mountain Daisy"', in Sergeant and Stafford, eds, *Burns and Other Poets*, pp. 67-79

Graham, James, *Poems, in English, Scotch, and Latin* (Paisley: Neilson, 1794)

Grant, Anne, *Poems on Various Subjects* (Edinburgh: the author, 1803)

Grenfell, Michael, 'Interest', in Michael Grenfell, ed., *Pierre Bourdieu: Key Concepts* (Durham: Acumen, 2011), pp. 153-70

Griffin, Dustin, *Patriotism and Poetry in Eighteenth-Century Britain* (Cambridge: Cambridge University Press, 2002)

Groom, Nick, *The Making of Percy's 'Reliques'* (Oxford: Oxford University Press, 1999)

Grose, Francis, *The Antiquities of Scotland*, 2 vols (London: Hooper, 1789-91), II

Grossman, Lev, 'Death of a Genius', *Time*, 18 September 2008, p. 56

Guillory, John, *Cultural Capital: The Problem of Literary Canon Formation* (Chicago: University of Chicago Press, 1993)

Harvie, Christopher, *Scotland and Nationalism: Scottish Society and Politics, 1707 to the Present* (New York: Routledge, 1998)

Henley, W. E., and T. F. Henderson, eds, *The Poetry of Robert Burns*, 4 vols (Edinburgh: Jack, 1896), II

Heron, Robert, *A Memoir of the Life of the Late Robert Burns* (Edinburgh: Brown, 1797)

Higgins, David, 'Celebrity, Politics and the Rhetoric of Genius', in Tom Mole, ed., *Romanticism and Celebrity Culture, 1750-1850* (Cambridge: Cambridge University Press, 2009), pp. 41-59

—— *Romantic Genius and the Literary Magazine: Biography, Celebrity and Politics* (London: Routledge, 2005)

Hogg, James, *Altrive Tales: Collected among the Peasantry of Scotland and from Foreign Adventurers*, ed. by Gillian Hughes, Stirling/South Carolina Research Edition of the Collected Works of James Hogg, 13 (Edinburgh: Edinburgh University Press, 2005)

—— *The Forest Minstrel*, ed. by Peter Garside and Richard Jackson, Stirling/South Carolina Research Edition of the Collected Works of James Hogg, 19 (Edinburgh: Edinburgh University Press, 2006)

—— *The Jacobite Relics of Scotland*, ed. by Murray G. H. Pittock, Stirling/South Carolina Research Edition of the Collected Works of James Hogg, 10, 12, 2 vols (Edinburgh: Edinburgh University Press, 2002-03)

—— *Mador of the Moor*, ed. by James E. Barcus, Stirling/South Carolina Research Edition of the Collected Works of James Hogg, 16 (Edinburgh: Edinburgh University Press, 2005)

—— *Memoir of the Author's Life and Familiar Anecdotes of Sir Walter Scott*, ed. by Douglas S. Mack (New York: Barnes and Noble, 1972)

—— *The Mountain Bard*, ed. by Suzanne Gilbert, Stirling/South Carolina Research Edition of the Collected Works of James Hogg, 20 (Edinburgh: Edinburgh University Press, 2007)

—— *The Pilgrims of the Sun: A Poem* (Edinburgh: Blackwood, 1815)

———— *The Poetic Mirror; or, The Living Bards of Britain* (Edinburgh: Ballantyne, 1816)

———— *The Private Memoirs and Confessions of a Justified Sinner*, ed. by P. D. Garside, Stirling/South Carolina Research Edition of the Collected Works of James Hogg, 9 (Edinburgh: Edinburgh University Press, 2001)

———— *The Queen's Wake: A Legendary Poem*, ed. by Douglas S. Mack, Stirling/South Carolina Research Edition of the Collected Works of James Hogg, 14 (Edinburgh: Edinburgh University Press, 2004)

———— 'Robin's Awa', in Ross, ed., *Round Burns' Grave*, pp. 91-92

———— *Scottish Pastorals* (Edinburgh: Taylor, 1801)

———— *The Spy*, ed. by Gillian Hughes, Stirling/South Carolina Research Edition of the Collected Works of James Hogg, 8 (Edinburgh: Edinburgh University Press, 2000)

Hogg, James, and William Motherwell, eds, *The Works of Robert Burns*, 5 vols (Glasgow: Fullerton, 1834-36), V

Horace, *Satires, Epistles and Ars Poetica*, trans. by H. Rushton Fairclough, Loeb Classical Library, 194 (Cambridge: Harvard University Press, 1999)

Hughes, Gillian, ed., *The Collected Letters of James Hogg*, 3 vols (Edinburgh: Edinburgh University Press, 2004-08), II (2006)

———— '"I think I shall soon be qualified to be my own editor": Peasant Poets and the Control of Literary Production', *John Clare Society Journal*, 22 (2003), 6-16

———— *James Hogg: A Life* (Edinburgh: Edinburgh University Press, 2007)

———— 'Magazines, Annuals, and the Press', in Ian Duncan and Douglas S. Mack, eds, *The Edinburgh Companion to James Hogg* (Edinburgh: Edinburgh University Press, 2012), pp. 31-37

Hume, David, *An Enquiry Concerning Human Understanding*, ed. by Stephen Buckle (Cambridge: Cambridge University Press, 2007)

———— *Essays: Moral, Political, and Literary*, ed. by Eugene F. Miller (Indianapolis: Liberty Fund, 1987)

———— *The History of England*, 6 vols (London: Cadell, 1778; repr. Indianapolis: Liberty Fund, 1983), I

———— *A Treatise of Human Nature*, ed. by L.A. Selby-Bigge, 2nd edn (Oxford: Clarendon, 1896)

Hyslop, E., 'Verses to the Memory of Burns', *The Star, Daily Evening Advertiser*, 25 August 1796, pp. 12-13

Irvine, Robert P., ed., *Robert Burns: Selected Poems and Songs* (Oxford: Oxford University Press, 2013)

Jack, R. D. S., 'Which Vernacular Revival? Burns and the Makars', *Studies in Scottish Literature*, 30 (1998), 9-18

Jauss, Hans, *Toward an Aesthetic of Reception*, trans. by Timothy Bahti (Minneapolis: University of Minnesota Press, 1982)

Johnson, James, Robert Burns, and Stephen Clark, *Scots Musical Museum*, 6 vols (Edinburgh: Johnson, 1787-1803)

Johnson, Randal, 'Editor's Introduction: Pierre Bourdieu on Art, Literature, and Culture', in Bourdieu, *The Field of Cultural Production*, pp. 1-28

Jones, Charles, *A Language Suppressed: The Pronunciation of the Scots Language in the Eighteenth Century* (Edinburgh: Donald, 1995)

'K', 'To Robert Burns', *Gazeteer and New Daily Advertiser*, 14 August 1790, pp. 29-30

Kames, Henry Home, Lord, *Elements of Criticism*, ed. by Peter Jones, 2 vols (Indianapolis: Liberty Fund, 2005)

—— *Essays on the Principles of Morality and Natural Religion*, ed. by Mary Catherine Moran (Indianapolis: Liberty Fund, 2005)

—— *Sketches of the History of Man*, ed. by James A. Harris, 3 vols (Indianapolis: Liberty Fund, 2007), I

Kidd, Colin, 'Burns and Politics', in Gerard Carruthers, ed., *The Edinburgh Companion to Robert Burns* (Edinburgh: Edinburgh University Press, 2009), pp. 61-73

King, Everard, *James Beattie's 'The Minstrel' and the Origins of Romantic Autobiography* (Lewiston: Mellen, 1992)

Kinghorn, A. M., 'The Literary and Historical Origins of the Burns Myth', *Dalhousie Review*, 39 (1959), 76-85

Kinsley, James, ed., *The Poems and Songs of Robert Burns*, 3 vols (Oxford: Clarendon, 1968)

Knight, Charles A., 'The Created World of the Edinburgh Periodicals', *Scottish Literary Journal*, 6.2 (1979), 20-36

Kord, Suzanne, *Women Peasant Poets in Eighteenth-Century England, Scotland, and Germany: Milkmaids on Parnassus* (Rochester, NY: Camden House, 2003)

Landry, Donna, *The Muses of Resistance: Laboring-Class Women's Poetry in Britain, 1739-1796* (Cambridge: Cambridge University Press, 1990)

Lapraik, John, *Poems on Several Occasions* (Kilmarnock: J. Wilson, 1788)

Leask, Nigel, *Robert Burns and Pastoral: Poetry and Improvement in Late Eighteenth-Century Scotland* (Oxford: Oxford University Press, 2010)

—— '"Their Groves of Sweet Myrtle": Robert Burns and the Scottish Colonial Experience', in Murray Pittock, ed., *Robert Burns and Global Culture* (Lewisburg: Bucknell University Press, 2011), pp. 172-88

Lindsay, Maurice, *The Burns Encyclopedia*, 3rd edn (New York: St. Martins, 1980)

Little, Janet, *The Poetical Works of Janet Little, the Scotch Milkmaid* (Air: J. & P. Wilson, 1792)

Lockhart, John Gibson, *Peter's Letters to his Kinsfolk*, ed. by William Ruddick (Edinburgh: Scottish Academic, 1977)

Low, Donald A., ed., *Robert Burns: The Critical Heritage* (London: Routledge and Kegan Paul, 1974)

Macaulay, James, *Poems on Various Subjects, in Scots and English* (Edinburgh: the author, 1788)

Mack, Douglas S., 'Hogg as Poet: A Successor to Burns?', in Kenneth Simpson, ed., *Love and Liberty, Robert Burns: A Bicentenary Celebration* (East Linton: Tuckwell, 1997), pp. 119-28

—— 'James Hogg's First Encounter with Burns's Poetry', in Patrick Scott and Kenneth Simpson, eds, *Burns and Friends: Essays by W. Ormiston Roy Fellows Presented to G. Ross Roy* (Columbia: University of South Carolina Press, 2012), pp. 122-30

Mackenzie, Henry, ed., *The Lounger* (Edinburgh: Creech, 1785-87)

—— *The Man of Feeling*, ed. by Brian Vickers (London: Oxford University Press, 1967)

Macpherson, James, *The Poems of Ossian and Related Works*, ed. by Howard Gaskill (Edinburgh: Edinburgh University Press, 1995)

Maginn, William, [Review of *Memoir of Burns*], *Fraser's Magazine*, 10 (1834), 10

Malcolmson, Bob, and Stephanos Mastoris, *The English Pig: A History* (London: Hambledon, 1998)

Maton, Karl, 'Habitus', in Michael Grenfell, ed., *Pierre Bourdieu: Key Concepts* (Durham: Acumen, 2011), pp. 49-68

Max, D. T., *Every Love Story is a Ghost Story: A Life of David Foster Wallace* (New York: Viking, 2012)

Maxwell, James, *Animadversions on Some Poets and Poetasters of the Present Age, Especially R—t B—s, and J—n L—k* (Paisley: Neilson, 1788)

Maynard, Luke R. J., 'Hoddin' Grey an' A' That: Robert Burns's Head, Class Hybridity, and the Value of the Ploughman's Mantle', in Aruna Krishnamurthy, ed., *The Working-Class Intellectual in Eighteenth- and Nineteenth-Century Britain* (Farnham: Ashgate, 2009), pp. 67-84

M'Bain, James, *Burns' Cottage: The Story of the Birthplace of Robert Burns* (Glasgow: Bryce, 1904)

McCrone, David, *Understanding Scotland: The Sociology of a Nation*, 2nd edn (New York: Routledge, 2001)

McCue, Kirsteen, 'Singing "more old songs than ever ploughman could"· The Songs of James Hogg and Robert Burns in the Musical Marketplace', in Sharon Alker and Holly Faith Nelson, eds, *James Hogg and the Literary Marketplace* (Farnham: Ashgate, 2009), pp. 123-37

McCulloch, Margery Palmer, 'The Lasses Reply to Mr. Burns: Women, Poetry and Song in the Scottish Lowlands', in Christopher MacLachlan, ed., *Crossing the Highland Line: Cross-Currents in Eighteenth-Century Scottish Writing* (Glasgow: Association for Scottish Literary Studies, 2009), pp. 137-52

McGinty, Walter J., *Robert Burns and Religion* (Aldershot: Ashgate, 2003)

McGuirk, Carol, 'Burns and Nostalgia', in Kenneth Simpson, ed., *Burns Now* (Edinburgh: Canongate, 1994), pp. 31-69

————— 'George Thomson and Robert Burns: With Friends Like These', *Eighteenth-Century Scotland*, 9 (1995), 16-20

————— 'James Currie and the Making of the Burns Myth', in Steven R. McKenna, ed., *Selected Essays on Scottish Language and Literature* (Lewiston: E. Mellen Press, 1992), pp. 149-62

————— *Robert Burns and the Sentimental Era* (Athens: University of Georgia Press, 1985)

————— ed., *Robert Burns: Selected Poems* (London: Penguin, 1993)

McIlvanney, Liam, *Burns the Radical: Poetry and Politics in Late Eighteenth-Century Scotland* (East Linton: Tuckwell, 2002)

————— 'Hugh Blair, Robert Burns, and the Invention of Scottish Literature', *Eighteenth-Century Life*, 29.2 (2005), 25-46

McLane, Maureen, *Balladeering, Minstrelsy, and the Making of British Romantic Poetry* (Cambridge: Cambridge University Press, 2011)

————— 'The Figure Minstrelsy Makes: Poetry and Historicity', *Critical Inquiry*, 29.3 (2003), 429-52

McLure, J. Derrick, *Language, Poetry and Nationhood* (East Linton: Tuckwell, 2000)

Millar, John, *Letters of Sidney, on Inequality of Property* (Edinburgh: Office of the Scots Chronicle, 1796)
—— *The Origin of the Distinction of Ranks*, ed. by Aaron Garrett (Indianapolis: Liberty Fund, 2006)
Mitchison, Rosalind, *A History of Scotland*, 2nd edn (London: Routledge, 1997)
Moffatt, Walter, 'Burns's Literary Reputation in England and Scotland, 1786-1834' (unpublished doctoral dissertation, Princeton University, 1941)
Moir, David Macbeth, *Sketches of the Poetical Literature of the Past Half-Century*, 3rd edn (Edinburgh: Blackwood, 1856)
Montesquieu, Charles-Louis de Secondat, Baron of la Brède and of, *My Thoughts*, ed. and trans. by Henry C. Clark (Indianapolis: Liberty Fund, 2012)
Moore, Robert, 'Capital', in Michael Grenfell, ed., *Pierre Bourdieu: Key Concepts* (Durham: Acumen, 2011), pp. 101-18
Mossner, E. C., and I. S. Ross, eds, *The Correspondence of Adam Smith*, 2nd edn (Oxford: Clarendon, 1987)
Nairn, Tom, *The Break-Up of Britain: Crisis and Neo-Nationalism* (London: NLB and Verso, 1981)
Nash, Andrew, 'The Cotter's Kailyard', in Robert Crawford, ed., *Robert Burns and Cultural Authority* (Edinburgh: Edinburgh University Press, 1997), pp. 180-97
—— *Kailyard and Scottish Literature* (Amsterdam: Rodopi, 2007)
Newman, Steve, *Ballad Collection, Lyric, and the Canon: The Call of the Popular from the Restoration to the New Criticism* (Philadelphia: University of Pennsylvania Press, 2007)
'Ninfeild', 'Elegy on the Death of R. Burns the Ayshire Plowman', *The Gentleman's Magazine*, 66 (1796), 684
Noble, Andrew, 'Burns and Scottish Nationalism', in Kenneth Simpson, ed., *Burns Now* (Edinburgh: Canongate, 1994), pp. 167-92
Noble, Andrew, and Patrick Scott Hogg, eds, *The Canongate Burns: The Complete Poems and Songs of Robert Burns* (Edinburgh: Canongate, 2003)
Patterson, Troy, 'Infinitely Sad: David Foster Wallace, Self-Absorbed Genius', *Slate*, 15 September 2008
<http://www.slate.com/articles/news_and_politics/obit/2008/09/ infinitely_sad.html> [accessed 7 January 2014]
Paul, Hamilton, ed., *The Poems and Songs of Robert Burns* (Air: J. Wilson, McCormick, & Carnie, 1819)
Peebles, William, *Burnomania: The Celebrity of Robert Burns Considered* (Edinburgh: Ogle, 1811)
Percy, Thomas, *Reliques of Ancient English Poetry*, ed. by J. V. Prichard, 2 vols (London: Bell, 1893), I
Peterkin, Alexander, *A Review of the Life of Robert Burns, and of Various Criticisms on his Character and Writings* (Edinburgh: Macredie, Skelly, and Muckersy, 1815)
Pittock, Murray, *Inventing and Resisting Britain: Cultural Identities in Britain and Ireland, 1685-1789* (New York: St. Martins, 1997)
—— '"A Long Farewell to All My Greatness": The History of the Reputation of Robert Burns', in Murray Pittock, ed., *Robert Burns and Global Culture* (Lewisburg: Bucknell University Press, 2011), pp. 25-46
—— *A New History of Scotland* (Stroud: Sutton, 2003)

———— *Scottish and Irish Romanticism* (Oxford: Oxford University Press, 2008)

Prandi, Julie, *The Poetry of the Self-Taught: An Eighteenth-Century Phenomenon* (New York: Peter Lang, 2008)

Radcliffe, David Hill, 'Completing James Beattie's *The Minstrel*', *Studies in Philology*, 100.4 (2003), 534-63

Rae, Thomas, ed., *Robert Burns: A Memoir* (Greenock: Signet Press, 1966)

Ramsay, Allan, *The Ever Green* (Edinburgh: the author, 1724)

Read, Dennis M., *R. H. Cromek, Engraver, Editor, and Entrepreneur* (Farnham: Ashgate, 2011)

Reid, J. B., ed., *A Complete Word and Phrase Concordance to the Poems and Songs of Robert Burns* (Glasgow: Kerr & Richardson, 1889; repr. New York: Franklin, 1969)

Reid, William, 'Monody on the Death of Robert Burns', *Scots Magazine*, 59 (1797), 337-38

Reid, William, and others, *Poetry: Selected and Original*, 4 vols (Glasgow: Brash & Reid, 1796-98), II (1797)

[Review of *The Forest Minstrel*], *Critical Review; or, Annals of Literature*, 22 (1811), 140-41

[Review of *The Mountain Bard*], in Arthur Aikin, ed., *Annual Review and History of Literature for 1807* (London: Longman, Hurst, Rees, and Orme, 1808), pp. 554-57

[Review of *The Mountain Bard*], *Critical Review; or, Annals of Literature*, 12 (1804), 237-44

[Review of *The Mountain Bard*], *Oxford Review*, 1 (1807), 541-48

[Review of *The Mountain Bard*], *Poetical Register*, 6 (1807), 548-49

[Review of *The Queen's Wake*], *Analectic Magazine*, 3 (1814), 104-25

[Review of *The Queen's Wake*], *Scots Magazine*, 75 (1813), 126-31

Riach, Alan, 'MacDiarmid's Burns', in Robert Crawford, ed., *Robert Burns and Cultural Authority* (Iowa City: University of Iowa Press, 1997), pp. 198-215

Richardson, Thomas C., 'James Hogg and *Blackwood's Edinburgh Magazine*: Buying and Selling the Ettrick Shepherd', in Sharon Alker and Holly Faith Nelson, eds, *James Hogg and the Literary Marketplace* (Farnham: Ashgate, 2009), pp. 185-200

Ricks, Christopher, *Allusion to the Poets* (Oxford: Oxford University Press, 2002)

Ringler, William, 'Poeta Nascitur Non Fit: Some Notes on the History of an Aphorism', *Journal of the History of Ideas*, 2.4 (1941), 497-504

Ritson, Joseph, *Observations on the First Three Volumes of the History of English Poetry* (London: Stockdale and Faulder, 1782)

Robertson, Joseph, *Lives of the Scottish Poets*, 3 vols (London: Boys, 1822), II

Robinson, Mairi, ed., *The Concise Scots Dictionary* (Edinburgh: Chambers, 1997)

Robotham, John, 'The Reading of Robert Burns', in Carol McGuirk, ed., *Critical Essays on Robert Burns* (London: Prentice Hall; New York: G.K. Hall, 1998), pp. 281-97

Rodden, John, *The Politics of Literary Reputation: The Making and Claiming of 'St. George' Orwell* (New York: Oxford University Press, 1989)

Rodger, Johnny, and Gerard Carruthers, 'Introduction', in Johnny Rodger and Gerard Carruthers, eds, *Fickle Man: Robert Burns in the 21st Century* (Dingwall: Sandstone, 2009), pp. 1-12

Roscoe, Henry, *Life of William Roscoe*, 2 vols (London: Cadell, 1833), I

Roscoe, William, 'Elegy on the Death of the Scottish Poet Burns', *Morning Chronicle*, 28 July 1800, pp. 12-14

———— 'Lines to the Memory of R. Burns', *Scots Magazine*, 59 (1797), 51-52

Ross, John D., ed., *Round Burns' Grave: The Paeans and Dirges of Many Bards* (Paisley: Gardner, 1891; repr. New York: AMS Press, 1973)

———— *Who's Who in Burns* (Stirling: Mackay, 1927)

Roy, G. Ross, 'Editing Robert Burns in the Nineteenth Century', in Kenneth Simpson, ed., *Burns Now* (Edinburgh: Canongate, 1994), pp. 129-49

———— '"The Mair They Talk, I'm Kend the Better": Poems about Robert Burns to 1859', in Kenneth Simpson, ed., *Love and Liberty, Robert Burns: A Bicentenary Celebration* (East Linton: Tuckwell, 1997), pp. 53-68

———— 'Robert Burns and the Brash and Reid Chapbooks of Glasgow', in Horst W. Drescher, ed., *Scottish Studies: Publications of the Scottish Studies Centre of the Johannes Gutenberg Universtät Mainz in Germershim* (Frankfurt am Main: Peter Lang, 1992), pp. 53-69

Rushton, Edward, *Poems* (London: Ostell, 1806)

Scott, Mary Jane, *James Thomson, Anglo-Scot* (Athens: University of Georgia Press, 1988)

Scott, Patrick, 'James Hogg's *Memoir of Burns*: Editing the Other, Editing the Self', in James Hogg, *Memoir of Burns*, ed. by Patrick Scott (Edinburgh: Edinburgh University Press, forthcoming), pp. 1-20

Scott, Walter, *Minstrelsy of the Scottish Border*, ed. by T. F. Henderson, 4 vols (Edinburgh: Blackwood, 1902; repr. Detroit: Singing Tree, 1968)

'Scotus, Thomas', 'To A' Scots Poets', *Morning Chronicle*, 6 September 1791, pp. 5-7

Sergeant, David, and Fiona Stafford, eds, *Burns and Other Poets* (Edinburgh: Edinburgh University Press, 2012)

Shaftesbury, Anthony Ashley Cooper, Third Earl of, *Characteristicks of Men, Manners, Opinions, Time*, ed. by Douglas den Uyl, 3 vols (Indianapolis: Liberty Fund, 2001)

Shanks, Henry, *The Peasant Poets of Scotland and Musings under the Beeches* (Bathgate: Gilbertson, 1881)

Sharpe, William, *A Dissertation upon Genius* (London: Bathurst, 1755)

Sher, Richard, *The Enlightenment and the Book* (Chicago: University of Chicago Press, 2006)

Siegel, Harry, 'Extremely Cloying and Incredibly False', *New York Press*, 20 April 2005   <http://nypress.com/extremely-cloying-incredibly-false> [accessed 7 January 2014]

Simpson, Kenneth, 'Robert Burns: "Heaven-taught ploughman"?', in Kenneth Simpson, ed., *Burns Now* (Edinburgh: Canongate, 1994), pp. 70-91

———— 'The Vernacular Enlightenment', in Johnny Rodger and Gerard Carruthers, eds, *Fickle Man: Robert Burns in the 21st Century* (Dingwall: Sandstone, 2009), pp. 91-103

Skoblow, Jeffrey, 'Dr. Currie, C'est Moi', *Studies in Scottish Literature*, 30 (1998), 109-15

———— 'Resisting the Powers of Calculation: A Bard's Politics', in Carol McGuirk, ed., *Critical Essays on Robert Burns* (London: Prentice Hall; New York: G.K. Hall, 1998), pp. 17-31

Smith, Adam, *Essays on Philosophical Subjects*, ed. by W. P. D. Wightman and J. C. Bryce (Indianapolis: Liberty Fund, 1982)

———— *Lectures on Jurisprudence*, ed. by R. L. Meek, D. D. Raphael, and P. G. Stein (Indianapolis: Liberty Fund, 1982)

———— *The Theory of Moral Sentiments*, ed. by D. D. Raphael and A. L. Macfie (Indianapolis: Liberty Fund, 1984)

———— *The Wealth of Nations*, ed. by R. H. Campbell and A. S. Skinner, 2 vols (Indianapolis: Liberty Fund, 1981), I

Smith, D. Nichol, ed., *Jeffrey's Literary Criticism* (London: Oxford University Press, 1910)

Snyder, Franklin B., *The Life of Robert Burns* (New York: Macmillan, 1932)

Stafford, Fiona, *The Sublime Savage: A Study of James Macpherson and the Poems of Ossian* (Edinburgh: Edinburgh University Press, 1988)

Starr, H. W., and J. R. Hendrickson, eds, *The Complete Poems of Thomas Gray: English, Latin, and Greek* (Oxford: Clarendon, 1966)

St. Clair, William, 'At the Boundaries of the Reading Nation', in Shafquat Towheed, Rosalind Cronc, and Katie Halsey, eds, *The History of Reading: A Reader* (London: Routledge, 2011), pp. 220-30

———— *The Reading Nation in the Romantic Period* (Cambridge: Cambridge University Press, 2004)

Sterling, Kirsten, *Bella Caledonia: Woman, Nation, Text* (Amsterdam: Rodopi, 2008)

Stevenson, Randall, and Cairns Craig, eds, *Twentieth-Century Scottish Drama: An Anthology*, (Edinburgh: Canongate, 1999)

Struthers, John, 'Dirge, to a Person Who Lamented that No Monument Had Been Erected on the Grave of Robert Burns', in *The Poor Man's Sabbath*, 3rd edn (Edinburgh: Constable and Murray, 1808), pp. 76-78

Sutherland, Kathryn, 'The Native Poet: The Influence of Percy's Minstrel from Beattie to Wordsworth', *Review of English Studies*, 33.132 (1982), 414-33

Taibbi, Matt, and others, '50 Most Loathsome New Yorkers — 2003', *New York Press*, 25 March 2003 <http://www.fineorsuperfine.com/newyorkpress5.html> [accessed 7 January 2014]

Tannahill, Robert, 'Dirge, Written on Reading an Account of Robert Burns's Funeral', *Scots Magazine*, 69 (1807), 526

———— 'Ode, Recited by the President of the Burns' Anniversary Society, Paisley', *Scots Magazine*, 72 (1810), 127

———— *Poems and Songs, Chiefly in the Scottish Dialect*, 4th edn (London: Cowie, 1817)

Thompson, Harold W., *A Scottish Man of Feeling* (London: Oxford University Press, 1931)

Thomson, George, and others, *Select Collection of Original Scottish Airs*, 5 vols (Edinburgh: the author, 1793-1818)

Thomson, James, 'Paisley Burns Club: A Sketch of its History', *Burns Chronicle*, 5 (1927), 131-34

Thomson, Patricia, 'Field', in Michael Grenfell, ed., *Pierre Bourdieu: Key Concepts* (Durham: Acumen, 2011), pp. 67-84

Thornton, Robert D., *James Currie, the Entire Stranger, and Robert Burns* (Edinburgh: Oliver & Boyd, 1963)

——— *William Maxwell to Robert Burns* (Edinburgh: Donald, 1979)

Trumpener, Katie, *Bardic Nationalism: The Romantic Novel and the British Empire* (Princeton: Princeton University Press, 1997)

Updike, John, 'Mixed Messages: "Extremely Loud and Incredibly Close"', *New Yorker*, 14 March 2005 <http://www.newyorker.com/archive/2005/03/14/050314crbo_books1> [accessed 7 January 2014]

van Deusen, Nancy, ed., *Dreams and Visions: An Interdisciplinary Enquiry* (Leiden: Brill, 2010)

'Verses to the Memory of R. Burns', *The Telegraph*, 29 July 1796, pp. 13-14

'Verses, Written in Broad Scotch, and Addressed to Robert Burns, the Air Shire Poet', *Literary Magazine and British Review*, 2 (1789), 297-98

Voltaire, *Candide and Other Stories*, trans. by Roger Pearson (Oxford: Oxford University Press, 2006)

Wadler, Joyce, 'Public Lives: Seeking Grandfather's Savior, and Life's Purpose', *New York Times,* 24 April 2002 <http://www.nytimes.com/2002/04/24/nyregion/public-lives-seeking-grandfather-s-savior-and-life-s-purpose.html> [accessed 7 January 2014]

Warton, Joseph, *An Essay on the Genius and Writings of Pope*, 4th edn, 2 vols (London: Dodsley, 1782)

'Wastle', 'Extracts from Wastle's Diary', *Blackwood's Edinburgh Magazine*, 7 (April-September 1820), 317-23

Watson, James, *Choice Collection of Comic and Serious Scots Poems*, 3 vols (Edinburgh: the author, 1706-1711)

Weinbrot, Howard, *Britannia's Issue: The Rise of British Literature from Dryden to Ossian* (Cambridge: Cambridge University Press, 1993)

Weisman, Karen, ed., *The Oxford Handbook of the Elegy* (Oxford: Oxford University Press, 2010)

Whatley, Christopher A., 'Robert Burns, Memorialization, and the "Heart-beatings" of Victorian Scotland', in Murray Pittock , ed., *Robert Burns and Global Culture* (Lewisburg: Bucknell University Press, 2011), pp. 204-28

Wickman, Matthew, 'Tonality and the Sense of Place in Fergusson's "Elegy, on the Death of Scots Music"', in Crawford, ed., *'Heaven-Taught Fergusson'*, pp. 163-78

Wilson, Fiona, 'Hogg as Poet', in Ian Duncan and Douglas S. Mack, eds, *The Edinburgh Companion to James Hogg* (Edinburgh: Edinburgh University Press, 2012), pp. 96-104

Wilson, John, *The Genius and Character of Burns* (New York: Wiley and Putnam, 1845)

Wood, Harriet Harvey, 'Burns and Watson's *Choice Collection*', *Studies in Scottish Literature*, 30 (1998), 19-30

Wordsworth, William, *The Complete Poetical Works of Wordsworth*, ed. by Andrew Jackson George, Cambridge Edition of the Poets (Boston: Houghton Mifflin, 1931)

——— *A Letter to a Friend of Burns* (London: Longman, Hurst, Rees, Orme, & Brown, 1816)

────── *Lyrical Ballads, with Pastoral and Other Poems*, 3rd edn, 2 vols (London: Longman and Rees, 1802), I

────── *The Poems of William Wordsworth* (London: Moxon, 1849)

'Written on a Blank Leaf of Burns' Poems', *Aberdeen Magazine*, October 1796, p. 247

Young, Ronnie, 'Genius, Men and Manners: Burns and Eighteenth-Century Scottish Criticism', *Scottish Studies Review*, 9.2 (2008), 129-47

────── 'James Beattie and the Progress of Genius in the Aberdeen Enlightenment', *Journal for Eighteenth-Century Studies*, 36.2 (2013), 245-61

Index